Family Circle®

ANNUAL recipes 2009

Pound Cake page 58

Meredith® Consumer Marketing
Des Moines, Iowa

Ice-Cream Cake Roll
Recipe page 33

WELCOME TO THE SECOND *FAMILY CIRCLE*® *ANNUAL RECIPES* COOKBOOK!

At *Family Circle*, we are well aware that one of the biggest challenges faced by everyone, every day, is what to have for dinner. Making a habit of eating out is hard on the budget and can be hard on your body, so that's not the answer. We're confident that in this book, you will find the answer—hundreds of them, in fact—taken from the pages of this year's *Family Circle* magazine.

As editors, it's our job to help make your life easier and better. One of the most delightful ways we do that is by coming up with fresh ideas for affordable, delicious and doable dinners to suit any occasion—whether that's a quick weeknight meal, a dinner party with friends or a holiday celebration.

The guiding principles of *Family Circle* food are convenience, speed, ease, economy, fun, flair, seasonality and—always—great taste. Each month offers a balanced diet of quick and leisurely cooking—and of healthfulness and indulgence. February features an array of fabulous ways with chocolate for Valentine's Day (see the recipe, left), as well as a fresh catch of quick and light fish dishes. In May, tap into a master cooking class with our food editors—and get ideas for money-saving meals that cost less than $2 per serving.

When you know the answer to the question "What's for dinner?," you're freed up to enjoy delicious food you've made yourself and the relationship-building connection that comes from gathering around your own table with family and friends. Happy cooking!

Linda

Linda Fears, Editor in Chief
Family Circle® magazine

Family Circle® Annual Recipes 2009

Meredith® Corporation Consumer Marketing
Vice President, Consumer Marketing: David Ball
Consumer Product Marketing Director: Steve Swanson
Consumer Marketing Product Manager: Wendy Merical
Business Director: Ron Clingman
Associate Director, Production: Douglas M. Johnston

Waterbury Publications, Inc.
Editorial Director: Lisa Kingsley
Associate Editor: Tricia Laning
Creative Director: Ken Carlson
Associate Design Director: Doug Samuelson
Contributing Copy Editors: Terri Fredrickson, Gretchen Kauffman, Peg Smith
Contributing Indexer: Elizabeth T. Parson

Family Circle® **Magazine**
Editor in Chief: Linda Fears
Creative Director: Karmen Lizzul
Food Director: Regina Ragone, M.S., R.D.
Senior Food Editor: Julie Miltenberger
Associate Food Editor: Michael Tyrrell
Assistant Food Editor: Cindy Heller
Editorial Assistant: Allison Baker

Meredith Publishing Group
President: Jack Griffin
Executive Vice President: Andy Sareyan
Vice President, Manufacturing: Bruce Heston

Meredith Corporation
Chairman of the Board: William T. Kerr
President and Chief Executive Officer: Stephen M. Lacy

In Memoriam: E.T. Meredith III (1933–2003)

Pictured on the front cover:
Chocolate-Peanut Butter Dream Bars
(recipe page 11)
Photography by Jason Donnelly

LET'S EAT! At the end of a long and busy day, sitting down at your own table to a fresh, flavorful home-cooked meal is satisfying in so many ways. This collection of *Family Circle* recipes from 2009 makes it simpler than ever to serve up delicious food you make yourself—whether it's a 30-minute weeknight dinner or a Saturday-night dinner party with friends. Recipes are organized by month to take advantage of what's in season and to make it easy to find just the right recipe for any craving or occasion. In addition to the hundreds of healthful, great-tasting recipes, you'll find dozens of tips, cooking tutorials and tantalizing photographs that will tempt you into the kitchen again and again.

Along with feature food stories from *Family Circle* in 2009, look for these regular installments:

▶ Healthy Family Dinners Look here to find a week's worth of easy-to-make, family-friendly meals.

▶ Quick and Easy Here are no-fuss recipes featuring a specific ingredient or cooking method.

▶ Slow-Cooker Solutions Learn to use your slow cooker to make effortless meals (and even desserts!).

▶ Food University Expand your cooking repertoire using step-by-step instructions to classic dishes.

Asian BBQ Chicken Thighs and Broccoli Slaw page 183

Smoky Mac and Cheese page 19

contents

Mustard Glazed Ribs
page 141

Layered Ice Cream Cake
page 205

Strawberry Waffle Sundaes
page 127

Chicken Parmesan page 251

Scallop and Orange Salad
page 17

Eye Round Roast with Shiitake Gravy
page 65

Ice Cream Sandwiches
page 242

january

Curried Lentil Soup
page 17

STAY WARM FROM THE INSIDE-OUT WITH ENTRÉES FEATURING HEALTHFUL SUPERFOODS, PLUS SIX FAMILY-FRIENDLY TAKES ON MAC 'N' CHEESE.

Chocolate-Peanut Butter Dream Bars
page 11

Cheesy Meximac
page 21

Cajun Pork Sandwiches
page 24

PEANUT BUTTER AND CHOCOLATE REACH FOR THE STARS.
BY KAREN TACK

chocolate-peanut butter dream bars

MAKES: 25 squares. **PREP:** 10 minutes. **BAKE:** at 350° for 42 minutes. **REFRIGERATE:** at least 2 hours.

- ¾ cup graham cracker crumbs
- 2 tablespoons granulated sugar
- 3 tablespoons unsalted butter, melted
- 1 box (18.2 ounces) brownie mix
- ½ cup chopped dry-roasted peanuts
- 4 ounces cream cheese, softened
- ½ cup creamy peanut butter
- ½ cup confectioners' sugar
- 3 tablespoons milk
- 1½ cups heavy cream
- 1 tablespoon light corn syrup
- ¾ cup semisweet chocolate chips
  Whipped cream, chopped peanuts, chocolate-peanut butter candies and caramel sauce, to garnish

1. Heat oven to 350°. Spray a 9-inch square baking pan with nonstick cooking spray. Line pan with foil, allowing sides to overhang; spray foil. In small bowl, combine graham cracker crumbs and granulated sugar. Mix in melted butter. Press crumb mixture into prepared pan. Bake until golden, about 5 to 7 minutes. Cool on wire rack.

2. Prepare brownie mix according to package directions for cakelike brownies (adding **¼ cup water, ⅓ cup oil** and **3 eggs**). Fold in chopped nuts. Pour batter into crust-lined pan. Return to 350° oven; bake until brownie is just set and a toothpick inserted in center comes out clean, 30 to 35 minutes. Cool completely in pan on a wire rack.

3. With electric mixer in medium bowl, beat cream cheese until smooth. Add peanut butter and confectioners' sugar; beat until just blended (it will look lumpy). Add milk; beat lightly to loosen mixture. In separate bowl, whip 1 cup of the cream and gently fold into peanut butter mixture. Spread mousse evenly over cooled brownie. Refrigerate 1 hour.

4. Heat remaining ½ cup cream in a small saucepan over medium heat until just boiling. Remove from heat; add corn syrup and chocolate chips. Cover and let stand 5 minutes. Stir until smooth. Pour glaze over chilled mousse and spread to cover completely. Return to refrigerator for at least 1 hour.

5. Run a small knife around inside of pan and lift out brownie. Heat knife under hot running water and trim edges. Slice brownie, rinsing knife after each cut, into 5 strips about 1½ inches wide. Cut each strip into 5 pieces about 1½ inches square. Transfer to a serving plate and garnish with whipped cream, nuts, candy and caramel sauce.

PER SERVING: 301 calories; 19 g fat (8 g sat.); 5 g protein; 31 g carbohydrate; 1 g fiber; 155 mg sodium; 30 mg cholesterol

Food styling: Charles Worthington. Prop styling: Sue Mitchell.

PHOTOGRAPHY BY JASON DONNELLY

dinner Rx

OUR PRESCRIPTION FOR GOOD HEALTH: DELICIOUS MEALS JAM-PACKED WITH OMEGA-3S, FIBER AND VITAMINS. BY COOKING WITH SUPERFOODS (THINK SPINACH, LENTILS AND WALNUTS), YOU CAN FIGHT DISEASE AND BOOST IMMUNITY RIGHT AT THE SUPPER TABLE. **BY CINDY HELLER**

Chicken and Soba Noodles (Recipe page 17)

PHOTOGRAPHY BY CHARLES SCHILLER

Curried Lentil Soup
(Recipe page 17)

A family favorite gets healthy with chicken breast, fat-free beans, and whole-wheat tortillas.

pork tenderloin with blueberry sauce

MAKES: 4 servings. **PREP:** 15 minutes.
ROAST: at 400° for 25 minutes.
COOK: 8 minutes.

- 1 pork tenderloin (about 1¼ pounds)
- 2 teaspoons sodium-free chicken grilling blend (such as Mrs. Dash)
- ½ teaspoon salt
- ½ teaspoon black pepper
- 12 ounces green beans, ends trimmed
- 1 tablespoon olive oil
- 1 small onion, chopped
- 1½ cups frozen blueberries, thawed
- ¼ cup cider vinegar
- 1 teaspoon sugar
- ½ teaspoon dried thyme

1. Heat oven to 400°. Rub pork with chicken seasoning and ¼ teaspoon each salt and pepper and place in a roasting pan. Roast at 400° for 25 minutes, until internal temperature registers 155°.
2. When 10 minutes of cooking time remain, remove pan and spread green beans around pork; drizzle with ½ tablespoon olive oil. Stir beans and return pan to oven.
3. Heat remaining ½ tablespoon olive oil in a small saucepan over medium-high heat. Cook onion 3 minutes. Add blueberries, vinegar, sugar, thyme and remaining ¼ teaspoon each salt and pepper to saucepan; cook for 5 minutes or until thickened. Serve pork with sauce.

PER SERVING: 269 calories; 9 g fat (2 g sat.); 32 g protein; 16 g carbohydrate; 5 g fiber; 368 mg sodium; 92 mg cholesterol

mushroom and chicken quesadillas

MAKES: 4 servings. **PREP:** 15 minutes.
COOK: 28 minutes.

- 1 pound chicken breast tenders
- 1 package (8 ounces) sliced mushrooms
- 4 8-inch whole-wheat tortillas
- 1 cup canned fat-free refried beans
- 1 cup reduced-fat shredded Mexican-blend cheese
- ½ cup prepared salsa

1. Fill a large skillet halfway with water; bring to a boil. Poach chicken 7 minutes or until cooked through. Let cool, then shred with two forks.
2. Remove skillet from heat and wipe clean. Coat skillet generously with nonstick cooking spray and place over medium-high heat. Cook mushrooms 5 minutes, stirring occasionally, or until softened.
3. Spread all 4 tortillas with ¼ cup refried beans. Divide cheese, chicken and mushrooms between 2 of the tortillas. Place remaining 2 tortillas on top, bean-side down.
4. Return skillet to medium-high heat. Coat skillet and tops of quesadillas with nonstick cooking spray. Cook one quesadilla 4 minutes per side or until cheese has melted, reducing heat to medium if tortilla becomes too brown. Repeat with remaining quesadilla. Cut both quesadillas in half and serve with salsa.

PER SERVING: 354 calories; 9 g fat (3 g sat.); 42 g protein; 26 g carbohydrate; 6 g fiber; 841 mg sodium; 86 mg cholesterol

Walnuts have the highest omega-3 content of all nuts—and they make a delicious crunchy crust on this fish.

walnut-crusted tilapia

MAKES: 4 servings. **PREP:** 15 minutes.
BAKE: at 425° for 15 minutes.
COOK: 11 minutes.

- ¾ cup chopped walnuts
- 1 tablespoon light mayonnaise
- 3 tablespoons Dijon mustard
- 4 tilapia fillets (about 6 ounces each)
- 1 teaspoon dried basil
- ¼ teaspoon salt
- ¼ teaspoon black pepper
- 1 tablespoon olive oil
- 1 small onion, chopped
- 2 bunches Swiss chard, stems removed and leaves cut into 1-inch pieces

1. Heat oven to 425°. Coat a baking sheet with nonstick cooking spray. In a small skillet over medium-high heat, toast ¼ cup walnuts for 5 minutes.

2. Stir together mayonnaise and 1 tablespoon of the mustard. Finely chop remaining ½ cup walnuts. Brush tilapia with mustard mixture, then sprinkle with ½ teaspoon basil and ⅛ teaspoon each salt and pepper. Press 2 tablespoons chopped walnuts onto one side of each fillet.

3. Place tilapia, walnut-side up, on baking sheet; bake at 425° for 15 minutes or until fish flakes easily.

4. Heat oil in a large skillet over medium-high heat. Add onion; cook 4 minutes. Stir in Swiss chard, remaining ½ teaspoon basil and ⅛ teaspoon each salt and pepper; cover. Cook, stirring, for 7 minutes or until tender. Add ¼ **cup water** if pan becomes dry. Stir in walnuts and remaining 2 tablespoons mustard.

PER SERVING: 404 calories; 21 g fat (2 g sat.); 44 g protein; 12 g carbohydrate; 2 g fiber; 569 mg sodium; 86 mg cholesterol

Spinach is rich in vitamin A, which promotes good cardiovascular health. Its iron content is better absorbed when paired with vitamin C, found in the fresh orange pieces in this salad.

scallop and orange salad

MAKES: 4 servings. **PREP:** 15 minutes.
COOK: 9 minutes.

- 2 small oranges
- 1 tablespoon olive oil
- 2 teaspoons low-sodium soy sauce
- 1 teaspoon honey
- ½ teaspoon salt
- ½ teaspoon black pepper
- ⅓ cup chopped walnuts
- 1 pound sea scallops
- 1 small red onion, thinly sliced
- 1 bag (6 ounces) baby spinach

1. Grate zest from 1 orange into a small bowl. Cut peel from both oranges and slice flesh into segments; set aside. Squeeze juice from membranes into bowl with zest. Whisk in ½ tablespoon olive oil, soy sauce, honey and ¼ teaspoon each salt and pepper.
2. Heat a large nonstick skillet over medium-high heat. Toast walnuts for 5 minutes or until fragrant; remove from heat.
3. Heat remaining ½ tablespoon olive oil in skillet over medium-high heat. Season scallops with remaining ¼ teaspoon each salt and pepper. Saute 3 to 4 minutes per side. Remove from skillet; keep warm.
4. Toss orange segments, walnuts, red onion and spinach with dressing. Place 1½ cups salad on each plate and top with scallops.

PER SERVING: 256 calories; 10 g fat (1 g sat.); 24 g protein; 19 g carbohydrate; 5 g fiber; 607 mg sodium; 37 mg cholesterol

chicken and soba noodles

MAKES: 6 servings. **PREP:** 10 minutes.
COOK: 8 minutes.

- 3 tablespoons low-sodium soy sauce
- 2 tablespoons rice vinegar
- 1 tablespoon sesame oil
- 2 teaspoons grated fresh ginger
- 2 teaspoons sugar
- 1 teaspoon lime juice
- ¼ teaspoon hot sauce (such as Tabasco)
- 1 pound boneless, skinless, thinly sliced chicken breasts
- 1 package (8.8 ounces) soba noodles
- 3 cups broccoli florets
- 1 small sweet red pepper, thinly sliced
- 1 tablespoon sesame seeds (optional)

1. In a small bowl, whisk together soy sauce, rice vinegar, sesame oil, ginger, sugar, lime juice and hot sauce.
2. Fill a large skillet halfway with water and bring to a boil over medium-high heat. Add chicken and cook 4 minutes or until cooked through; set aside. When cool enough to handle, shred chicken using two forks and place pieces in a large serving bowl.
3. Bring a large pot of lightly salted water to a boil. Cook noodles following package directions. Add broccoli florets to pot for final 4 minutes of cooking time. Drain noodles and rinse with cold water.
4. Place noodle mixture and red pepper in serving bowl with chicken. Drizzle soy sauce mixture on top and toss well to coat. Sprinkle sesame seeds on top, if desired, and serve at room temperature or cold.

PER SERVING: 267 calories; 4 g fat (1 g sat.); 25 g protein; 36 g carbohydrate; 1 g fiber; 585 mg sodium; 44 mg cholesterol

curried lentil soup

MAKES: 4 servings. **PREP:** 10 minutes.
COOK: 55 minutes.

- 1 tablespoon olive oil
- 1 large onion, chopped
- 1 large carrot, peeled and chopped
- 2 teaspoons curry powder
- 1 can (14.5 ounces) diced tomatoes, drained
- 1 cup dried lentils, picked over
- 4½ cups low-sodium chicken broth
- 1 cup water
- ½ teaspoon black pepper
- ¼ teaspoon salt
- 1 bunch (about ¾ pound) fresh kale, rinsed, tough stems removed, leaves coarsely chopped (about 8 cups)
- ¼ cup 2% Greek yogurt

1. Heat olive oil in a large pot over medium-high heat. Cook onion and carrot, stirring occasionally, 5 minutes. Stir in curry powder and cook 1 minute more.
2. Add tomatoes, lentils, broth, water and ¼ teaspoon pepper to pot. Bring to a boil, then partially cover. Reduce heat to medium-low and simmer for 45 minutes or until lentils are tender.
3. In batches, puree soup in a blender until smooth; return to pot and gently reheat. Stir in remaining ¼ teaspoon pepper, salt and kale. Cook 5 minutes or until kale is wilted and tender. Dollop each serving with 1 tablespoon yogurt.

PER SERVING: 314 calories; 4 g fat (1 g sat.); 22 g protein; 50 g carbohydrate; 11 g fiber; 1,028 mg sodium; 7 mg cholesterol

mac 'n' cheese please

SIX NEW COMBOS THAT ARE FAST ENOUGH FOR WEEKNIGHTS AND WILL HAVE EVERYONE FIGHTING OVER THE SERVING SPOON. **BY JULIE MILTENBERGER**

Instead of the usual bread crumbs, panko provides a lighter, crispier topping.

PHOTOGRAPHY BY LUCY SCHAEFFER

smoky mac and cheese

MAKES: 8 servings. **PREP:** 10 minutes. **COOK:** 7 minutes. **MICROWAVE:** 3 minutes at 50% power.

- 8 ounces shell macaroni or mini wheels
- 8 ounces mild Cheddar cheese, shredded
- 6 slices American cheese
- ¼ to ½ teaspoon mesquite flavoring
- 1 teaspoon smoked paprika
- 1½ teaspoons smoked sweet pepper seasoning blend (such as McCormick)
- ½ to 1 cup 2% milk
- 6 slices hickory-smoked bacon, crisply fried and broken into pieces

1. Cook macaroni in large pot of lightly salted water according to package directions. Drain and put in large baking dish.

2. Mix in Cheddar cheese, American cheese, mesquite flavoring, paprika and sweet pepper seasoning blend. Stir until cheese melts, adding milk for desired creaminess.

3. Sprinkle bacon on top. Cover and vent in the corners. Microwave 3 minutes at 50% power. Serve warm.

PER SERVING: 397 calories; 20 g fat (13 g sat.); 20 g protein; 33 g carbohydrate; 2 g fiber; 690 mg sodium; 67 mg cholesterol

READER RECIPE

"I made this for our church carry-in dinner. It was a big hit."

Ruthanne Kiozel
Spring Hill, FL

four-cheese classic mac

MAKES: 12 servings. **PREP:** 10 minutes. **COOK:** 14 minutes. **BROIL:** 3 minutes.

- 1 box (16 ounces) cavatappi or cellentani (corkscrew-shaped pasta)
- 3 tablespoons plus 1 teaspoon unsalted butter
- 3 tablespoons all-purpose flour
- 2½ cups 2% milk
- 1 teaspoon onion powder
- ½ teaspoon salt
- ¼ teaspoon black pepper
- 8 ounces Gouda cheese, grated
- 4 ounces sharp Cheddar cheese, grated
- 4 ounces Swiss cheese, grated
- ½ cup grated Parmesan cheese
- ⅔ cup plain panko bread crumbs
  Chopped fresh parsley (optional)

1. Heat broiler. Coat a 9 × 9-inch broiler-safe baking dish or six 1-cup ramekins with nonstick cooking spray. Bring a large pot of lightly salted water to a boil. Add pasta and cook 11 minutes, following package directions. Drain and transfer to bowl.

2. Heat 3 tablespoons of the butter in a medium-size saucepan over medium heat until melted. Add flour, whisking to blend. Gradually add milk; whisk until smooth. Bring to a simmer over medium to medium-high heat, stirring, then add onion powder, salt and pepper. Simmer 3 minutes, then remove from heat.

3. Stir in Gouda, Cheddar, Swiss and ¼ cup of the Parmesan until cheeses are melted and sauce is smooth. Mix into cooked pasta and pour mixture into prepared dish(es).

4. In medium-size microwave-safe bowl, melt remaining 1 teaspoon butter. Stir in panko and remaining ¼ cup Parmesan. Divide evenly over pasta. Broil 3 minutes or until browned. Garnish with parsley, if desired.

PER SERVING: 448 calories; 20 g fat (12 g sat.); 22 g protein; 45 g carbohydrate; 2 g fiber; 525 mg sodium; 66 mg cholesterol

This rich and creamy dish made with truffle oil and wild mushrooms is fancy enough for company.

reduced-fat mac

MAKES: 6 servings. **PREP:** 5 minutes.
COOK: 13 minutes.

1 box (13.25 ounces) whole-grain penne pasta
4 cups broccoli florets (about 2 stalks)
1 cup skim milk
1 tablespoon all-purpose flour
1 teaspoon Dijon mustard
½ teaspoon salt
¼ teaspoon black pepper
  Pinch cayenne pepper
8 ounces 2% sharp Cheddar cheese, grated (2 cups)

1. Heat large pot of lightly salted water to boiling. Add pasta and cook 6 minutes. Add broccoli and cook an additional 4 minutes. Drain.
2. Meanwhile, whisk milk and flour together in a small saucepan. Bring to a simmer over medium heat, then simmer 3 minutes, until thickened. Remove from heat and whisk in mustard, salt, pepper and cayenne.
3. Add grated Cheddar, whisking constantly until melted. Transfer pasta and broccoli to serving bowl. Pour cheese sauce over pasta-broccoli mixture and stir until coated.

PER SERVING: 294 calories; 8 g fat (4 g sat.); 18 g protein; 37 g carbohydrate; 4 g fiber; 449 mg sodium; 21 mg cholesterol

penne with fontina and mushrooms

MAKES: 6 servings. **PREP:** 10 minutes. **COOK:** 20 minutes. **BAKE:** at 350° for 20 minutes.

1 box (16 ounces) calcium-and-fiber-fortified penne pasta (such as Ronzoni)
4 teaspoons olive oil flavored with white truffles or herbs
1 package (4 ounces) assorted sliced wild mushrooms
12 ounces Fontina cheese (rind discarded), cubed
½ package (4 ounces) cream cheese, cut into chunks
½ cup milk
½ teaspoon salt
⅛ teaspoon black pepper
  Pinch ground nutmeg
1 teaspoon unsalted butter
2 ounces (about 2 slices) Italian bread

1. Heat oven to 350°. Coat a 2-quart baking dish with nonstick cooking spray. Heat large pot of lightly salted water to boiling. Add pasta and cook 11 minutes, according to package directions.

2. Meanwhile, heat 3 teaspoons of the oil in a 10-inch nonstick skillet over medium-high heat. Add mushrooms and cook 4 minutes. Pour into large bowl; drain pasta and add to same bowl.
3. Combine Fontina, cream cheese and milk in the pasta pot over medium to medium-high heat. Cook 3 to 5 minutes, until cheeses are melted and sauce is smooth. Stir in salt, pepper and nutmeg. Remove from heat; pour into bowl with mushrooms and pasta. Stir to combine, then pour into prepared baking dish.
4. Melt butter and remaining 1 teaspoon oil in mushroom skillet over medium-high heat. Pulse bread in food processor until crumbs are formed. Add crumbs (about 1 cup) to butter mixture in skillet. Cook 2 minutes, stirring, until crumbs are just browned. Sprinkle over pasta. Bake at 350° for 20 minutes. Serve warm.

PER SERVING: 453 calories; 23 g fat (12 g sat.); 20 g protein; 49 g carbohydrate; 6 g fiber; 581 mg sodium; 68 mg cholesterol

cheesy meximac

MAKES: 10 servings. **PREP:** 10 minutes. **COOK:** 11 minutes. **BAKE:** at 350° for 25 minutes.

1 box (16 ounces) rotini pasta
2 scallions, trimmed and sliced
1 tablespoon unsalted butter
1 tablespoon all-purpose flour
1½ cups milk
¼ teaspoon salt
⅛ teaspoon black pepper
16 ounces Pepper-Jack cheese, grated
1 can (10 ounces) Mexican-flavored corn, drained
Pinch chili powder

1. Heat oven to 350°. Coat an 11×7×2-inch baking pan with nonstick cooking spray. Bring large pot of lightly salted water to a boil. Add rotini and cook 5 minutes. Add scallions and cook an additional 2 minutes. Drain and set aside.

2. In a medium-size saucepan, melt butter over medium heat. Whisk in flour until smooth. Gradually add milk, whisking constantly, until smooth. Stir in salt and pepper; bring to a simmer. Cook, simmering, 4 minutes. Remove from heat.

3. Add half of the grated cheese to milk mixture; whisk until smooth. Stir in corn, then combine in large bowl with pasta and scallions. Pour half into prepared dish; top with half of remaining cheese. Repeat, ending with cheese.

4. Bake at 350° for 25 minutes. Cool slightly before serving.

PER SERVING: 401 calories; 17 g fat (10 g sat.); 18 g protein; 43 g carbohydrate; 2 g fiber; 507 mg sodium; 55 mg cholesterol

kiddie mac 'n' cheese

MAKES: 8 servings. **PREP:** 5 minutes. **COOK:** 12 minutes.

1 box (16 ounces) small macaroni or shells
1 cup milk
8 ounces sliced American cheese, cut up
1 cup shredded Cheddar cheese
Pinch salt

1. Heat large pot of lightly salted water to boiling. Add pasta and cook 11 minutes, according to package directions. Drain.

2. Add milk to pasta pot and heat over medium heat. Sprinkle in American and Cheddar cheeses and the salt and whisk until melted and smooth.

3. Return macaroni to pot with cheese sauce and stir to combine. Serve warm.

PER SERVING: 388 calories; 14 g fat (8 g sat.); 18 g protein; 47 g carbohydrate; 2 g fiber; 379 mg sodium; 36 mg cholesterol

slow-cooker solutions

GREAT-TASTING RECIPES FOR EFFORTLESS MEALS. **BY CINDY HELLER**

Food styling: Toni Brogan. Prop styling: Deborah Williams.

barbecue chili

MAKES: 6 servings. **PREP:** 10 minutes. **SLOW COOK:** 4½ hours on HIGH or 6½ hours on LOW.

- 2 cans (15.5 ounces each) kidney beans, rinsed and drained
- 2 cans (15.5 ounces each) pinto beans, rinsed and drained
- 1 large onion, chopped
- 1 green bell pepper, chopped
- 3 tablespoons chili powder
- 1 tablespoon ground cumin
- 1 can (14.5 ounces) diced tomatoes with jalapeños, drained
- ⅓ cup low-sodium chicken broth
- 1½ cups frozen corn, thawed
- 1 bag (12 ounces) frozen meatless soy crumbles

- ¾ cup barbecue sauce
  Fresh cilantro leaves, shredded cheese and reduced-fat sour cream, for serving (optional)

1. Stir together kidney and pinto beans, onion, green pepper, chili powder, cumin, diced tomatoes and broth in slow cooker bowl. Cover and cook on HIGH for 4 hours or LOW for 6 hours.

2. Remove cover and mash beans gently with a potato masher until liquid has thickened slightly. Stir in corn, meat crumbles and barbecue sauce and cook

an additional 30 minutes or until heated through. Top with cilantro, cheese and sour cream, if desired. Serve immediately.

PER SERVING 360 calories; 5 g fat (1 g sat.); 22 g protein; 59 g carbohydrate; 16 g fiber; 923 mg sodium; 0 mg cholesterol

PHOTOGRAPHY BY TINA RUPP

chicken and bean stew

MAKES: 6 servings. **PREP:** 15 minutes.
SLOW COOK: 3½ hours on HIGH or 5½ hours on LOW.

- 1 **pound boneless, skinless chicken thighs, trimmed**
- 1 **large onion, sliced**
- 1 **can (14.5 ounces) diced tomatoes with peppers, celery and onions (such as Hunt's), drained**
- ¾ **cup low-sodium chicken broth**
- ⅛ **teaspoon cayenne**
- ½ **teaspoon salt**
- ½ **teaspoon black pepper**
- ¾ **cup frozen corn**
- ¾ **cup frozen lima beans**
- 1 **tablespoon Dijon mustard**
- 4 **cups prepared mashed potatoes (optional)**

1. Stir together chicken, onion, tomatoes, broth, cayenne and ¼ teaspoon each salt and pepper in slow cooker bowl. Cover and cook on HIGH for 3 hours or LOW for 5 hours.
2. Remove chicken from slow cooker and cut into 1-inch pieces. Return chicken to slow cooker and stir in remaining ¼ teaspoon each salt and pepper, frozen corn and lima beans (no need to thaw) and the mustard. Cook 30 minutes more.
3. Serve with mashed potatoes, if desired.

PER SERVING: 158 calories; 4 g fat (1 g sat.); 17 g protein; 12 g carbohydrate; 3 g fiber; 588 mg sodium; 74 mg cholesterol

beef with mushrooms and red wine

MAKES: 4 servings. **PREP:** 15 minutes. **COOK:** 13 minutes. **SLOW COOK:** 5½ hours on HIGH or 7½ hours on LOW.

- 1 **tablespoon olive oil**
- 1 **pound chuck steak (1 inch thick), trimmed and cut into 1-inch pieces**
- 1 **package (10 ounces) cremini mushrooms, cleaned and quartered**
- 2 **cloves garlic, chopped**
- ½ **teaspoon salt**
- ½ **teaspoon black pepper**
- 2 **tablespoons tomato paste**
- 3 **tablespoons all-purpose flour**
- 1 **package (1 pound) frozen pearl onions**
- 1½ **cups low-sodium beef broth**
- ¾ **cup dry red wine**
- ¾ **teaspoon dried thyme**
- 8 **ounces green beans, trimmed**
- 6 **ounces cholesterol-free egg noodles, cooked (optional)**

1. Heat oil in a large nonstick skillet over medium-high heat. Add steak to skillet and cook 5 minutes, stirring occasionally, until browned. Remove with a slotted spoon to slow cooker bowl.
2. Add mushrooms and garlic to skillet and sprinkle with ¼ teaspoon each salt and pepper. Cook, stirring occasionally, 5 minutes. Stir in tomato paste and cook, stirring, 2 minutes. Add flour and cook, stirring constantly, 1 minute.
3. Scrape contents of skillet into slow cooker bowl with beef. Stir in onions, broth, red wine and ½ teaspoon of the thyme. Cover and cook on HIGH for 5 hours or LOW for 7 hours.
4. Remove lid and stir in remaining ¼ teaspoon each salt and pepper, ¼ teaspoon dried thyme and green beans. Cover and cook an additional 30 minutes. Serve on top of egg noodles, if desired.

PER SERVING: 383 calories; 16 g fat (5 g sat.); 28 g protein; 23 g carbohydrate; 4 g fiber; 420 mg sodium; 75 mg cholesterol

chicken with cashews

MAKES: 6 servings. **PREP:** 15 minutes.
SLOW COOK: 3½ hours on HIGH or 5½ hours on LOW.

- 1 **pound boneless, skinless chicken breasts, cut into 1-inch chunks**
- 2 **cups baby carrots**
- ½ **cup low-sodium chicken broth**
- 4 **tablespoons ginger-flavored soy sauce (such as House of Tsang) or regular low-sodium soy sauce**
- 8 **ounces snow peas, trimmed**
- 2 **cans (8 ounces each) pineapple tidbits, drained, and 2 tablespoons juice reserved**
- 1 **sweet red pepper, seeded and thinly sliced**
- 3 **tablespoons cornstarch**
- ½ **cup roasted cashews**
- 3 **cups cooked brown rice (optional)**

1. Stir together chicken, carrots, broth and 2 tablespoons soy sauce in slow cooker bowl. Cover and cook for 3 hours on HIGH or 5 hours on LOW.
2. Remove cover and stir in snow peas, pineapple and red pepper and cook an additional 20 minutes.
3. In small bowl, stir together remaining 2 tablespoons soy sauce, 2 tablespoons pineapple juice and cornstarch. Stir into liquid in slow cooker bowl. Stir in cashews and cook an additional 10 minutes or until liquid has thickened. Serve over rice, if desired.

PER SERVING 249 calories; 7 g fat (1 g sat.); 22 g protein; 23 g carbohydrate; 3 g fiber; 366 mg sodium; 44 mg cholesterol

cajun pork sandwiches

MAKES: 8 servings. **PREP:** 15 minutes. **SLOW COOK:** 6 hours on HIGH or 8 hours on LOW.
COOK: 1 minute.

- 1 **boneless pork butt or shoulder (about 2½ pounds), trimmed**
- 1½ **tablespoons sodium-free steak seasoning blend (such as Mrs. Dash)**
- 1 **large onion, chopped**
- 3 **ribs celery, sliced**
- ¼ **cup plus 2 tablespoons red wine vinegar**
- 2 **tablespoons cornstarch**
- 2½ **tablespoons Cajun seasoning blend (such as McCormick)**
- 6 **tablespoons light mayonnaise**
- 6 **whole-wheat hamburger buns**

1. Rub pork with steak seasoning.
2. Place pork in slow cooker bowl. Scatter onion and celery around pork and pour ¼ cup of the vinegar over top. Cover and cook on HIGH for 6 hours or LOW for 8 hours.
3. Remove pork from slow cooker and cut into chunks. Let stand until cool enough to handle.
4. While pork is cooling, strain contents of slow cooker over a fat separator, setting vegetables aside. Pour defatted liquid into a small saucepan.
5. In a small bowl, stir together remaining 2 tablespoons vinegar with cornstarch. Bring defatted liquid to a boil over medium-high heat. Whisk in vinegar mixture and 1 tablespoon of the Cajun seasoning. Boil 1 minute, or until thickened.
6. Using two forks or your hands, pull pork into shreds, discarding excess fat. Place meat in a bowl and stir in vegetables. Add thickened liquid and toss to combine.
7. Stir together remaining 1½ tablespoons Cajun seasoning and mayonnaise. To serve, place ½ cup pork mixture on each bun and top with 1 tablespoon spiced mayo.

PER SERVING: 329 calories; 13 g fat (4 g sat.); 30 g protein; 22 g carbohydrate; 3 g fiber; 856 mg sodium; 89 mg cholesterol

mediterranean pork roast

MAKES: 8 servings. **PREP:** 15 minutes.
SLOW COOK: 3 hours on HIGH or 6 hours on LOW. **COOK:** 1 minute.

- 2 **fennel bulbs, trimmed and sliced**
- 1 **boneless pork loin roast (about 3 pounds), trimmed**
- 4 **teaspoons Greek seasoning mix (such as McCormick)**
- 4 **plum tomatoes, chopped**
- ⅓ **cup plus 2 tablespoons low-sodium chicken broth**
- ¾ **teaspoon salt**
- ½ **teaspoon black pepper**
- 2 **tablespoons cornstarch**
- 1½ **teaspoons Worcestershire sauce**
- ¼ **cup chopped black olives (optional)**

1. Place fennel in slow cooker bowl. Rub pork with 1 teaspoon of the Greek seasoning and place in bowl on top of fennel.

2. Scatter tomatoes around pork. Pour ⅓ cup of the broth in bowl; top with 2 teaspoons Greek seasoning, ½ teaspoon of the salt and ¼ teaspoon of the pepper. Cook 3 hours on HIGH or 6 hours on LOW.

3. Blend remaining 2 tablespoons broth, the cornstarch and Worcestershire. Remove pork to a serving platter; keep warm. Strain liquid from slow cooker into a small saucepan; place vegetables around pork.

4. Bring liquid to a boil over medium-high heat. Whisk in cornstarch mixture, remaining 1 teaspoon Greek seasoning and ¼ teaspoon each salt and black pepper; cook 1 minute. Spoon sauce over pork. Sprinkle with olives, if desired.

PER SERVING: 241 calories; 6 g fat (2 g sat.); 37 g protein; 8 g carbohydrate; 3 g fiber; 390 mg sodium; 111 mg cholesterol

EASY PREP Not sure how to trim fennel? Here's a quick rundown on the easiest way to slice and dice it.

1. Cut stalks and fronds off fennel bulbs. (Reserve fronds for garnish.)

2. Using tip of knife, cut through bottom of bulb to remove the conelike core.

3. Cut bulb in half from top to bottom.

4. Cut halves into wedges or slices.

You know you can depend on this go-to appliance for easy suppers, but a slow cooker can also help you save at the supermarket. These hearty dinners top out at $5 a serving.

food **university**

THIS BASIC TOMATO SAUCE IS THE CULINARY EQUIVALENT OF THE LITTLE BLACK DRESS. IT'S ALWAYS IN STYLE—AND IN SEASON, AS IT MAKES PERFECTLY DELICIOUS USE OF CANNED TOMATOES. **BY JULIE MILTENBERGER**

All this yummy comfort-food dish needs is a dusting of freshly grated Parmesan.

basic marinara

MAKES: 4 cups. **PREP:** 5 minutes. **COOK:** 30 minutes.

- 2 tablespoons olive oil
- 1 medium-size onion, peeled and chopped
- 2 cloves garlic, peeled and chopped
- 1 can (28 ounces) whole tomatoes
- 1 can (8 ounces) no-salt-added tomato sauce
- 1 teaspoon Italian seasoning (or ½ teaspoon dried oregano plus ½ teaspoon dried basil)
- 1 teaspoon sugar
- ½ teaspoon salt
- ¼ teaspoon black pepper
- 1 pound spaghetti

PER 1 CUP MARINARA: 148 calories; 7 g fat (1 g sat.); 3 g protein; 17 g carbohydrate; 3 g fiber; 690 mg sodium; 0 mg cholesterol

Variations: If you prefer a sugar-free version, replace the 1 teaspoon sugar with ¼ cup peeled, chopped carrot stirred into the oil along with onion and garlic. For a spicier sauce, add ¼ teaspoon red pepper flakes before simmering. For a meaty take, cook 1 pound lean ground beef or pork along with onion and garlic.

1. Heat oil in medium-size saucepan over medium-low heat. Add onion and garlic and cook, stirring occasionally, 10 minutes.

2. Add tomatoes and their liquid, tomato sauce, dried herbs, sugar, salt and pepper. Using clean kitchen scissors, cut tomatoes into bite-size chunks in pan (see second illustration).

3. Bring sauce to a simmer over medium-high heat, then reduce heat to medium and simmer 20 minutes (see last illustration). Meanwhile, in large pot of lightly salted water, cook spaghetti according to package directions. Drain pasta and serve topped with marinara sauce.

Chop garlic cloves into equal-size pieces so they cook evenly and don't burn.

Keep your hands clean by using kitchen scissors to cut canned tomatoes into bite-sized chunks.

Gently simmer sauce for 20 minutes over medium heat. If it boils vigorously, sauce may stick to the pan.

february

Ice-Cream Cake Roll
page 33

GET MORE DELICIOUS FISH IN YOUR DIET
WITH OUR FRESH CATCHES, THEN GIVE
YOUR SWEET TOOTH (AND YOUR SWEETIE)
A SUMPTUOUS CHOCOLATE TREAT.

Oreos 'n' Cream Cake
page 31

Turkey Cheeseburgers
page 46

**Teriyaki Tuna
and Soba Noodles**
page 43

HAVE YOUR CAKE—AND A FEW COOKIES, TOO.
BY KAREN TACK

oreos 'n' cream cake
MAKES: 16 servings. **PREP:** 20 minutes. **BAKE:** at 350° for 36 minutes. **CHILL:** 20 minutes.

Cake:
- 1¾ cups all-purpose flour
- ⅔ cup Dutch-process cocoa powder
- 1½ teaspoons baking soda
- ½ teaspoon baking powder
- ½ teaspoon salt
- ¾ cup (1½ sticks) unsalted butter, softened
- 1½ cups granulated sugar
- 1 teaspoon vanilla extract
- 3 large eggs, at room temperature
- 1¼ cups buttermilk

Filling:
- 4 ounces cream cheese, softened
- ½ cup (1 stick) unsalted butter, softened
- 1 box (16 ounces) confectioners' sugar
- 3 to 4 tablespoons milk

Frosting:
- 1½ cups heavy cream
- ¼ cup granulated sugar
- 1 teaspoon vanilla extract
- 3 cups crushed Oreos

1. Heat oven to 350°. Coat two 8-inch round cake pans with nonstick cooking spray and dust with flour; shake out any excess flour.

2. Cake: In a medium-size bowl, mix flour, cocoa powder, baking soda, baking powder and salt together until well blended; set aside.

3. In a large bowl, with mixer on medium speed, beat butter, sugar and vanilla for 3 minutes or until light and fluffy. Add eggs, one at a time, beating well after each addition.

4. On low speed, beat flour mixture into butter mixture in three additions, alternating with buttermilk, beginning and ending with flour; beat 1 minute. Divide batter evenly between prepared pans. Bake at 350° for about 36 minutes or until toothpick inserted in centers comes out clean. Cool cakes in pans on wire racks for 10 minutes. Turn cakes out onto racks; let cool completely.

5. Filling: In a large bowl, with mixer on medium speed, beat cream cheese and butter until smooth. Gradually add confectioners' sugar, then milk. Beat for 2 minutes or until light and fluffy.

6. When layers have cooled, trim off any crowned cake from the tops and discard. Cut each layer in half horizontally with a serrated knife. Place one cut layer on a cake stand and top with one-third of filling; spread evenly over top. Repeat with 2 more cake layers. Place last layer on top, cut side down. Refrigerate for 20 minutes or until filling is set.

7. Frosting: In a large bowl, with mixer on high, beat heavy cream, sugar and vanilla until soft peaks form. Generously spread whipped cream all over cake, using the back of a spoon to make swirls and peaks on top. Place chopped cookies in a large bowl and carefully hold cake stand over bowl. With cupped hands, gently press cookie crumbs onto the sides of the cake to cover. Brush excess crumbs off stand before serving.

PER SERVING: 551 calories; 29 g fat (17 g sat.); 5 g protein; 71 g carbohydrate; 2 g fiber; 323 mg sodium; 117 mg cholesterol

Oreo is a registered trademark of Kraft and is used with permission.

Food styling: Karen Tack. Prop styling: Leslie Siegel.

PHOTOGRAPHY BY RITA MAAS

how
sweet
it is

WE DARE ANYONE TO EVEN TRY TO
RESIST THESE CHOCOLATE DESSERTS.
THEY'RE PERFECT FOR VALENTINE'S
DAY— OR ANY OF THE OTHER 364.

BY CINDY HELLER

PHOTOGRAPHY BY TINA RUPP

These recipes celebrate chocolate in all of its fabulous forms—from an all-in-one frozen Ice-Cream Cake Roll to warm and gooey Chocolate-Marshmallow Sandwiches.

ice-cream cake roll

MAKES: 10 servings. **PREP:** 20 minutes.
BAKE: at 350° for 12 minutes.
FREEZE: 4 hours.

- ¾ cup all-purpose flour
- ⅓ cup cocoa powder
- 1 teaspoon baking powder
  Pinch salt
- 4 eggs
- ¾ cup granulated sugar
- 2 teaspoons vanilla extract
- 2 tablespoons confectioners' sugar
- 3 cups mint chip ice cream, softened
  Chocolate syrup, for serving

1. Heat oven to 350°. Coat a 15 × 10 × 1-inch jelly-roll pan with nonstick cooking spray. Line bottom of pan with waxed paper. Spray paper.

2. Stir together flour, cocoa powder, baking powder and salt. In a large bowl, beat eggs with an electric mixer on medium speed for 5 minutes, until very light yellow. Gradually add granulated sugar, beating until smooth. Beat in vanilla extract.

3. Fold flour mixture into egg mixture until no lumps remain. Pour into prepared pan, spreading level. Bake at 350° for 12 minutes or until cake springs back when lightly touched.

4. Dust a clean kitchen towel with confectioners' sugar. Turn cake out onto towel. Roll up towel and cake from short end; cool completely.

5. Unroll; spread with softened ice cream to within 1 inch of edges. Reroll cake without towel; wrap in plastic wrap. Freeze at least 4 hours or overnight. If frozen overnight, let stand at room temperature 20 minutes before serving. To serve, carefully remove plastic wrap and drizzle cake with chocolate syrup.

PER SERVING: 316 calories; 14 g fat (8 g sat.); 7 g protein; 41 g carbohydrate; 2 g fiber; 120 mg sodium; 148 mg cholesterol

the lowdown on chocolate

Can't decide what type of chocolate to fall in love with? Well, we've simplified things for you. It's the variety of cocoa beans, the amount of cocoa solids (which make it taste "chocolatey") and the types of additives that affect the final flavor.

white chocolate: Not technically chocolate, as it contains no solid cocoa content. Made from cocoa butter, sugar, milk and vanilla, it's creamy and sweet.

dark chocolate: Mildly sweet chocolate with a high amount of cocoa solids and little or no milk solids. Comes in varying intensities.

milk chocolate: A variety that contains 10% to 20% cocoa solids, 12% milk solids and a moderate amount of sugar.

bittersweet: Containing 60% to 85% cocoa solids and a very low sugar content, this one's for serious chocoholics!

unsweetened: Contains almost 100% cocoa solids. This chocolate is for baking, not snacking, as it is very bitter.

semisweet: The classic baking chocolate found in grocery stores in chips or bar form. Often contains 40% to 60% cocoa solids.

chocolate-walnut turnovers

MAKES: 18 turnovers. **PREP:** 15 minutes. **BAKE:** at 400° for 14 minutes.

- 2 eggs
- ½ cup part-skim ricotta cheese
- ⅓ cup plus 1 tablespoon granulated sugar
- 2 teaspoons vanilla extract
- 1 tablespoon cocoa powder
- 1 tablespoon all-purpose flour
- 2 ounces semisweet chocolate, finely chopped
- ⅔ cup chopped walnuts
- 1 package (17.3 ounces) puff pastry sheets, thawed
  Confectioners' sugar, for dusting

1. Heat oven to 400°. In small bowl, whisk together 1 egg and **1 tablespoon water;** set aside.

2. In large bowl, mix ricotta, ⅓ cup of the sugar, vanilla and remaining egg. Stir in cocoa powder and flour, then chocolate and walnuts.

3. On a lightly floured surface, roll out puff pastry sheets into 12-inch squares. With a sharp knife, cut each sheet into 9 equal squares (each 4 inches per side).

4. Spoon 1½ tablespoons chocolate-walnut filling into the center of one square. Brush edges with egg mixture; fold in half diagonally to form a triangle. Press well to seal edges; transfer to an ungreased baking sheet. Repeat with remaining pastry squares and filling.

5. Brush tops with egg mixture and sprinkle with remaining 1 tablespoon sugar. Bake at 400° for 14 minutes or until browned on top. Cool turnovers on rack. To serve, dust with confectioners' sugar.

PER TURNOVER: 100 calories; 6 g fat (2 g sat.); 3 g protein; 9 g carbohydrate; 1 g fiber; 39 mg sodium; 26 mg cholesterol

coconut-cream-filled cupcakes

MAKES: 18 cupcakes. **PREP:** 15 minutes. **BAKE:** at 350° for 17 minutes.

Cupcakes:
- 1½ cups all-purpose flour
- 1 cup unsweetened cocoa powder
- 2 teaspoons baking powder
- ½ teaspoon salt
- 1 cup plus 2 tablespoons (2¼ sticks) unsalted butter, softened
- 1½ cups granulated sugar
- 3 eggs
- ¾ cup milk

Filling and Frosting:
- ¼ cup (½ stick) unsalted butter, softened
- ¼ cup shortening
- 2 cups confectioners' sugar
- 2 tablespoons milk
- 1 tablespoon coconut extract
- 1 container (1 pound) prepared dark chocolate frosting

1. Cupcakes: Heat oven to 350°. Generously coat 18 indents in two cupcake pans with nonstick cooking spray. In a bowl, whisk together flour, cocoa powder, baking powder and salt.

2. Beat butter and sugar in a large bowl on medium speed for 2 minutes, until light and fluffy. Add eggs, one at a time, beating well after each. On low speed, add flour mixture, alternating with milk, in two additions. Divide batter among indents, ⅓ cup each.

3. Bake at 350° for 17 minutes or until toothpick inserted in centers comes out clean. Cool cupcakes in pan on rack for 10 minutes. Remove cupcakes to rack and let cool completely.

4. Filling and Frosting: Beat butter, shortening, confectioners' sugar and milk until smooth. Mix in coconut extract. Transfer cream filling to a pastry bag and fit with a small tip. Insert tip deep into cupcake and fill with cream until you can see top bulging. Spread cupcakes with prepared frosting and serve.

PER CUPCAKE: 483 calories; 27 g fat (13 g sat.); 4 g protein; 59 g carbohydrate; 2 g fiber; 224 mg sodium; 73 mg cholesterol

These decadent little cakes have a pleasant surprise inside—a creamy coconut-flavored filling.

chocolate-marshmallow sandwiches

MAKES: 4 sandwiches. **PREP:** 15 minutes. **MICROWAVE:** 1 minute. **COOK:** 16 minutes.

⅔ cup semisweet chocolate chips
4 tablespoons marshmallow creme (such as Fluff)
8 slices white bread
2 tablespoons unsalted butter, melted

1. In a glass bowl, microwave chips on 50% power for 1 minute; stir until completely melted and smooth. Let cool slightly.

2. On one piece of bread, spread 1 tablespoon chocolate. On another slice of bread, spread 1 tablespoon marshmallow creme. Join slices and brush top with a little of the melted butter. Repeat with remaining slices of bread.

3. Heat a medium-size nonstick skillet over medium heat. Place sandwich, butter-side down, in pan and brush top with butter.

4. Cook for about 2 minutes, or until golden brown. Flip and cook an additional 2 minutes. Remove from skillet and serve immediately. Repeat with remaining sandwiches.

PER SANDWICH: 383 calories; 16 g fat (9 g sat.); 7 g protein; 55 g carbohydrate; 2 g fiber; 409 mg sodium; 15 mg cholesterol

raspberry-chocolate fondue

MAKES: 10 ¼-cup servings.
PREP: 10 minutes. **COOK:** 3 minutes.

- ¾ cup heavy cream
  Pinch salt
- 6 ounces milk chocolate, chopped
- 6 ounces semisweet chocolate, chopped
- 2½ tablespoons raspberry extract
- 1 tablespoon corn syrup
  Assorted pound cake cubes and cut-up fruit, such as strawberries, raspberries, banana and pineapple, for dipping

1. Bring cream and salt to a boil in a small saucepan over medium heat. Remove from heat and add both kinds of chocolate to saucepan; cover and let sit for 3 minutes. Remove cover and whisk until smooth.

2. Whisk in raspberry extract and corn syrup. Serve immediately with pound cake and fruit. Stir often and reheat over low heat as necessary.

PER SERVING: 253 calories; 17 g fat (10 g sat.); 2 g protein; 22 g carbohydrate; 2 g fiber; 22 mg sodium; 28 mg cholesterol

Be sure to use unsalted butter—not margarine—to make these cookies crisp and delicate.

chocolate-toffee cookies

MAKES: 48 cookies. **PREP:** 10 minutes.
BAKE: at 375° for 12 minutes.

- 2⅓ cups all-purpose flour
- ¾ teaspoon baking soda
- ¼ teaspoon salt
- 1 cup (2 sticks) unsalted butter, softened
- 1 cup packed light-brown sugar
- ½ cup granulated sugar
- 1 egg
- 2 teaspoons vanilla extract
- 1 cup semisweet chocolate chips
- 1 bag (8 ounces) chopped milk chocolate toffee pieces (such as Hershey's Heath Bar baking pieces)

1. Heat oven to 375°. Coat baking sheets with nonstick cooking spray; set aside.

2. Stir together flour, baking soda and salt in a medium-size bowl; set aside.

3. In a large bowl, beat together butter and both sugars until light and fluffy, about 3 minutes. Beat in egg and vanilla.

4. On low speed, gradually add in flour mixture. Beat for 2 minutes or until blended. Stir in chocolate chips and toffee pieces.

5. Drop batter by tablespoonfuls onto prepared baking sheets and bake at 375° for 12 minutes or until golden. Cool baking sheets on wire racks for 5 minutes. Transfer cookies to wire rack to cool completely.

PER COOKIE: 125 calories; 6 g fat (4 g sat.); 1 g protein; 16 g carbohydrate; 0 g fiber; 55 mg sodium; 16 mg cholesterol

catch of the day

YOU'RE OFF THE HOOK FOR DINNER TONIGHT, THANKS TO THESE DELICIOUS (AND HEART-HEALTHY) FISH RECIPES. **BY MICHAEL TYRRELL**

**Teriyaki Tuna
and Soba Noodles
(Recipe page 43)**

PHOTOGRAPHY BY CHARLES SCHILLER

Try using the sauce from Cajun Catfish and Remoulade to spice up shrimp, too! (Recipe page 43)

This lip-tingling recipe calls for hot curry powder. You can also use milder Madras curry, if you like.

panko-crusted tilapia and bow ties

MAKES: 4 servings. **PREP:** 15 minutes.
COOK: 9 minutes. **BAKE:** at 450° for
10 minutes. **BROIL:** 2 minutes.

- 4 U.S. farm-raised tilapia fillets, about 5 ounces each
- ½ teaspoon salt
- ¼ teaspoon black pepper
- ½ cup Italian-seasoned panko bread crumbs (such as Progresso)
- ½ pound bow tie pasta
- 1 container (10 ounces) Brussels sprouts, trimmed and halved
- 3 tablespoons olive oil
- 4 cloves garlic, peeled and chopped
- ⅛ teaspoon red pepper flakes
- ¼ cup grated Parmesan cheese

1. Heat oven to 450°. Bring a large pot of water to boiling. Coat a broiler-safe baking pan with nonstick cooking spray. Place tilapia fillets in pan, skin-side down, and coat lightly with cooking spray. Season fish with ¼ teaspoon of the salt and black pepper. Sprinkle 2 tablespoons panko crumbs over each fillet. Bake at 450° for 10 minutes.
2. While fish is baking, boil bow ties for 4 minutes. Add Brussels sprouts and cook an additional 5 minutes. Drain, reserving ½ cup cooking liquid.
3. In a large skillet, heat olive oil over medium-high heat. Add garlic and red pepper flakes and cook 30 seconds. Add bow ties, Brussels sprouts, reserved cooking liquid and remaining ¼ teaspoon salt. Cook 1 minute until heated through. Stir in cheese.
4. Turn oven to broil. Broil fillets 1 to 2 minutes, until browned and crisp. Serve with bow ties.

PER SERVING: 497 calories; 16 g fat (4 g sat.); 40 g protein; 50 g carbohydrate; 3 g fiber; 587 mg sodium: 78 mg cholesterol

curried salmon and mint raita

MAKES: 4 servings. **PREP:** 15 minutes. **COOK:** 15 minutes. **BAKE:** at 450° for 15 minutes.

- ½ cup reduced-fat plain yogurt
- ½ cucumber, peeled and seeds removed, diced
- 2 tablespoons chopped fresh mint
- ⅛ teaspoon salt
- 1 cup long-grain white rice
- 1 can (14.5 ounces) vegetable broth
- 4 Alaskan wild salmon fillets, about 5 ounces each
- 1 tablespoon canola oil
- 1 teaspoon hot curry powder
- ¼ teaspoon cinnamon
- ¼ teaspoon ground ginger
- ⅛ teaspoon garlic powder
  Pinch salt

1. For raita, in a small bowl, mix together yogurt, cucumber, mint and salt. Cover and refrigerate until ready to serve.

2. In a medium saucepan cook the rice, following package directions, substituting vegetable broth for water.
3. Heat oven to 450°. Coat a glass 13 × 9 × 2-inch baking dish with nonstick cooking spray. Place salmon fillets, skin-side down, in dish. In a small bowl, mix together oil, curry powder, cinnamon, ginger, garlic powder and salt. Spoon curry mixture over salmon. Bake at 450° for 15 minutes or until fish flakes easily when tested with a fork.
4. Serve salmon with raita and rice.

PER SERVING: 479 calories; 15 g fat (2 g sat.); 38 g protein; 45 g carbohydrate; 1 g fiber; 667 mg sodium; 91 mg cholesterol

Serve this aromatic fish dish with a crisp green salad and some crusty bread.

mediterranean fish casserole

MAKES: 4 servings. **PREP:** 10 minutes. **BAKE:** at 400° for 1 hour.

- 2 tablespoons olive oil
- 1 pound small white potatoes, cut into quarters
- 2 large Italian frying peppers, thinly sliced
- ¼ teaspoon salt
- ¼ teaspoon black pepper
- 3 cloves garlic, peeled and chopped
- 4 ¾-inch-thick U.S. Pacific-caught cod or halibut fillets, about 5 ounces each
- ¼ cup pitted kalamata olives, chopped
- 2 plum tomatoes, seeded and cut into ¼-inch wedges
- 2 tablespoons lemon juice
- ¼ cup flat-leaf parsley, chopped

1. Heat oven to 400°. Grease an oval 2-quart casserole dish with 1 tablespoon of the olive oil. Spread potatoes and peppers over bottom of the dish. Season with ⅛ teaspoon each of the salt and pepper. Bake at 400° for 35 minutes or until potatoes are tender, stirring occasionally.

2. Scatter garlic over potatoes and peppers. Season fish with remaining ⅛ teaspoon each salt and pepper and place on top of the potatoes. Distribute olives and tomatoes over the casserole. Drizzle with lemon juice and remaining 1 tablespoon olive oil. Sprinkle with parsley.

3. Bake at 400° for 25 minutes or until fish flakes easily when tested with a fork.

PER SERVING: 272 calories; 8 g fat (1 g sat.); 26 g protein; 26 g carbohydrate; 4 g fiber; 417 mg sodium; 54 mg cholesterol

READER RECIPE

"We serve these to friends as an appetizer. Mango-lime margaritas make this meal even better!"

Christina Soave
Boynton Beach, FL

shrimp quesadillas with mango

MAKES: 5 quesadillas. **PREP:** 15 minutes.
MARINATE: 15 minutes. **COOK:** 40 minutes.

- 2 tablespoons olive oil
- 1 large sweet red pepper, seeded and sliced
- 1 large yellow pepper, seeded and sliced
- 1 large Vidalia onion (about 12 ounces), peeled and sliced
- ⅛ teaspoon salt
- ¾ pound U.S. farm-raised medium-size shrimp, shelled and deveined
- 2 cloves garlic, peeled and chopped
- 2 limes
- 2 teaspoons chili powder
- 1 large ripe mango, pitted and peeled
- 1 package fajita-size flour tortillas (10 tortillas)
- 1¼ cup shredded Monterey Jack cheese
- ½ cup sour cream

1. Heat 1 tablespoon of the olive oil in a large nonstick skillet over medium heat. Add peppers, onion and salt. Cook for 20 minutes, stirring occasionally, until vegetables are soft and slightly browned. Remove to a bowl.
2. Meanwhile, place shrimp in a resealable bag and add garlic, remaining olive oil, juice of ½ lime and chili powder. Shake bag and marinate for 15 minutes.
3. Puree mango with the juice from 1 lime in a food processor. Set aside.
4. In same skillet, cook shrimp, 2 minutes per side, and remove to a bowl.
5. Wipe out skillet and spray with nonstick cooking spray. Top a tortilla with one-fifth of the shrimp, onions and peppers. Sprinkle with ¼ cup of cheese. Place another tortilla on top and cook in skillet 1 to 2 minutes per side until lightly browned. Repeat with remaining tortillas. Serve with sour cream, mango puree and remaining lime.

PER QUESADILLA: 547 calories; 25 g fat
(11 g sat.); 29 g protein; 52 g carbohydrate;
5 g fiber; 918 mg sodium; 145 mg cholesterol

teriyaki tuna and soba noodles

MAKES: 4 servings. **PREP:** 15 minutes.
MARINATE: 15 minutes. **COOK:** 10 minutes.

- ¼ cup reduced-sodium teriyaki sauce
- 2 tablespoons rice vinegar
- 1 tablespoon chopped fresh ginger
- 1 teaspoon sugar
- 2 cloves garlic, peeled and chopped
- 4 U.S. Pacific-caught tuna steaks, about 6 ounces each
- 6 ounces soba noodles
- ½ pound sugar snap peas, strings removed
- 1 sweet red pepper, seeded and thinly sliced
- 2 scallions, thinly sliced
  Additional teriyaki sauce for noodles, optional

1. In a small bowl, stir together teriyaki sauce, vinegar, ginger, sugar and garlic. Reserve 3 tablespoons for the noodles. Marinate tuna in the remaining teriyaki sauce mixture for 15 minutes.
2. Prepare soba noodles following package directions, adding snap peas during the last 3 minutes of cooking. Drain and place in a medium-size bowl. Toss with red pepper slices and reserved teriyaki sauce mixture. Let stand at room temperature.
3. Coat a grill pan with nonstick cooking spray and heat over medium-high heat. Grill tuna for 3 minutes. Turn and grill for an additional 2 minutes for medium doneness. Serve with soba noodles and garnish with scallions. Toss noodles with additional teriyaki sauce, if desired.

PER SERVING: 389 calories; 2 g fat (1 g sat.);
47 g protein; 44 g carbohydrate; 3 g fiber;
730 mg sodium; 80 mg cholesterol

cajun catfish and remoulade

MAKES: 4 servings. **PREP:** 10 minutes.
BAKE: at 450° for 20 minutes.

- ½ cup light mayonnaise
- 1 tablespoon capers, drained and chopped
- 2 teaspoons spicy brown mustard
- 1 teaspoon cider vinegar
- ¼ teaspoon hot sauce
- 4 U.S. farm-raised catfish fillets, about 6 ounces each
- 2 teaspoons Cajun seasoning (such as McCormick)
- 1 lemon, thinly sliced
  Cooked brown rice and steamed zucchini, optional

1. In a small bowl, mix together mayonnaise, capers, mustard, vinegar and hot sauce. Cover and refrigerate remoulade.
2. Heat oven to 450°. Coat a glass 13 × 9 × 2-inch baking dish with nonstick cooking spray. Place one fish fillet in prepared dish and sprinkle ¼ teaspoon of the seasoning. Flip one long end over the other like a book. Sprinkle another ¼ teaspoon seasoning over top of fillet. Repeat with remaining fillets. Top each with a slice of lemon.
3. Bake at 450° for 18 to 20 minutes or until fish flakes easily when tested with a fork. Serve with remoulade sauce, brown rice and zucchini, if desired.

PER SERVING: 368 calories; 22 g fat (6 g sat.);
35 g protein; 3 g carbohydrate; 0 g fiber;
703 mg sodium; 111 mg cholesterol

dinner rush

RUNNING LATE (AGAIN)? NO NEED TO SETTLE FOR TAKEOUT FOR THE UMPTEENTH TIME—THESE FAST, FRESH MEALS GET A JUMP START FROM GREAT-TASTING PREPARED INGREDIENTS. **BY JULIE MILTENBERGER**

**Tomato-Vegetable Bisque,
opposite page.**

PHOTOGRAPHY BY ALISON MIKSCH

penne pesto with chicken

MAKES: 6 servings. **PREP** 10 minutes. **COOK:** 19 minutes.

- 1 large bunch broccoli rabe, trimmed slightly and cut into 1½-inch pieces
- 1 box (16 ounces) penne pasta
- 2 cloves garlic, peeled and sliced
- 1 package (9 ounces) fully cooked grilled chicken strips (such as Purdue Short Cuts), cut into bite-size pieces
- 1 container (7 ounces) Buitoni Reduced-Fat Basil Pesto

1. Bring a large pot of lightly salted water to a boil. Add broccoli rabe and cook 3 minutes. Scoop into bowl with a slotted spoon and add pasta to boiling water. Cook 9 minutes.

2. Meanwhile, drain water from broccoli rabe. Heat **2 tablespoons olive oil** in a large skillet over medium heat. Add garlic and cook 2 minutes. Stir in broccoli rabe; cook 3 minutes more. Season with **⅛ teaspoon salt** and **¼ teaspoon pepper.**

3. Drain pasta. Stir chicken, pasta and pesto into skillet. Cook 2 minutes to heat through. Serve warm.

PER SERVING: 530 calories; 17 g fat (3 g sat.); 28 g protein; 67 g carbohydrate; 3 g fiber; 675 mg sodium; 32 mg cholesterol

tomato-vegetable bisque

MAKES: 10 cups. **PREP:** 10 minutes. **COOK:** 21 minutes.

- 2 tablespoons olive oil
- 1 medium-size onion, peeled and chopped
- 3 large carrots, peeled and cut into coins
- 3 medium-size parsnips, peeled and cut into coins
- ½ teaspoon dried oregano
- ½ teaspoon black pepper
- 2 cans (28 ounces each) fire-roasted diced tomatoes, drained
- 1 box (32 ounces; 4 cups) Pacific Natural Foods Organic Vegetable Broth
- ⅔ cup heavy cream
  Hot sauce, seasoned croutons, optional

1. Heat oil in a large pot over medium heat. Add onion and cook 6 minutes. Stir in carrots, parsnips, oregano and pepper. Cook an additional 3 minutes.

2. Add drained tomatoes and 2 cups of the broth. Increase heat to medium-high and partially cover pot. Bring to a simmer, then reduce heat to medium and continue to simmer 10 minutes, until all vegetables are cooked.

3. Ladle half of the mixture into a blender; carefully purée. While blending, add 1 cup of the remaining vegetable broth. Repeat with remaining tomato mixture and remaining broth. Return to pot, stir in cream and heat gently until warm, about 2 minutes. Add hot sauce and croutons to taste.

PER CUP: 150 calories; 9 g fat (4 g sat.); 2 g protein; 16 g carbohydrate; 3 g fiber; 594 mg sodium; 22 mg cholesterol

Shredded zucchini adds moistness and texture to these cheesy burgers.

beef stir-fry

MAKES: 6 servings. **PREP:** 5 minutes.
COOK: 20 minutes.

- 1½ cups uncooked white rice
- 1 flank steak (about 1¼ pounds)
- 1 package (about ¾ pound) assorted sweet pepper strips
- 1 package (about ¾ pound) broccoli florets
- ¾ cup House of Tsang's Sweet Ginger Grill Sauce or other stir-fry sauce

1. Bring **3 cups water** to a boil; stir in rice. Reduce heat, cover and cook 20 minutes.
2. Meanwhile, slice beef across the grain into thin strips, each about 3 inches long. Heat **2 tablespoons oil** in a large skillet over medium-high heat. Add beef and stir-fry for 3 minutes. Remove to a platter with a slotted spoon.
3. Stir pepper strips, broccoli and ⅓ **cup water** into pan. Cover and cook 4 minutes. Uncover, add beef and stir-fry sauce. Cook 1 minute. Serve with rice on the side.

PER SERVING: 470 calories; 13 g fat (2 g sat.); 26 g protein; 63 g carbohydrate; 3 g fiber; 891 mg sodium; 31 mg cholesterol

turkey cheeseburgers

MAKES: 4 servings. **PREP:** 15 minutes. **BROIL:** 12 minutes.

- 1 package (about 1¼ pounds) ground turkey
- 1 medium-size zucchini, trimmed and grated (about 1 cup)
- 1 cup shredded Cheddar cheese
- ½ teaspoon salt
- ½ teaspoon onion powder
- ½ teaspoon dried basil
- ¼ teaspoon black pepper
- 4 Arnold's Multi-Grain Sandwich Thins or multigrain rolls
  Lettuce leaves (optional)
  Sliced tomato (optional)

1. Heat broiler, arranging rack so burgers will be about 2 inches from heat.

2. In a large bowl, combine turkey, zucchini, cheese, salt, onion powder, basil and pepper. Mix well and form into four flat patties, each about 5 inches.
3. Place burgers on a broiler pan and broil 6 minutes. Carefully flip burgers and continue to broil an additional 6 minutes, or until burgers register 165° on an instant-read thermometer.
4. Toast rolls, if desired. Stack rolls with burgers, lettuce leaves and sliced tomato. Serve warm.

PER SERVING 417 calories; 19 g fat (9 g sat.); 40 g protein; 25 g carbohydrate; 6 g fiber; 803 mg sodium; 112 mg cholesterol

pork schnitzel

MAKES: 6 servings. **PREP:** 10 minutes. **COOK:** 8 minutes.

- 6 thin boneless center-cut pork chops (about 1¼ pounds total)
- ½ teaspoon salt
- ¼ teaspoon black pepper
- ⅓ cup all-purpose flour
- 1 egg, beaten with ¼ cup water
- ⅔ cup plain dry bread crumbs
- ½ package medium egg noodles
- 4 tablespoons unsalted butter
  Chopped fresh parsley, to garnish

1. Place one pork chop between two sheets of waxed paper and pound to ⅛-inch thickness. Repeat with all chops.
2. Bring a large pot of lightly salted water to boiling. Season pork chops on both sides with salt and pepper. Spread flour on a dinner plate. Place egg mixture in a shallow dish or pie plate. Place bread crumbs on a third plate.

3. Add noodles to boiling water and cook 7 minutes. Meanwhile, melt 2 tablespoons of the butter in a large nonstick skillet over medium heat. Coat a pork chop with flour, dip in egg mixture, then coat with bread crumbs. Repeat with all chops.
4. Cook 3 pork chops in skillet for 2 minutes. Flip and cook an additional 1 to 2 minutes. Transfer to a platter; add remaining 2 tablespoons butter to skillet. Repeat cooking with remaining 3 chops.
5. Drain noodles; place on platter with cutlets and sprinkle with parsely. Serve immediately.

PER SERVING: 412 calories; 13 g fat (6 g sat.); 30 g protein; 39 g carbohydrate; 1 g fiber; 480 mg sodium; 151 mg cholesterol

cassoulet

MAKES: 8 servings. **PREP:** 10 minutes. **COOK:** 20 minutes.

- 6 slices bacon, chopped
- 1 boneless pork roast (2 pounds), trimmed of fat and cut into 1-inch cubes
- 1 medium onion, chopped
- ½ teaspoon salt
- ½ teaspoon black pepper
- ½ teaspoon Italian seasoning
- 8 ounces (½ package) reduced-fat kielbasa, cut into coins
- ¾ cup red wine
- 1 can (14.5 ounces) diced tomatoes with garlic and onions, drained
- 2 cans (15 ounces each) butter beans, drained and rinsed

1. Heat a heavy pot or Dutch oven over medium heat. Add bacon and cook 6 minutes, until browned and crispy.
2. Add pork, onion, salt, pepper and Italian seasoning to pot, cooking 4 minutes, until pork is no longer pink. Stir in kielbasa and cook 2 minutes more.
3. Increase heat to medium-high and add wine. Simmer 4 minutes. Stir in tomatoes and continue to simmer 3 minutes. Stir in beans; heat through, about 1 minute. Serve warm.

PER SERVING: 331 calories; 14 g fat (5 g sat.); 35 g protein; 19 g carbohydrate; 5 g fiber; 847 mg sodium; 87 mg cholesterol

food **university**

IT'S SUPEREASY TO MAKE PANCAKES FROM A MIX. BUT ODDS ARE YOU
HAVE EVERYTHING YOU NEED TO MAKE THESE BREAKFAST (OR ANYTIME!)
CROWD-PLEASERS FROM SCRATCH. **BY JULIE MILTENBERGER**

**Add-in Ideas: Drop
6 blueberries onto each
round just before you
flip it. Or sprinkle with
a little ground flaxseed
for a nutrient boost.**

PHOTOGRAPHY BY ALISON MIKSCH

perfect pancakes

MAKES: 16 4-inch pancakes. **PREP:** 10 minutes. **COOK:** 2 minutes per batch.

1½ cups all-purpose flour
 3 tablespoons granulated sugar
 4 teaspoons baking powder
 ⅛ teaspoon salt
 ⅛ teaspoon ground allspice
 2 eggs
 1 cup milk
 ¼ cup vegetable oil
   Butter, maple or pancake syrup,
   confectioners' sugar, for serving

1. Heat a griddle or large pan to medium heat. Heat oven to warm (180°) and place a foil-lined baking sheet inside.
2. In a large bowl, whisk together flour, granulated sugar, baking powder, salt and allspice. Separate eggs (see first illustration) and whisk egg yolks in small bowl with milk and oil.
3. With an electric mixer, beat egg whites to stiff peaks, about 1 minute. Stir milk mixture into flour mixture just until combined. Fold in egg whites (second illustration) in two additions, until no white streaks remain.

4. Using a ladle, drop ¼ to ⅓ cup batter onto heated griddle. Repeat, spacing at least 1 inch apart. Cook 1 minute, or until bubbles in batter pop and remain open (see third illustration). Carefully flip pancakes and cook an additional 30 seconds to 1 minute.
5. Transfer to baking sheet in warm oven; repeat with remaining batter. Serve warm with butter and syrup or confectioners' sugar, if desired.

PER PANCAKE: 101 calories; 5 g fat (1 g sat.); 2 g protein; 12 g carbohydrate; 0 g fiber; 133 mg sodium; 28 mg cholesterol

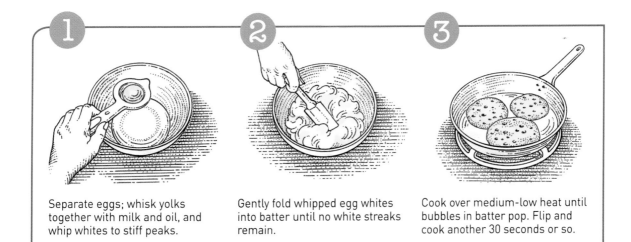

Separate eggs; whisk yolks together with milk and oil, and whip whites to stiff peaks.

Gently fold whipped egg whites into batter until no white streaks remain.

Cook over medium-low heat until bubbles in batter pop. Flip and cook another 30 seconds or so.

march

Blueberry Muffins
page 55

AS THE MARCH WINDS BLOW, STAY WARM
WITH HOME-BAKED GOODS FRESH FROM
THE OVEN—AND CELEBRATE ST. PADDY'S
DAY WITH A SLOW-COOKED FEAST.

Creamy Rotini and Salmon
page 65

Spinach and Chicken Pie
page 67

Loaded Potato Skins
page 73

bake it easy

HOW TO BEAT, FOLD AND FROST
YOUR WAY TO THE CLASSICS—
CHEESECAKE, BLUEBERRY
MUFFINS, BROWNIES AND MORE.

BY JULIE MILTENBERGER

PHOTOGRAPHY BY TINA RUPP

Food styling: Liza Jernow. Prop styling: Leslie Siegel.

double-chocolate brownies

MAKES: 24 brownies. **PREP:** 20 minutes. **MICROWAVE:** 2 minutes. **BAKE:** at 350° for 35 minutes.

- ¾ cup (1½ sticks) unsalted butter
- 4 ounces (4 squares) unsweetened chocolate
- 2 cups sugar
- 4 large eggs
- 1¼ cups all-purpose flour
- 2 teaspoons vanilla extract
- 1 cup chopped pecans
- 1 bag (12 ounces) chocolate chips (2 cups)

1. Heat oven to 350°. Line 13 × 9 × 2-inch baking pan with nonstick foil (step A, below), leaving overhang.
2. In large glass bowl, heat butter and chocolate in microwave on HIGH for 2 minutes; stir until smooth (step B, below). Let stand 5 minutes to cool slightly. Whisk in sugar, eggs, flour and vanilla. Stir in pecans and half of the chocolate chips (1 cup). Transfer batter to prepared pan. Sprinkle with remaining 1 cup chocolate chips (step C, below).
3. Bake at 350° for 35 minutes, until top is dry to the touch. Let cool completely in pan on wire rack. Lift brownie from pan with foil. Cut into squares and serve.

PER BROWNIE: 279 calories; 17 g fat (8 g sat.); 4 g protein; 33 g carbohydrate; 2 g fiber; 14 mg sodium; 50 mg cholesterol

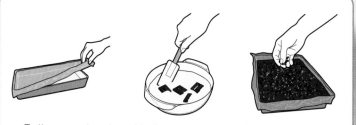

a To line pan, place it upside down on counter and shape foil over outside. Flip pan over and tuck shaped piece inside. **b** No need to chop chocolate before microwaving—though squares will look solid after heating. Stir until smooth and lump-free. **c** Scatter remaining chips over batter for double the chocolate in every bite!

Add an ice-cold glass of milk and you have one of the most delectable combos in dessert history. Sweet bonus: Only one bowl to wash.

ILLUSTRATIONS BY KATE FRANCIS

blueberry muffins

MAKES: 10 muffins. **PREP:** 10 minutes.
BAKE: at 375° for 25 minutes.

- 2 cups all-purpose flour
- ¾ cup plus 5 teaspoons sugar
- ¾ teaspoon baking powder
- ½ teaspoon baking soda
- ½ teaspoon salt
- ½ cup milk
- 2 eggs
- ½ cup vegetable oil
- 1 teaspoon grated orange zest
- 1 cup fresh blueberries

1. Heat oven to 375°. Coat a standard-size muffin pan with nonstick cooking spray.

2. In large bowl, whisk flour, ¾ cup of the sugar, baking powder, baking soda and salt. Make a well in the center (step A, page 56).

3. In small bowl, whisk together milk, eggs, oil and orange zest (step A, below). Pour milk mixture into well in flour mixture, then stir just until combined. Fold in blueberries (step B, below).

4. Spoon batter into prepared muffin pan, ⅓ cup batter in each cup (step C, below). Each muffin cup should be about ¾ full. Fill the two empty muffin cups with water, so muffins bake evenly.

5. Sprinkle each muffin with ½ teaspoon sugar. Bake muffins at 375° for 23 to 25 minutes, until crowned and lightly brown. Remove from pan and cool on wire rack. Serve warm or at room temperature.

PER MUFFIN: 286 calories; 13 g fat (1 g sat.); 4 g protein; 39 g carbohydrate; 1 g fiber; 229 mg sodium; 44 mg cholesterol

Pair a hit of fresh orange flavor—courtesy of grated zest—with a crunchy, sugary top crust for a phenomenal morning pick-me-up.

a To finely grate orange zest, we recommend a Microplane zester. This utensil—originally designed to mimic a woodworking tool—does the best job separating flavorful rind from bitter pith. **b** Gently fold berries into batter, taking care not to crush the fragile fruit. **c** Pour a scant ⅓ cup batter into each prepared muffin cup, dividing equally.

Extra-ripe fruit makes for an extra-moist loaf—ripen bananas on the countertop for about four days, until their skins are fairly well-spotted all over.

banana bread

MAKES: 2 loaves (20 slices). **PREP:** 15 minutes.
BAKE: at 350° for 35 minutes.

2½	cups all-purpose flour
1½	teaspoons baking soda
¼	teaspoon cinnamon
¼	teaspoon ground nutmeg
¼	teaspoon salt
3	large ripe bananas, peeled
2	large eggs
¾	cup sugar
½	cup (1 stick) unsalted butter, melted and cooled
¾	cup chopped walnuts Confectioners' sugar, for dusting (optional)

1. Heat oven to 350°. Coat two 8½ × 4½ × 2⅝-inch loaf pans with nonstick cooking spray. Set aside.
2. In large bowl, combine flour, baking soda, cinnamon, nutmeg and salt. Make a well in the center (step A, below). Mash bananas in medium-size bowl (step B, below). Add eggs, sugar and butter and beat until fairly smooth (step C, below).
3. Pour banana mixture into well in dry ingredients and stir just until blended. Fold in walnuts, then divide batter evenly between prepared loaf pans.
4. Bake loaves at 350° for 35 minutes, until browned and tops spring back lightly when gently pressed. Remove to wire rack to cool, dust with confectioners' sugar, if desired, and serve.

PER SLICE: 180 calories; 8 g fat (3 g sat.); 3 g protein; 25 g carbohydrate; 1 g fiber; 132 mg sodium; 33 mg cholesterol

a After blending the flour, baking soda, spices and salt (a whisk works best), make a well in the center by pressing dry ingredients up against side of bowl. **b** Mash the banana in a second bowl—a potato masher comes in handy here. **c** With an electric mixer on medium speed, beat eggs, sugar and melted butter into bananas until smooth.

new york-style cheesecake

MAKES: 16 servings. **PREP:** 25 minutes.
BAKE: at 325° for 1 hour.
REFRIGERATE: overnight.

Crust:

- 9 **graham cracker boards (4 crackers each)**
- 1 **tablespoon sugar**
  Pinch salt
- 5 **tablespoons unsalted butter, melted**

Filling:

- 4 **packages (8 ounces each) cream cheese, softened**
- 1¼ **cups sugar**
- 3 **large eggs**
- 3 **tablespoons all-purpose flour**
- 1 **tablespoon vanilla extract**

1. Heat oven to 325°.

2. Crust: Place graham crackers in large resealable plastic bag and crush with a rolling pin. Transfer crumbs to small bowl and add sugar and salt. Stir in melted butter until all crumbs are evenly moistened. Transfer crumbs to 9-inch springform pan and press onto bottom and ½ inch up sides (step A, below). Place sheet of extra-wide heavy-duty foil on countertop; place pan in center and fold foil up around pan (step B, below).

3. Filling: In large bowl, beat cream cheese until smooth. Add sugar and beat on low speed until blended. Add eggs, one at a time, beating well after each. Beat in flour and vanilla. Pour filling into crust. Place cheesecake in large roasting pan and fill pan with enough hot water to come halfway up side of springform pan (step C, below).

4. Bake cheesecake at 325° for 1 hour. Turn oven off, prop door open and let cool in oven for 30 minutes. Remove from oven and cool completely. Refrigerate overnight. To serve, release and remove side of pan before slicing.

PER SERVING: 349 calories; 25 g fat (15 g sat.); 6 g protein; 26 g carbohydrate; 0 g fiber; 241 mg sodium; 109 mg cholesterol

*TIP If you don't have a large enough roasting pan to set up a water bath, simply place a pan of water on the bottom of your oven before turning it on. Then bake cheesecake on the lowest rack. This should prevent cracks from forming on the top, but if they do, just cover them with whipped cream or fruit.

This creamy New York classic is too good to save for special occasions—it just takes a little extra time and the right tools: a 9-inch springform pan, some extra-wide heavy-duty foil and a large roasting pan.

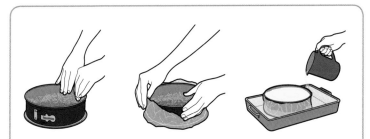

a With your fingers, press crumb mixture into bottom and slightly up side of springform pan. **b** Fold heavy-duty foil around outside of pan to form a watertight seal. **c** Place cheesecake in large roasting pan; fill pan with hot water until it comes halfway up side of springform pan.

Pound cake got its name from the weight of the ingredient in the recipe: 1 pound each of butter, flour, sugar and eggs. We've lightened it up a bit, but ours is still buttery heaven!

pound cake

MAKES: 16 servings. **PREP:** 30 minutes.
BAKE: at 350° for 1 hour.

- 1 cup (2 sticks) unsalted butter, softened
- 2¾ cups all-purpose flour, plus more for dusting pan
- ½ teaspoon baking soda
- ½ teaspoon salt
- 1¾ cups sugar
- 6 large eggs
- 1 tablespoon vanilla extract
- 1 cup sour cream (reduced fat is okay) blended with ¼ cup milk
- 1 cup confectioners' sugar

1. Heat oven to 350°. Grease a 12-cup capacity fluted tube pan with 1 tablespoon of the butter. Add a little flour, tilting pan so flour sticks to butter (step A, below).
2. Measure 2¾ cups flour (step B, below); pour into small bowl; add baking soda and salt. Whisk together to blend.
3. In large bowl, beat remaining butter and the sugar on high speed just until pale and fluffy (step C, below). Beat in eggs, one at a time, until smooth. Add vanilla.
4. On low speed, beat in half of the flour mixture, then sour cream mixture. Beat in remaining flour mixture just until blended.
5. Spoon batter into prepared pan. Bake at 350° for 1 hour, until cake springs back when pressed. Cool in pan on rack for 10 minutes. Place rack over cake, carefully flip to release cake from pan; cool.
6. Blend confectioners' sugar and 1 to 2 tablespoons water until smooth. Place cake on rack over parchment paper. Pour glaze over, letting it drip down side.

PER SERVING: 347 calories; 15 g fat (9 g sat.); 6 g protein; 47 g carbohydrate; 1 g fiber; 151 mg sodium; 118 mg cholesterol

a After greasing the baking pan, sprinkle with about 2 tablespoons flour. Working over the sink or a garbage can, tilt and turn pan, tapping gently, and coat butter with flour. Discard excess. **b** Spoon flour into a measuring cup and then level by sweeping a knife or spoon handle across top. This ensures that your flour doesn't get packed in, which can make the cake too dense. **c** Beat butter and sugar on high speed just until they turn pale and fluffy but are still grainy, about 3 to 5 minutes.

moist lemon cake

MAKES: 16 servings. **PREP:** 25 minutes.
BAKE: at 350° for 35 minutes.

Cake:
- 1 lemon
- 3 cups all-purpose flour
- 2 teaspoons baking powder
- ½ teaspoon salt
- 1 cup milk
- 1 container (6 ounces) lemon yogurt
- 1 teaspoon vanilla extract
- 1 cup (2 sticks) unsalted butter, softened
- 1¾ cups sugar
- 3 large eggs

Frosting:
- ¾ cup (1½ sticks) unsalted butter, softened
- 1 box (16 ounces) confectioners' sugar
- 2 tablespoons lemon juice (from Cake)
- Yellow food coloring (optional)

1. Cake: Heat oven to 350°. Coat two 9-inch round cake pans with nonstick cooking spray. Line pans with waxed paper (step A, below); spray paper.

2. Zest lemon peel (about 2 teaspoons; see step A, page 55). Juice lemon (step B, below).

3. In medium-size bowl, combine flour, baking powder and salt. In a measuring cup, whisk together milk, yogurt and vanilla. In large bowl, beat butter and sugar together on medium speed until light and fluffy. Beat in eggs, one at a time, beating well after each.

4. On low speed, beat flour mixture into butter mixture in three additions, alternating with milk mixture. Beat well after each addition. Fold in zest. Divide batter evenly between prepared pans.

5. Bake layers at 350° for 35 minutes or until cake springs back when pressed lightly. Cool in pans on wire rack for 10 minutes. Carefully invert cake layers directly onto racks, remove and discard waxed paper and let layers cool completely.

6. Frosting: Once layers are cool, beat butter, 1 cup of the confectioners' sugar, the reserved lemon juice (about 2 tablespoons) and 2 tablespoons water in a large bowl until smooth. Gradually beat in remaining confectioners' sugar until good spreading consistency. Tint with a few drops of food coloring, if desired. To frost cake, place one layer on a plate or stand. Spread top of layer with 1 cup frosting. Stack second cake layer on first and begin frosting side of cake (step C, right). Continue around side of cake, then finish top, swirling decoratively. Serve immediately or refrigerate before slicing and serving.

PER SERVING: 491 calories; 22 g fat (13 g sat.);
5 g protein; 71 g carbohydrate; 1 g fiber; 152 mg sodium;
95 mg cholesterol

This cake can be adapted for different tastes. Omit lemon peel, juice and food coloring (and use vanilla yogurt) for a vanilla flavor, or sub coffee for the juice and use coffee yogurt for a cappuccino cake.

a Trace cake pan on waxed paper. Cut out circle; repeat for second pan. Fit waxed paper circles into bottoms of greased pans, then spray paper. **b** After grating the peel, slice lemon in half and juice it. Set juice aside for frosting. **c** Spread a generous amount of frosting on side of stacked layers—an offset (angled) spatula works well.

eat right tonight

IT'S AS EASY AS PICKING A LEAN PROTEIN, ADDING A HANDFUL OF WHOLE GRAINS OR CHOOSING A DIFFERENT KIND OF PASTA. FINALLY—PROOF POSITIVE THAT HEALTHY DOESN'T HAVE TO BE BORING. **BY MICHAEL TYRRELL**

Fat-free half-and-half makes Creamy Rotini and Salmon (recipe page 65) taste rich without being loaded with fat and calories.

You can enjoy the rich taste of beef and still eat healthfully—just be sure it's a lean cut, such as this Eye Round Roast with Shiitake Gravy (recipe page 65).

PHOTOGRAPHY BY LUCY SCHAEFFER

Look for quinoa—a high-fiber source of complete protein— in the rice and dried-bean aisle of the supermarket.

gingersnap apple crisp

MAKES: 8 servings **PREP:** 20 minutes
BAKE: at 375° for 1 hour

4	Fuji apples, peeled, cored and cut into ¼-inch-thick slices (about 5 cups)
⅓	cup sweetened dried cranberries
2	tablespoons lemon juice
2	tablespoons light-brown sugar
2	tablespoons cornstarch
12	gingersnap cookies, coarsely chopped
⅓	cup quick-cook oats
2	tablespoons unsalted butter, softened

1. Heat oven to 375°. Coat 2½-quart baking dish with nonstick cooking spray.
2. In large bowl, combine apples, dried cranberries, lemon juice, brown sugar and cornstarch. Toss to combine and spoon into prepared dish.
3. In medium-size bowl, stir together cookie crumbs and oats. Mix in softened butter until mixture is crumbly. Sprinkle evenly over the apple mixture. Cover with aluminum foil.
4. Bake at 375° for 30 minutes. Remove foil and bake 30 minutes more, until apples are tender. Allow to cool 15 minutes before serving.

PER SERVING: 175 calories; 5 g fat (2 g sat.); 1 g protein; 33 g carbohydrate; 2 g fiber; 37 mg sodium; 8 mg cholesterol

quinoa and red bean burritos

MAKES: 8 burritos. **PREP:** 15 minutes. **COOK:** 15 minutes. **MICROWAVE:** 45 seconds.
BAKE: at 350° for 12 minutes.

1	cup quinoa
2	teaspoons McCormick smoky sweet pepper blend
1	can (15 ounces) red kidney beans, drained, rinsed and lightly mashed
1½	cups jarred salsa
8	whole-wheat tortillas
1	cup shredded Mexican-cheese blend

1. Place quinoa and pepper blend in a saucepan and cook following package directions. Once cooked, stir in beans and 1 cup of the salsa.
2. While quinoa is cooking, heat oven to 350°. Coat a large baking sheet with nonstick cooking spray.

3. Heat tortillas in microwave for 45 seconds to soften. Place ½ cup of the quinoa mixture in center of each tortilla and fold like a package. Place seam-side down on baking sheet.
4. Lightly coat burritos with nonstick cooking spray and top with remaining salsa and cheese, dividing equally. Bake burritos at 350° for 12 minutes until heated through, with cheese melted. Serve with additional salsa.

PER BURRITO: 315 calories; 8 g fat (4 g sat.); 14 g protein; 47 g carbohydrate; 8 g fiber; 734 mg sodium; 13 mg cholesterol

Next time you want something sweet, sprinkle berries on your salad, or feature apples or pears in your dessert.

The generous amount of olive oil in this salad is a good thing. Olive oil contains monounsaturated fat, which can lower your risk of heart disease by reducing the bad cholesterol (LDL) levels in your blood.

composed tuna salad

MAKES: 4 servings. **PREP:** 15 minutes.

2 tablespoons sherry-wine vinegar
1 teaspoon spicy brown mustard
⅛ teaspoon salt
⅛ teaspoon black pepper
¼ cup extra-virgin olive oil
1 large head Boston lettuce, leaves separated, rinsed and dried
2 cans (6 ounces each) high-quality tuna packed in oil, drained (such as Progresso)
½ pound steamed green beans
1 bunch radishes, trimmed and washed

4 hard-cooked eggs, peeled and quartered
⅓ cup pitted kalamata olives

1. In a small bowl, whisk together vinegar, mustard, salt and pepper. Slowly drizzle in olive oil, whisking continuously, until mixture is evenly blended (see photo above). Set aside.
2. Arrange lettuce over the bottom of a large serving platter. Break up tuna and place in the middle of lettuce. Arrange

green beans, radishes, egg quarters and olives around tuna in a decorative fashion.
3. To serve, drizzle half of the dressing over the components of the salad. Serve remaining dressing on the side.

PER SERVING: 423 calories; 29 g fat (5 g sat.); 33 g protein; 9 g carbohydrate; 3 g fiber; 683 mg sodium; 227 mg cholesterol

Switch from refined
carbohydrates like white
bread to fiber-packed
complex carbs like
vegetables, sweet potatoes
and brown rice.

pork and sweet potato stir-fry

MAKES: 4 servings. **PREP:** 15 minutes.
COOK: 17 minutes.

- ½ cup beef broth
- 2 tablespoons reduced-sodium soy sauce
- 1 tablespoon ketchup
- 1 tablespoon rice vinegar
- 2 teaspoons cornstarch
- ¼ teaspoon red pepper flakes
- 2 tablespoons olive oil
- 1 pound thin boneless pork chops, cut, across grain, ¼ inch thick
- ⅛ teaspoon salt
- 1½ pounds sweet potatoes (about 2 large), peeled, quartered lengthwise and sliced crosswise ¼ inch thick
- 2 green peppers, cored, seeded and cut into ½-inch-thick strips

1. In bowl, mix broth, soy sauce, ketchup, vinegar, cornstarch and red pepper flakes until smooth. Set aside.
2. Heat 1 tablespoon of the oil in a large nonstick skillet over medium-high heat. Add pork and stir-fry for 2 minutes. Season with salt. Remove to plate and keep warm.
3. Add remaining 1 tablespoon oil to skillet; sauté sweet potatoes and peppers over medium-high heat for 8 minutes. Add 1 cup water and simmer, covered, on medium-low for 6 minutes, until sweet potato is tender, stirring occasionally.
4. Stir in broth mixture and cooked pork and bring to a boil. Reduce heat and simmer for 1 minute, until sauce is thickened and meat is heated through. Serve immediately.

PER SERVING: 355 calories; 10 g fat (2 g sat.); 37 g carbohydrate; 30 g protein; 6 g fiber; 787 mg sodium; 62 mg cholesterol

eye round roast with shiitake gravy

MAKES: 8 servings. **PREP:** 15 minutes.
ROAST: at 450° for 30 minutes, then at 350° for 20 minutes. **COOK:** 9 minutes.

- 2 tablespoons olive oil
- 1 eye round roast (about 3 pounds)
- ¼ teaspoon salt
- ¼ teaspoon plus pinch black pepper
- 1 small onion, finely chopped
- ½ pound sliced shiitake mushrooms
- ⅓ cup dry red wine
- 1 tablespoon all-purpose flour
- ¼ teaspoon ground nutmeg
- 1 can (14½ ounces) beef broth

1. Heat oven to 450°. Brush 1 tablespoon of the oil over eye round and season with salt and ¼ teaspoon of the pepper. Roast at 450° for 30 minutes, turning over halfway through. Reduce temperature to 350° and roast for an additional 15 to 20 minutes or until internal temperature registers 130° on an instant-read thermometer for medium rare. Remove from oven and allow to rest, tented with foil, 10 minutes.
2. Heat remaining 1 tablespoon olive oil in a large nonstick skillet over medium-high heat. Add onion and mushrooms and cook for 7 minutes, stirring occasionally, until lightly browned. Stir in wine and cook 1 minute.
3. In small bowl, whisk flour, nutmeg and pinch of black pepper into broth. Stir broth into onion-mushroom mixture. Simmer for 1 minute, until thickened.
4. To serve, slice the roast as thinly as possible. Serve gravy on the side, with mashed potatoes, if desired.

PER SERVING: 283 calories; 9 g fat (2 g sat.); 40 g protein; 7 g carbohydrate; 1 g fiber; 381 mg sodium; 70 mg cholesterol

creamy rotini and salmon

MAKES: 6 servings. **PREP:** 10 minutes.
BAKE: at 450° for 12 minutes.
COOK: 15 minutes.

- ½ pound salmon fillet (1 piece)
- 1 box (14½ ounces) omega-3-enriched rotini pasta (such as Barilla)
- 2 cups fat-free half-and-half
- 2 teaspoons cornstarch
- ¼ teaspoon salt
- ¼ teaspoon ground nutmeg
- ⅛ teaspoon cayenne pepper
- 1 box (10 ounces) frozen peas, thawed
- ½ cup grated Parmesan cheese
- ⅓ cup toasted walnuts, coarsely chopped

1. Heat oven to 450°. Coat a small baking pan with nonstick cooking spray. Add salmon to pan and bake at 450° for 12 minutes or until fish flakes easily when tested with a fork. Keep warm.
2. Meanwhile, cook pasta following package directions. Drain and return to pot.
3. While pasta is cooking, whisk together half-and-half, cornstarch, salt, nutmeg and cayenne. Place in medium-size saucepan and bring to a boil. Simmer on low for 1 minute, until sauce thickens. Add peas and simmer for an additional minute, until peas are heated through. Remove from heat; stir in ¼ cup of the Parmesan cheese.
4. Stir sauce into drained pasta. Remove skin from salmon and discard. Flake salmon into bite-size pieces and gently stir into pasta; top with remaining ¼ cup cheese and the nuts to serve.

PER SERVING: 479 calories; 11 g fat (2 g sat.); 29 g protein; 63 g carbohydrate; 8 g fiber; 359 mg sodium; 30 mg cholesterol

1-dish **wonders**

OUR DELICIOUS CASSEROLES ARE JUST LIKE THE ONES YOU WERE RAISED ON—BUT WAY BETTER. AND AT LESS THAN $3 A SERVING, THEY'LL BE TWICE AS TEMPTING.

Our Seafood Lasagna is as delicious as it is nutritious—it's filled with vitamin-packed veggies. (Recipe, opposite page)

spinach and chicken pie

MAKES: 8 servings. **PREP:** 30 minutes. **COOK:** 18 minutes. **BAKE:** at 375° for 45 minutes.

- 2 tablespoons unsalted butter
- 1 large onion, chopped
- 2¼ pounds ground chicken
- 3 packages (10 ounces each) frozen chopped spinach, thawed and squeezed dry
- 1½ teaspoons salt
- 1 teaspoon black pepper
- ½ teaspoon ground nutmeg
- ¼ teaspoon red pepper flakes
- 1½ cups (12 ounces) crumbled feta cheese
- 4 eggs, lightly beaten
- 1 tablespoon chopped fresh oregano
- 8 sheets (18 x 13 inches) phyllo dough, thawed, halved crosswise (13 × 9 inches)

1. Heat oven to 375°. Coat 13 × 9 × 2-inch baking pan with nonstick cooking spray.

Melt butter in large skillet over high heat. Add onion and reduce heat to medium; cook 5 minutes. Add chicken and cook 8 minutes, until no longer pink. Add spinach, salt, pepper, nutmeg and red pepper flakes; cook 5 minutes. Transfer to large bowl. Stir in cheese, eggs and oregano.

2. Place a half sheet of phyllo in bottom of pan. Coat with cooking spray. Repeat with 7 more half sheets, coating each sheet. Spread spinach mixture over top. Repeat with remaining 8 half sheets. Cut top layer in 8 equal pieces.

3. Bake at 375° for 45 minutes, until top is browned. Recut to serve.

PER SERVING: 424 calories; 26 g fat (11 g sat.); 32 g protein; 17 g carbohydrate; 3 g fiber; 994 mg sodium; 287 mg cholesterol

seafood lasagna

MAKES: 12 servings. **PREP:** 20 minutes. **BAKE:** at 350° for 55 minutes.

- 1 pound reduced-fat cream cheese
- 3 scallions, trimmed and chopped
- ¼ cup milk
- 2 teaspoons Old Bay seasoning or Creole seasoning
- 2 sweet red peppers, cored, seeded and finely diced
- 2 boxes (10 ounces each) frozen chopped broccoli, thawed, squeezed dry
- ¾ pound imitation crabmeat, shredded
- 2 eggs
- ½ teaspoon salt
- ¼ teaspoon black pepper
- 1 jar (1 pound) alfredo pasta sauce
- 12 no-boil lasagna noodles
- ¼ cup grated Parmesan cheese

1. Heat oven to 350°. Coat a 13 × 9 × 2-inch baking dish with nonstick spray. Stir cream cheese, scallions, milk and Old Bay seasoning in bowl until smooth. Stir in peppers, reserving ½ cup, and broccoli, reserving 1 cup. Add crabmeat, 1 egg, salt and pepper. Whisk remaining egg into alfredo sauce.

2. Spread ⅓ cup alfredo sauce into baking dish. Top with 3 noodles, one-third of the crab mixture and one-fourth of alfredo sauce. Repeat layering twice. Top with 3 noodles; sprinkle with reserved red peppers and broccoli. Pour on remaining alfredo sauce. Sprinkle with Parmesan.

3. Bake, covered, at 350° for 30 minutes. Uncover; bake an additional 20 to 25 minutes, until browned and bubbly. Let stand 10 minutes.

PER SERVING: 321 calories; 16 g fat (10 g sat.); 16 g protein; 28 g carbohydrate; 2 g fiber; 999 mg sodium; 87 mg cholesterol

We added ground chicken to this Mediterranean classic to make it a protein-rich all-in-one meal.

Food styling: Megan Schlow. Prop styling: Megan Hedgpeth.

You can assemble this dish ahead of time, then refrigerate. When ready to cook, just add 10 minutes to the baking time.

nacho casserole

MAKES: 8 servings. **PREP:** 10 minutes.
COOK: 5 minutes. **BAKE:** at 375° for 35 minutes.

- 2 tablespoons olive oil
- ½ pound pre-sliced sweet peppers (about ½-inch-wide strips)
- 1 pound lean ground beef
- ½ teaspoon garlic salt
- 2 tubes (10 ounces each) refrigerated pizza dough
- 1 jar (16 ounces) medium-hot salsa
- 3 cups shredded taco-cheese blend
- 1 can (2.2 ounces) sliced black olives, drained (about ¼ cup)
- 3 large scallions, trimmed and sliced

1. Heat oven to 375°. Coat 13 × 9 × 2-inch baking dish with nonstick cooking spray.
2. In large skillet, heat oil over medium-high heat. Add peppers, ground beef and garlic salt; cook, stirring to break up clumps of beef, until the peppers are soft and beef is no longer pink, about 5 minutes. Drain off any excess fat from skillet.
3. Remove pizza dough from tubes. Cut the dough crosswise into ½-inch-wide slices, then cut each slice into quarters.
4. In large bowl, toss together dough pieces and salsa. Add cooked meat mixture, 2 cups of the taco-cheese blend and olives. Scrape mixture into baking dish. Sprinkle the remaining 1 cup taco-cheese blend over the top.
5. Bake at 375° for 30 minutes. Sprinkle scallions evenly over the top. Bake an additional 5 minutes.

PER SERVING: 502 calories; 25 g fat (9 g sat.); 31 g protein; 40 g carbohydrate; 3 g fiber; 1,181 mg sodium; 51 mg cholesterol

seven-layer gratin

MAKES: 6 servings. **PREP:** 15 minutes.
BAKE: at 350° for 50 minutes.

- 3 medium zucchini, cut diagonally into ¼-inch-thick slices
- 1 yellow squash, cut diagonally into ¼-inch-thick slices
- ¼ cup plus 2 tablespoons dried bread crumbs
- ½ teaspoon dried sage
- 1 tablespoon flour
- 1¼ teaspoons salt
- ½ teaspoon black pepper
- 1 can (8.5 ounces) artichoke hearts, drained
- 1 scallion, trimmed and minced
- 1½ cups shredded Swiss cheese
- ¾ cup light cream
- ½ pound ground turkey
- 2 tablespoons grated Parmesan cheese

1. Heat oven to 350°. In large bowl, mix zucchini, yellow squash, ¼ cup of the bread crumbs, sage, flour, 1 teaspoon of the salt, and pepper. In blender, puree artichoke hearts, scallion, ½ cup of the Swiss cheese, ¼ cup of the cream, the remaining salt and a pinch of pepper.
2. Spread one-third of the squash mixture over bottom of a shallow 2-quart baking dish. Spread half of the artichoke puree over squash.
Top with half of the turkey. Repeat layering; top with the remaining squash mixture.
3. Toss together the remaining 1 cup Swiss cheese, remaining bread crumbs and the Parmesan. Sprinkle evenly over gratin. Drizzle with the remaining ½ cup light cream.
4. Bake at 350° for 50 minutes or until squash is tender and top is golden. Let stand 10 minutes before serving.

PER SERVING: 299 calories; 18 g fat (10 g sat.); 20 g protein; 16 g carbohydrate; 2 g fiber; 1,039 mg sodium; 79 mg cholesterol

cheese and onion bread casserole

MAKES: 8 servings. **PREP:** 10 minutes.
LET: STAND: 30 minutes. **COOK:** 15 minutes.
BAKE: at 350° for 45 minutes.

- 4 eggs
- 3 cups low-fat (1%) milk
- ¼ teaspoon ground nutmeg
- 1 loaf French bread (about 16 inches long), cubed (about 8 cups)
- 2 tablespoons olive oil
- 3 large onions (about 1½ pounds), sliced
- ½ teaspoon sugar
- ½ teaspoon salt
- ¼ teaspoon black pepper
- 2 cups shredded Cheddar cheese

1. Whisk together eggs, milk and nutmeg in large bowl. Add bread cubes. Let mixture stand 30 minutes, stirring occasionally.

2. Heat oil in large nonstick skillet. Add onion, sugar, salt and pepper; cook over medium-low heat until onion is very tender, 15 minutes.

3. Heat oven to 350°. Coat 13 × 9 × 2-inch baking dish with nonstick cooking spray.

4. Spoon half of bread mixture into baking dish. Top with half of onion mixture. Repeat with the remaining bread and onion. Sprinkle with cheese.

5. Bake at 350° for 45 minutes or until puffed and golden. Let cool slightly before serving.

PER SERVING: 397 calories; 18 g fat (8 g sat.); 19 g protein; 40 g carbohydrate; 3 g fiber; 733 mg sodium; 141 mg cholesterol

Keep this dish interesting by substituting different cheeses—try Pepper Jack for some added heat, or a rich and creamy Fontina.

slow-cooker solutions

GREAT-TASTING RECIPES FOR EFFORTLESS MEALS. **BY CINDY HELLER**

Food styling: Michael Pederson. Prop styling: Lynda White.

spicy beef stew

MAKES: 6 servings. **PREP:** 15 minutes. **COOK:** 13 minutes. **SLOW-COOK:** 4½ hours on HIGH or 6½ hours on LOW.

1 tablespoon olive oil
1 pound chuck steak, trimmed and cut into ¾-inch pieces
1 large onion, chopped
2 tablespoons tomato paste
3 tablespoons flour
1½ cups low-sodium beef broth
2 teaspoons dried oregano
1 teaspoon cumin
2 plum tomatoes, chopped
2 cans (15 ounces each) white hominy, drained and rinsed
1 each green and yellow bell pepper, chopped

1 chipotle pepper in adobo sauce (from a 7-ounce can), seeded and chopped, plus 1 tablespoon of the adobo sauce
2 tablespoons lime juice
Sour cream (optional)

1. Heat oil in a nonstick skillet over medium-high heat. Add steak and cook 7 minutes. Remove to slow cooker bowl.
2. Add onion to skillet. Cook 3 minutes. Stir in tomato paste; cook 2 minutes. Add flour and cook, stirring, 1 minute.

3. Scrape onion mixture into slow cooker bowl. Stir in broth, oregano and cumin; cook on HIGH for 3 hours or LOW for 5 hours.
4. Stir in tomatoes, hominy, peppers, chipotle and adobo sauce. Cook 1½ hours more. Stir in lime juice. Serve with sour cream, if desired.

PER SERVING: 223 calories; 7 g fat (2 g sat.); 21 g protein; 22 g carbohydrate; 4 g fiber; 925 mg sodium; 33 mg cholesterol

PHOTOGRAPHY BY ALEXANDRA GRABLEWSKI

pork goulash

MAKES: 6 servings. **PREP:** 15 minutes.
SLOW-COOK: 3½ hours on HIGH or 5 hours on LOW.

- 1 boneless pork loin roast (about 1¾ pounds), trimmed and cut into ½-inch pieces
- 3 medium-size parsnips, peeled and cut into ½-inch coins
- 2 large carrots, peeled and cut into ½-inch coins
- 1 large onion, chopped
- 4 tablespoons sweet paprika
- 2 cups low-sodium chicken broth
- ½ pound green beans, trimmed and cut into 1-inch pieces
- ½ cup reduced-fat sour cream
- 2 tablespoons cornstarch
- ½ teaspoon salt
- ½ teaspoon black pepper

1. Place pork, parsnips, carrots and onion in slow cooker. Sprinkle with 2 tablespoons of the paprika; stir to coat. Pour in broth. Cover and cook on HIGH for 3 hours or LOW for 4½ hours.
2. Add green beans; cook 30 minutes.
3. In a small bowl, blend remaining 2 tablespoons paprika, sour cream, cornstarch, salt and pepper. Stir into slow cooker bowl until thickened.

PER SERVING: 274 calories; 6 g fat (3 g sat.); 34 g protein; 21 g carbohydrate; 6 g fiber; 678 mg sodium; 85 mg cholesterol

corned beef and cabbage

MAKES: 10 servings. **PREP:** 15 minutes. **SLOW-COOK:** 8 hours on LOW.

- 8 whole cloves
- 1 medium yellow onion, halved
- 1 lean center-cut corned beef brisket* (about 2 pounds)
- 3 large carrots, peeled and quartered lengthwise and cut into 2-inch pieces
- ½ pound new potatoes, halved
- ½ pound boiling onions, peeled
- 1 small head cabbage, outer leaves removed, cut into 6 wedges

1. Stick cloves in onion. Place onion and beef in slow cooker and add enough water to cover ingredients plus 3 more inches. Cover and cook on LOW for 5 hours.

2. Add carrots, potatoes, onions and cabbage to slow cooker and cook an additional 3 hours.
3. Remove corned beef from slow cooker and slice. Place on large platter with vegetables. Drizzle with the broth to moisten and serve.

PER SERVING: 238 calories; 14 g fat (4 g sat.); 15 g protein; 13 g carbohydrate; 3 g fiber; 1,026 mg sodium; 49 mg cholesterol

*Corned beef brisket labeled "flat" has fewer calories—and about 30% less fat—than the "point" variety.

MADE WITH TURKEY BACON, LOWER-FAT CHEESE, AND REDUCED-FAT SOUR CREAM, THIS SPORTS-BAR CLASSIC HAS BEEN REVAMPED FOR THE HOME KITCHEN WITH BETTER HEALTH IN MIND. **BY JULIE MILTENBERGER**

The texture of russet potato skins makes them ideal for making Loaded Potato Skins— broiling makes them nice and crisp.

PHOTOGRAPHY BY ALEXANDRA GRABLEWSKI

loaded potato skins

MAKES: 5 servings (2 skins each). **PREP:** 10 minutes. **MICROWAVE:** 16 minutes. **COOK:** 5 minutes. **BROIL:** 7 minutes.

 5   **large russet potatoes (12 ounces each)**
10   **slices turkey bacon**
 ½   **teaspoon salt**
 ¼   **teaspoon black pepper**
2½ **cups shredded 2% Cheddar cheese**
     (about 10 ounces)
 3   **scallions, trimmed and sliced**
 ½   **cup reduced-fat sour cream**

1. Scrub potatoes; pierce with a fork (see first illustration). Place on paper towels. Microwave on HIGH 16 minutes.

2. In large skillet over medium heat cook bacon until crisp, 5 minutes.

3. Position rack 6 inches from oven top and heat broiler. Line a baking sheet with nonstick foil. Slice potatoes in half lengthwise; scoop out flesh, leaving about ¼-inch edge (second illustration), reserving flesh for another use. Place skins, cut-side down, on sheet; coat with nonstick cooking spray. Broil 4 minutes.

4. Remove potato skins from oven. Flip over (cut-side up). Season with salt and pepper. Sprinkle each with 2 tablespoons of the cheese and 1 slice bacon, crumbled. Top bacon with an additional 2 tablespoons cheese per skin.

5. Return to broiler; broil 3 minutes, until cheese melts (third illustration). Top with scallions and serve with sour cream.

PER 2 SKINS: 364 calories; 21 g fat (11 g sat.);
22 g protein; 25 g carbohydrate; 3 g fiber;
1,077 mg sodium; 74 mg cholesterol

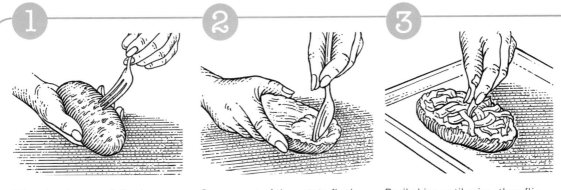

After cleaning, carefully pierce potatoes with a fork so they don't burst in the microwave.

Scoop most of the potato flesh from the skin; reserve for mashed potatoes.

Broil skins until crisp, then flip over. Fill with toppings and broil again to heat through and melt cheese.

april

Spring Cupcakes
page 77

SPRING IS OFFICIALLY HERE!
GARDEN-FRESH RECIPES FEATURING
VITAMIN-PACKED VEGGIES BRING GOOD TASTE
AND HEALTH TO YOUR FAMILY'S TABLE.

Lemon Poppy Seed Cake
page 86

Tropical Pizza
page 89

Grilled Balsamic Asparagus
page 103

These cheery cakes can be frozen, unfrosted, and then thawed for an anytime treat.

WE LOVE CLASSIC BUTTERCREAM FROSTING, BUT IF YOU WANT
TO TRY A LIGHTER MARSHMALLOW FROSTING, WE'VE INCLUDED
A RECIPE FOR THAT AS WELL. **BY KAREN TACK**

spring cupcakes

MAKES: 24 cupcakes. **PREP:** 15 minutes. **BAKE:** at 350° for 25 minutes.

⅓ cup unsweetened cocoa powder
2 tablespoons canola oil
3½ cups all-purpose flour
1 tablespoon baking powder
½ teaspoon salt
1½ cups (3 sticks) unsalted butter, softened
1½ cups granulated sugar
4 eggs
1½ cups milk
2 teaspoons vanilla extract
Frosting:
3 sticks (1½ cups) unsalted butter, softened
6 cups confectioners' sugar
½ cup milk
½ teaspoon vanilla extract
Assorted pastel food colorings

1. In a small bowl, blend cocoa powder and oil until smooth. Set aside. Heat oven to 350°. Place liners in two standard-size muffin pans, for a total of 24 cupcakes. In a medium-size bowl, whisk flour, baking powder and salt.

2. With electric mixer, beat butter and sugar in large bowl until light-colored and smooth. Add eggs, one at a time, beating well after each addition. On low speed, add flour mixture, alternating with milk. Stir in vanilla. Divide batter in half. Stir cocoa mixture into one half. Spoon both batters into prepared liners, ⅓ cup in each (12 chocolate, 12 vanilla).

3. Bake at 350° for 25 minutes or until firm to the touch. Let cupcakes cool in pan on rack for 5 minutes, then transfer cakes directly to rack; cool completely.

4. Frosting: Beat butter, sugar, milk and vanilla on low speed to blend, then on high speed for 2 minutes, until good spreading consistency. Divide frosting into bowls and tint to desired colors. Transfer frosting to plastic bags and snip off one corner. Pipe in swirled pattern onto cooled cupcakes.

PER CUPCAKE WITH FROSTING: 472 calories; 26 g fat (15 g sat.); 4 g protein; 58 g carbohydrate; 1 g fiber; 118 mg sodium; 98 mg cholesterol

Marshmallow Frosting: In a large metal bowl, whisk together **3 egg whites, 2 cups granulated sugar, ¼ cup cool water** and **½ teaspoon cream of tartar.** Place over a pot of simmering water; beat until mixture registers 160° on an instant-read thermometer, about 7 minutes. Tint and pipe onto cupcakes as in step 4.

PER CUPCAKE WITH FROSTING: 317 calories; 14 g fat (8 g sat.); 4 g protein; 45 g carbohydrate; 1 g fiber; 121 mg sodium; 67 mg cholesterol

PHOTOGRAPHY BY RITA MAAS

coffee
crumb
cakes

cream-
filled
cupcakes

devilish
cocoa
sandwiches

snowy
coconut
rounds

double takes

THESE LUSCIOUS
LOOK-ALIKES TASTE
JUST LIKE THE
OLD-SCHOOL FAVES
THAT INSPIRED THEM—
ONLY BETTER BECAUSE
THEY'RE HOMEMADE!

BY KAREN TACK

vanilla
sponge
cakes

PHOTOGRAPHY BY RITA MAAS

Food styling: Karen Tack. Prop styling: Leslie Siegel.

cream-filled cupcakes

MAKES: 24 servings. **PREP:** 20 minutes.
BAKE: at 350° for 20 minutes

    2 cups all-purpose flour
    1 cup unsweetened cocoa powder
 1½ teaspoons baking soda
    ½ teaspoon salt
 1½ cups buttermilk
    1 teaspoon vanilla extract
    ½ cup (1 stick) unsalted butter, softened
 1½ cups sugar
    3 large eggs
Filling and Swirl:
    4 tablespoons unsalted butter, softened
 1½ cups confectioners' sugar
    2 to 3 tablespoons milk
Glaze:
    ½ cup heavy cream
    1 tablespoon light corn syrup
    1 cup semisweet chocolate chips

1. Heat oven to 350°. Line 24 muffin cups
with paper liners.
2. Combine the flour, cocoa, baking soda
and salt in a medium bowl. Whisk to
blend. Combine the buttermilk and the
vanilla in a measuring cup.
3. Beat the butter and the sugar in a
medium mixing bowl with an electric
mixer on medium high speed until light
and fluffy. Add the eggs one at a time,
beating well after each addition. Add the
flour mixture alternating with the
buttermilk mixture, starting and ending
with the flour mixture.
4. Divide the batter among the prepared
muffin pans. Bake until a toothpick
inserted in centers comes out clean,
18 to 20 minutes. Transfer to a wire rack
and cool 10 minutes. Invert and cool
completely.
5. Filling and Swirl: Beat butter in a
medium-size bowl until light and fluffy.
Gradually add confectioners' sugar. Add
2 tablespoons of the milk and beat
5 minutes until almost white and light
and fluffy. Add additional milk if mixture
is too thick. Spoon frosting into a pastry

bag fitted with a medium-size plain
round tip. Remove cakes from pan. Insert
tip of pastry bag into top of cakes, about
½ inch deep, and squeeze.
6. Glaze: Heat the cream and corn syrup
in a small saucepan over medium heat
until it just comes to a boil. Remove from
heat and stir in the chocolate chips.
Cover and let stand 5 minutes. Whisk
until smooth.
7. Dip the tops of the filled cupcakes into
the chocolate glaze. Place on a cooling
rack to set for 10 minutes.
8. Change the piping tip for the vanilla
frosting to a smaller round tip. Pipe
decorative swirls on top of the glazed
cupcakes.

PER CUPCAKE: 256 calories; 12 g fat (7 g sat.);
4 g protein; 37 g carbohydrate; 2 g fiber;
156 mg sodium; 49 mg cholesterol

coffee crumb cakes

MAKES: 12 servings. **PREP:** 10 minutes.
BAKE: at 350° for 20 minutes.

 1½ cups all-purpose flour
    1 teaspoon baking powder
    ⅛ teaspoon salt
    ½ cup (1 stick) unsalted butter, softened
    ⅔ cup sugar
    2 large eggs
    ⅓ cup whole milk
    ½ teaspoon vanilla extract
Topping:
    ¼ cup packed dark-brown sugar
    ¼ cup granulated sugar
    ½ teaspoon cinnamon
       Pinch salt
    ⅓ cup unsalted butter, melted
    1 cup all-purpose flour

1. Heat oven to 350°. Coat 12 muffin cups
with nonstick spray and dust with flour.
2. Combine flour, baking powder and salt
in a medium-size bowl. Whisk to blend.
Beat butter and sugar in a large bowl
until light and fluffy, about 3 minutes.
Add eggs, one at a time, and continue

beating until smooth. Add flour mixture
alternating with milk until just blended.
Stir in vanilla.
3. Divide batter evenly among indents of
prepared pan (about ¼ cup in each).
4. Topping: Combine sugars, cinnamon
and salt in a medium-size bowl. Stir in
melted butter. Add flour and rub mixture
with hands to make crumb topping.
Mixture should clump together and form
little balls. Sprinkle topping over batter
in the cups, about 1 heaping tablespoon
for each.
5. Bake until a toothpick inserted in
centers comes out clean; 15 to 20
minutes. Cool completely on wire rack.

PER CRUMB CAKE: 299 calories; 14 g fat (8 g sat.);
4 g protein; 40 g carbohydrate; 1 g fiber;
76 mg sodium; 69 mg cholesterol

devilish cocoa sandwiches

MAKES: 12 servings. **PREP:** 10 minutes.
BAKE: at 350° for 14 minutes.

    2 cups all-purpose flour
    1 cup packed light-brown sugar
    ½ cup unsweetened cocoa powder
    1 teaspoon baking soda
    ¼ teaspoon salt
    1 cup buttermilk
    1 large egg, lightly beaten
    6 tablespoons unsalted butter, melted
    1 can (12 ounces) whipped vanilla
       frosting

1. Line 2 sheet pans with parchment.
Heat oven to 350°.
2. Combine flour, brown sugar, cocoa
powder, baking soda and salt in a
medium-size bowl. Whisk to blend. Stir in
buttermilk, egg and melted butter. Stir
with a wooden spoon until just blended.
3. Spoon some of the mixture into a large
resealable plastic bag. Snip a ½-inch
corner from the bag. Pipe 3½ × 1-inch
logs, about 2 inches apart, on prepared
pans, about 12 per pan. Bake until firm to
the touch, 12 to 14 minutes. Transfer to

wire rack and let cool completely.

4. Spoon the frosting into a second resealable bag. Snip a ½-inch corner from the bag. Pipe some of the frosting onto the flat side of half of the cookies. Sandwich with another cookie, flat side against frosting. Continue with remaining cookies and frosting.

PER SANDWICH: 348 calories; 14 g fat (5 g sat.); 4 g protein; 53 g carbohydrate; 2 g fiber; 219 mg sodium; 33 mg cholesterol

snowy coconut rounds

MAKES: 8 servings. **PREP:** 20 minutes.
BAKE: at 350° for 22 minutes.
MICROWAVE: 20 seconds.

- 1 **cup all-purpose flour**
- ¾ **cup sugar**
- ½ **cup unsweetened cocoa powder**
- ¾ **teaspoon baking soda**
- ¼ **teaspoon baking powder**
- ¼ **teaspoon salt**
- ¾ **cup buttermilk**
- ⅓ **cup vegetable oil**
- 1 **large egg**

Marshmallow Topping:
- 1 **envelope unflavored gelatin**
- 3 **tablespoons egg white powder**
- ¾ **cup sugar**
- 2 **cups sweetened flake coconut**
  Red food coloring (optional)

1. Heat oven to 350°. Grease and flour eight, 8-ounce ovenproof glass bowls or round ramekins.

2. Combine flour, sugar, cocoa, baking soda, baking powder and salt in a medium-size bowl. Whisk to blend. In another bowl, combine buttermilk, oil and egg.

3. Add buttermilk mixture to the flour mixture. Mix until just blended. Divide batter evenly among prepared bowls, a generous ¼ cup in each. Place in oven on a baking sheet. Bake at 350° for 18 to 22 minutes or until a toothpick inserted in centers comes out clean. Transfer to a

wire rack; cool 10 minutes. Invert, remove bowls; cool completely.

4. Marshmallow Topping: Sprinkle gelatin over 2 tablespoons cool water. Let stand 5 minutes.

5. Combine egg white powder and ½ cup warm water in a large bowl. Whisk to blend. Beat mixture with an electric mixer on high until foamy. Gradually add sugar, 1 tablespoon at a time, and beat until thick and glossy.

6. Heat gelatin mixture in microwave until dissolved, about 15 to 20 seconds. Pour dissolved gelatin into whipped egg whites, and stir to combine.

7. Place coconut in a small bowl. (Tint half pink with food coloring, if desired.) Spread an even layer of frosting all over the rounded side of cakes. Press the coconut onto the sides and to cover. Continue with remaining cakes.

PER ROUND: 443 calories; 19 g fat (9 g sat.); 8 g protein; 65 g carbohydrate; 3 g fiber; 213 mg sodium; 27 mg cholesterol

vanilla sponge cakes

MAKES: 16 cakes. **PREP:** 15 minutes.
BAKE. at 350° for 17 minutes.

- 1½ **cups all-purpose flour**
- 1½ **teaspoons baking powder**
- ¼ **teaspoon salt**
- 5 **tablespoons unsalted butter**
- 3 **large eggs**
- 1 **cup plus 2 tablespoons sugar**

Filling:
- 6 **tablespoons unsalted butter, softened**
- 2 **cups confectioners' sugar**
- 1 **to 2 tablespoons milk**

1. Heat oven to 350°. Grease and flour Canoe pan; set aside.

2. Combine flour, baking powder and salt in a small bowl. Whisk to blend. Heat ½ cup water and the butter in a small saucepan until the water just boils and the butter melts. Remove from heat.

3. Beat the eggs with an electric mixer on high for 2 minutes. Gradually add the sugar and beat until thick and golden, 4 to 5 minutes longer. Fold in the flour mixture until just blended. Add the water and melted butter and stir until just blended.

4. Divide half of the batter evenly among the prepared pan indents, a scant ¼ cup per cake.

5. Bake until cakes are golden and a toothpick inserted in centers comes out clean, about 15 to 17 minutes. Invert cakes onto a wire rack to cool. Wash pan and repeat with the remaining batter. Transfer to a wire rack and cool completely.

6. Filling: Beat butter in a medium-size bowl until light and fluffy. Gradually add confectioners' sugar. Add 1 tablespoon of the milk and beat 5 minutes until almost white and light and fluffy. Add extra milk if filling is too stiff. Spoon frosting into a pastry bag fitted with a small round tip (or use the decorating set supplied with pan). Remove cakes from pan. Insert tip of the pastry bag into the center of the flat side of the cakes and squeeze. Repeat on either side for a total of 3 spots of frosting piped into the base of each cake, resembling the classic cream-filled treats. Flip over, so cake sits flat-side down. Repeat with all cakes and filling and serve.

PER CAKE: 238 calories; 9 g fat (5 g sat.); 3 g protein; 38 g carbohydrate; 0 g fiber; 89 mg sodium; 60 mg cholesterol

Look for the Canoe pan plus 9-piece decorating kit from Norpro at kitchenstoreon10th .com or amazon.com; $25.

sweet
inspiration

FAMILY CIRCLE AND **SHARE OUR STRENGTH** ARE TEAMING UP AGAIN THIS YEAR TO FIGHT CHILDHOOD HUNGER. HELP US OUT BY HOSTING A BAKE SALE—THESE GOODIES ARE GUARANTEED TO RAKE IN THE DOUGH. **BY JULIE MILTENBERGER**

Lemon Poppy Seed Cake
(Recipe page 86)

Food styling: Michael Pederson. Prop styling: Megan Hedgpeth.

READER RECIPE

"These pretzels were a great success. I'd recommend selling two small rods per package."

Terri Tomlinson
Sterling Heights, MI

chocolate-covered pretzel rods

Heat 10 ounces chopped semisweet chocolate bars in the microwave in 30-second increments until melted. Ladle chocolate over ¾ of each pretzel rod (you will need one 12-ounce bag). Tap or scrape off excess chocolate, then roll pretzel in sprinkles, crushed cookies, toffee bits or mini M&M's (you will need 1½ cups assorted toppings). Dry on a cooling rack until set.

PER SERVING: 118 calories; 5 g fat (1 g sat.); 1 g protein; 19 g carbohydrate; 1 g fiber; 98 mg sodium; 0 mg cholesterol

PHOTOGRAPHY BY ALEXANDRA GRABLEWSKI

"These bars are delicious, chewy and easy to make, and have a rich butterscotch flavor."

Margaret Grubb
North Charleston, SC

grannie's old-fashioned butterscotch bars

MAKES: 24 bars. **PREP:** 10 minutes. **BAKE:** at 350° for 25 minutes.

½ cup (1 stick) unsalted butter
1¾ cups packed light-brown sugar
2 eggs
2 cups self-rising flour
1 teaspoon butter rum extract
1 cup chopped pecans
Confectioners' sugar, for dusting

1. Heat oven to 350°. Coat a 13 × 9 × 2-inch baking dish with nonstick cooking spray; set aside.
2. Melt butter in a medium-size saucepan. Add sugar, eggs and flour to saucepan and mix until well blended. Stir in butter rum extract and pecans.
3. Pour into prepared baking dish and bake at 350° for about 25 minutes or until toothpick inserted into center comes out clean.
4. Cool completely on a wire rack and dust with confectioners' sugar. Cut into 24 squares and serve.

PER SERVING: 172 calories; 8 g fat (3 g sat.); 2 g protein; 25 g carbohydrate; 1 g fiber; 143 mg sodium; 28 mg cholesterol

"These muffins sold like hotcakes at a local craft fair."

Melissa Dunstatter
Rocky Point, NY

zucchini-nut chocolate muffins

MAKES: 24 servings. **PREP:** 15 minutes. **BAKE:** at 325° for 28 minutes.

2½ cups all-purpose flour
4 tablespoons cocoa powder
1 teaspoon baking soda
½ teaspoon ground cinnamon
½ teaspoon salt
½ cup milk
¼ teaspoon white vinegar
½ cup (1 stick) unsalted butter, softened
½ cup vegetable oil
1¾ cups granulated sugar
2 eggs
2 teaspoons vanilla extract
2 cups peeled, finely grated zucchini
1 cup semisweet chocolate chips

¼ cup chopped pecans or walnuts

1. Heat oven to 325°. Line 2 cupcake pans with foil liners.
2. In medium-size bowl, blend flour, cocoa powder, baking soda, cinnamon and salt; set aside. Stir together milk and vinegar in a small bowl; set aside.
3. In large bowl, beat butter, oil and sugar on medium-high speed for 3 minutes or until light and fluffy. Add eggs and vanilla; beat until combined. Add milk mixture and beat well.

4. On low speed, gradually add flour mixture; beat until just combined. Stir in zucchini and ½ cup of the chips. Fill prepared indents ⅔ full (a generous ¼ cup) and sprinkle with remaining ½ cup chips and the nuts.
5. Bake at 325° for 20 to 28 minutes or until toothpick inserted in centers comes out clean. Cool completely on a wire rack.

PER SERVING: 238 calories; 12 g fat (4 g sat.);
3 g protein; 30 g carbohydrate; 1 g fiber;
112 mg sodium; 28 mg cholesterol

lemon poppy seed cake

MAKES: 16 servings. **PREP:** 20 minutes. **BAKE:** at 350° in large pan for 65 minutes or in smaller paper pans for 35 minutes.

- 3 **cups all-purpose flour**
- 1 **tablespoon baking powder**
- 1 **teaspoon salt**
- 1 **small jar (1.25 ounces) poppy seeds**
- 1 **cup (2 sticks) unsalted butter, softened**
- 2 **cups sugar**
- 4 **eggs**
- ½ **teaspoon vanilla extract**
- 1½ **cups milk, blended with 2 tablespoons fresh lemon juice (milk may curdle)**
- 2 **teaspoons grated fresh lemon peel**

1. Heat oven to 350°. Grease and flour a removable-bottom tube pan, or have two 7⅞ × 2⅜-inch paper tube pans ready. In a medium-size bowl, whisk together flour, baking powder, salt and poppy seeds. Set aside.
2. In a large bowl, beat butter and sugar until fluffy, 2 minutes. Add eggs, one at a time, until incorporated and mixture is smooth. Beat in vanilla. Add half the flour mixture, then the milk–lemon juice mixture. Beat on low speed until smooth. Add remaining flour mixture and beat until just blended. Stir in lemon peel.
3. Transfer batter to pan(s) and at 350° bake large tube pan for 65 minutes or small pans for 33 to 35 minutes, until top is dry and lightly browned. Cool cake(s) in pan on wire rack for 15 minutes, then remove large cake from pan (if using). Leave smaller cakes in their paper pans. Cool completely.
4. Slice large cake into 16 slices and package individually. Wrap smaller cakes in festive plastic wrap.

PER SERVING: 327 calories; 14 g fat (8 g sat.); 5 g protein; 45 g carbohydrate; 1 g fiber; 243 mg sodium; 85 mg cholesterol

Note: Paper baking pans (such as the tube pans) are great for packaging whole cakes in decorative containers. Simply prep the batter for this lemon poppy seed cake, and divide into two paper pans. To order pans, visit thepeppermillinc.com, $10 for 12 pans, or bakedeco.com, $13.50 for a pack of 25.

"Our Great American Bake Sale was a hit, and the one-day event raised over $1,200."

Carron Findley
Los Gatos, CA

carron's "killer" cookies

MAKES: 4½ dozen. **PREP:** 15 minutes.
BAKE: at 350° for 10 minutes.

- 1½ **cups all-purpose flour**
- 1 **teaspoon baking soda**
- 1 **teaspoon baking powder**
- 1 **teaspoon salt**
- 1 **cup vegetable shortening**
- 1 **cup granulated sugar**
- 1 **cup light-brown sugar**
- 2 **eggs**
- 1 **teaspoon vanilla extract**
- 2 **cups old-fashioned oats**
- 2 **cups Rice Krispies cereal**
- 1 **cup sweetened flake coconut**
- 1 **bag (6 ounces) semisweet chocolate chips**

1. Heat oven to 350°. Place parchment paper on 4 baking sheets and set aside.
2. In small bowl, blend flour, baking soda, baking powder and salt with a whisk; set aside.
3. In large bowl, beat shortening and both sugars on medium-high speed about 3 minutes or until light and fluffy. Add eggs, one at a time, beating well after each addition. Beat in vanilla.
4. On low speed, gradually add flour mixture and beat until just combined. Stir in oats, Rice Krispies, coconut and chocolate chips.
5. Form balls with 2 tablespoons of dough and place 2 inches apart on prepared sheets. Bake at 350° for 10 minutes. Cool on sheets for 5 minutes then transfer to cooling rack to cool completely.

PER SERVING: 131 calories; 6 g fat (2 g sat.); 2 g protein; 18 g carbohydrate; 1 g fiber; 94 mg sodium; 8 mg cholesterol

vegging out

THESE DAYS EVEN DIE-HARD MEAT-EATERS ARE OPTING FOR MORE VEGETABLES—WHETHER TO CUT CALORIES OR SAVE MONEY. EITHER WAY, NO ONE WILL HAVE A BEEF WITH THESE GREAT-TASTING RECIPES!

BY MICHAEL TYRRELL

Spinach is an inexpensive form of hard-to-get iron.

Tortellini provide a satisfying pasta hit without too many calories.

Mushrooms add a meaty flavor and texture.

Chickpeas pack fiber and are naturally rich in protein.

Cheese, such as flavored feta, is an easy, convenient way to infuse bold flavor.

Edamame, or fresh soybeans, contain all nine essential amino acids.

Soy crumbles can be substituted for ground meat in most recipes.

Food styling: Toni Brogan. Prop styling: Christina Lane.

PHOTOGRAPHY BY JAMES BAIGRIE

tropical pizza

MAKES: 8 slices. **PREP:** 10 minutes.
BAKE: at 450° for 12 minutes.

- 1 **large whole-wheat or regular Boboli pizza crust (14 ounces)**
- 1 **cup pineapple mango chipotle salsa (such as Pace)**
- 1 **cup shredded Monterey Jack cheese**
- ½ **cup shredded Swiss cheese**
- ½ **green pepper, seeded and thinly sliced**
- ½ **red pepper, seeded and thinly sliced**
- ½ **small onion, peeled and thinly sliced**

1. Heat oven to 450°.
2. Place pizza crust on a large baking sheet. Spread ⅔ cup of the salsa over the crust. Sprinkle the cheeses over the salsa. Spoon remaining ⅓ cup salsa over cheese; scatter pepper and onion over the top.
3. Bake at 450° for 10 to 12 minutes or until heated through and cheese is melted. Allow to cool slightly. Cut into 8 slices.

PER SLICE: 227 calories; 9 g fat (4 g sat.); 12 g protein; 28 g carbohydrate; 5 g fiber; 581 mg sodium; 19 mg cholesterol

Tortellini Soup
(Recipe opposite page)

Ingredients such as cheese-filled tortellini, canned beans, and frozen edamame provide the protein in these meatless, veggie-packed dishes.

tortellini soup

MAKES: 4 servings. **PREP** 15 minutes.
COOK: 9 minutes.

- 3 **cups vegetable broth**
- 3 **cups water**
- ½ **teaspoon dried Italian seasoning**
- 1 **package (9 ounces) cheese-filled spinach tortellini**
- 3 **large carrots, peeled and sliced into thin coins**
- 3 **ribs celery, thinly sliced**
- ¾ **pound ripe plum tomatoes (about 4), seeded and chopped**
- 1 **bag (6 ounces) baby spinach Grated Parmesan cheese (optional)**

1. In a large pot, bring broth, water and Italian seasoning to a boil. Add the tortellini and simmer for 3 minutes. Add carrots and celery and simmer for an additional 4 minutes. Stir in the tomatoes and spinach and simmer for 2 more minutes or until vegetables are tender and the spinach is wilted.
2. Ladle soup into bowls and serve with Parmesan cheese, if desired.

PER SERVING: 215 calories; 4 g fat (3 g sat.); 9 g protein; 37 g carbohydrate; 6 g fiber; 1,006 mg sodium; 15 mg cholesterol

taco-night pasta

MAKES: 6 servings. **PREP:** 10 minutes. **COOK:** 12 minutes.

- 1 **pound wagon wheel-shaped pasta**
- 1 **can (15 ounces) Great Northern beans, drained and rinsed**
- 1 **can (14/2 ounces) no-salt-added stewed tomatoes**
- 1 **can (10 ounces) mild enchilada sauce (such as Old El Paso)**
- 1 **teaspoon hot chili powder**
- ½ **teaspoon ground cumin**
- ¼ **teaspoon salt**
- 1 **package (12 ounces) soy crumbles (such as Morningstar Farms)**
- 1 **cup shredded reduced-fat sharp cheddar cheese**

1. Cook pasta following package directions. Drain and return to pot.
2. While pasta is cooking, prepare sauce. In a large skillet, stir together beans, tomatoes, enchilada sauce, chili powder, cumin and salt. Break up

tomatoes with a wooden spoon. Simmer over medium heat for 3 minutes, stirring occasionally. Add the soy crumbles and simmer for an additional 3 minutes, stirring occasionally.
3. Stir the sauce into pot with pasta. Add half of the cheese and stir to blend.
4. Spoon pasta into a large serving bowl and sprinkle remaining ½ cup cheese over the top. Serve immediately.

PER SERVING: 518 calories; 9 g fat (3 g sat.); 30 g protein; 79 g carbohydrate; 10 g fiber; 842 mg sodium; 14 mg cholesterol

edamame and mushroom risotto

MAKES: 4 servings. **PREP:** 15 minutes. **COOK:** 47 minutes.

- **2 tablespoons olive oil**
- **8 ounces white button mushrooms, trimmed and sliced**
- **1 pound frozen edamame**
- **3 cups vegetable broth mixed with 1½ cups water**
- **1 small onion, peeled and finely chopped**
- **1⅓ cups arborio rice**
- **¼ cup white wine**
- **⅛ teaspoon black pepper**
- **½ cup shredded Parmesan cheese**

1. Heat 1 tablespoon of the olive oil in a large nonstick skillet over medium-high heat. Add mushrooms and cook for 5 minutes, stirring occasionally. Set aside.

2. Cook edamame, about 5 minutes, following package directions. Drain, cool and remove beans from shells. Add beans to mushrooms in skillet. Discard shells.

3. Place broth and water in a medium-size saucepan and bring to a simmer.

4. In a large saucepan, heat remaining tablespoon oil over medium heat. Add onion and cook 5 minutes, stirring occasionally. Add rice and stir until rice is coated with oil. Cook for 1 minute, stirring. Add wine and cook until wine is absorbed—about 1 minute.

5. Add ½ cup of the simmering broth mixture. Cook over medium-low heat, stirring, until broth is absorbed. Add remaining broth mixture, ½ cup at a time, cooking in the same manner. This should take about 30 minutes.

6. Gently heat mushrooms and edamame. Stir into rice and remove from heat. Stir in the pepper and ¼ cup of the cheese.

7. Divide among 4 bowls and sprinkle with remaining Parmesan cheese.

PER SERVING: 495 calories; 18 g fat (4 g sat.); 24 g protein; 60 g carbohydrate; 6 g fiber; 978 mg sodium; 15 mg cholesterol

veggie gyro

MAKES: 4 servings. **PREP:** 15 minutes.
REFRIGERATE: 30 minutes.
MICROWAVE: 20 seconds.

- 1 container (6 ounces) plain, low-fat yogurt, liquid drained (if any)
- ½ cucumber, peeled, seeded and diced
- 1 clove garlic, finely chopped
- 1 tablespoon lemon juice
- 1 tablespoon fresh dill, chopped
  Pinch salt and pepper
- 4 whole-wheat pitas
- ½ head iceberg lettuce, sliced
- ½ small red onion, peeled and thinly sliced
- 2 large plum tomatoes (about ½ pound), sliced
- 1 package (8 ounces) garlic-and-herb flavored feta cheese, crumbled

1. To make sauce: Stir together yogurt, cucumber, garlic, lemon juice, dill, salt and pepper in a small bowl. Cover and chill 30 minutes.

2. Assemble gyros: Wrap pitas in damp paper towel and microwave for 20 seconds. Place puffed-side down on plates. Down the middle of each, evenly layer lettuce, sauce, onion, tomato slices and feta. Fold up both sides like a taco.

PER SERVING: 393 calories; 17 g fat (10 g sat.); 21 g protein; 46 g carbohydrate; 7 g fiber; 1,111 mg sodium; 43 mg cholesterol

zucchini and chickpea ratatouille

MAKES: 4 servings. **PREP:** 10 minutes. **BAKE:** at 425° for 30 minutes. **COOK:** 11 minutes.

- 2 medium-size zucchini, about 1¼ pounds, quartered lengthwise and cut into ½-inch pieces
- 1 large red pepper, cored, seeded and cut into ½-inch pieces
- 2 tablespoons olive oil
- 4 cloves garlic, finely chopped
- 2 cans (14½ ounces) Italian-seasoned diced tomatoes
- 1 can (15½ ounces each) chickpeas, drained and rinsed
- ¼ teaspoon salt
- ⅛ teaspoon black pepper
- ⅛ teaspoon red pepper flakes
- 3 cups cooked brown rice

1. Heat oven to 425°.

2. Coat a baking sheet with nonstick cooking spray. Add zucchini and red pepper; toss with 1 tablespoon olive oil. Bake at 425° for 30 minutes or until tender.

3. Heat remaining 1 tablespoon oil in a large nonstick skillet over medium-high heat. Add garlic, cook 30 seconds to 1 minute. Stir in tomatoes and cook for 5 minutes, stirring occasionally. Add zucchini, peppers, chickpeas, salt, pepper and red pepper flakes. Cook an additional 5 minutes, stirring occasionally. Serve with cooked brown rice.

PER SERVING: 402 calories; 9 g fat (1 g sat.); 16 g protein; 67 g carbohydrate; 10 g fiber; 855 mg sodium; 0 mg cholesterol

pasta pronto

YOU ALREADY KNOW THIS QUICK-COOK, BUDGET-FRIENDLY PANTRY STAPLE IS PERFECT FOR WEEKNIGHTS. HERE'S A HALF-DOZEN RECIPES TO REV UP YOUR REPERTOIRE. **BY CINDY HELLER**

Gnocchi with Creamy
Tomato Sauce
(Recipe page 99)

$2.70
per serving

PHOTOGRAPHY BY TINA RUPP

$1.95
per serving

Spaghetti with Spinach
(Recipe page 99)

$2.00
per serving

bow ties with tuna

MAKES: 6 servings. **PREP:** 15 minutes.
COOK: 12 minutes.

    12 ounces bowtie pasta
     2 garlic cloves, chopped
     1 jar (24 ounces) roasted red peppers,
        drained and chopped
     1 small onion, chopped
     1 tablespoon olive oil
     1 tablespoon capers
     1 tablespoon balsamic vinegar
     1 tablespoon Italian seasoning
     ½ cup tomato juice
     ¼ teaspoon salt
     ¼ teaspoon black pepper
     3 cans (6 ounces each) albacore tuna
        packed in water, drained

1. Bring a large pot of salted water to a
boil. Cook pasta according to package
directions, about 12 minutes, reserving
¼ cup of pasta water. Return pasta
to pot.
2. Meanwhile, place garlic, roasted red
peppers, onion, olive oil, capers, vinegar,
Italian seasoning and tomato juice in a
blender. Puree until smooth, then pour
into a small saucepan. Stir in salt
and pepper.
3. Simmer over medium heat for
5 minutes. Pour over pasta and stir to
combine. Gently stir in tuna; serve
immediately.

PER SERVING: 451 calories; 7 g fat (1 g sat.);
25 g protein; 70 g carbohydrate; 7 g fiber;
747 mg sodium; 24 mg cholesterol

$2.55
per serving

sausage, broccoli and noodles

MAKES: 4 servings. **PREP:** 10 minutes. **COOK:** 11 minutes

     3 packages (3 ounces each) ramen
        noodle soup, chicken flavor
     ¼ cup reduced-fat sour cream
     1 tablespoon cornstarch
     3 links sweet Italian turkey sausage,
        casings removed
     3 cups frozen baby broccoli flowerets,
        thawed

1. Bring a large pot of salted water to a
boil. Cook noodles for 2 minutes,
reserving seasoning packets for later;
drain and set aside. In a small bowl, stir
together sour cream and cornstarch;
set aside.
2. Cook sausage in a large nonstick
skillet over medium heat, breaking up

with a spoon, for 5 minutes or until
cooked through.
3. Add broccoli, 1 cup water and
1½ teaspoons of the ramen chicken
seasoning to skillet. Cover and simmer
over medium heat for 3 minutes or until
broccoli is cooked through.
4. Remove cover and stir sour cream
mixture into skillet. Cook for 1 minute or
until sauce has thickened. Add noodles to
skillet and toss to coat with sauce. Serve
immediately.

PER SERVING: 392 calories; 11 g fat (2 g sat.);
19 g protein; 55 g carbohydrate; 6 g fiber;
886 mg sodium; 45 mg cholesterol

$1.00 per serving

cellentani with ham and greens

MAKES: 8 servings. **PREP:** 10 minutes. **COOK:** 12 minutes.

1 **pound cellentani (such as Barilla)**
2 **tablespoons unsalted butter**
1 **medium-size onion, chopped**
⅓ **pound thinly sliced Virginia ham, cut into ½ × 2-inch ribbons**
1 **package (10 ounces) frozen chopped kale, thawed according to package directions**
3 **tablespoons flour**
1 **can (14 ounces) low-sodium chicken broth**
   Grated Romano cheese (optional)

1. Bring a large pot of salted water to a boil. Cook cellentani according to package directions, about 12 minutes. Drain and return to pot.
2. Meanwhile, melt butter in a large nonstick skillet over medium-high heat. Cook the onion, ham and kale for 8 minutes. Reduce heat to medium and add flour to skillet. Cook, stirring constantly, for 1 minute.
3. Add chicken broth to skillet and cook, stirring occasionally, for 3 minutes or until sauce has thickened slightly. Pour contents of skillet over pasta and stir to combine. Top with Romano cheese, if desired.

PER SERVING: 282 calories; 4 g fat (2 g sat.); 12 g protein; 49 g carbohydrate; 3 g fiber; 345 mg sodium; 16 mg cholesterol

$1.80
per serving

Egg Drop Soup with
Chicken & Noodles
(Recipe opposite page)

egg drop soup with chicken & noodles

MAKES: 6 servings. **PREP:** 10 minutes.
COOK: 15 minutes.

- 4 cups low-sodium chicken broth
- 3 tablespoons low-sodium soy sauce
- 3 garlic cloves, smashed
- 1½ teaspoons ground ginger
- 4 ounces wide rice noodles or pad thai noodles, broken into 3-inch pieces
- 2 tablespoons cornstarch
- 2 eggs, lightly beaten
- 1½ cups cooked, shredded chicken
- 3 scallions, thinly sliced (optional)

1. Bring the broth, 1½ cups water, soy sauce, garlic and ginger to a boil over medium-high heat in a medium-size saucepan. Reduce heat to medium and cook broth mixture for 10 minutes.
2. Remove the garlic cloves with a slotted spoon and add noodles to pot; cook for 4 minutes or until tender.
3. Meanwhile, stir together the cornstarch and 2 tablespoons water in a small bowl; whisk into broth and cook for 1 minute or until thickened.
4. Stir the soup so it is moving in a circular direction. Pour in the beaten eggs in a slow, steady stream. Stir in chicken and garnish with scallions, if desired. Serve immediately.

PER SERVING: 155 calories; 2 g fat (1 g sat.); 14 g protein; 18 g carbohydrate; 0 g fiber; 644 mg sodium; 96 mg cholesterol

gnocchi with creamy tomato sauce

MAKES: 6 servings. **PREP:** 15 minutes.
COOK: 8 minutes.

- 2 packages (17.5 ounces each) potato gnocchi (such as De Cecco)
- 1 tablespoon olive oil
- 3 cups sliced white mushrooms
- ½ teaspoon salt
- ½ teaspoon black pepper
- 1¼ cups no-salt-added tomato sauce
- 1¼ cups frozen peas, thawed
- 1 teaspoon dried basil
- ½ cup ricotta cheese

1. Bring a large pot of salted water to a boil. Add gnocchi to pot; cook about 2 minutes or until gnocchi rise to the top of water. Remove with a slotted spoon to a large bowl.
2. Meanwhile, heat olive oil in a large nonstick skillet over medium-high heat. Add mushrooms to skillet; sprinkle with ¼ teaspoon each salt and pepper. Cook 3 minutes.
3. Add tomato sauce, peas and basil to skillet and reduce heat to medium; simmer for 5 minutes. Stir in ricotta cheese and remaining ¼ teaspoon each salt and pepper; pour over gnocchi. Stir to combine.

PER SERVING: 365 calories; 6 g fat (2 g sat.); 10 g protein; 69 g carbohydrate; 5 g fiber; 825 mg sodium; 11 mg cholesterol

spaghetti with spinach

MAKES: 6 servings. **PREP:** 10 minutes.
COOK: 12 minutes.

- 12 ounces spaghetti
- 4 tablespoons extra-virgin olive oil
- ½ cup panko bread crumbs
- 4 garlic cloves, minced
- ¼ teaspoon red pepper flakes
- 1 bag (6 ounces) baby spinach
- ½ cup grated Parmesan cheese

1. Bring a large pot of salted water to a boil. Cook spaghetti according to package directions, about 12 minutes. Drain, reserving ¼ cup of the water; return pasta to pot.
2. Meanwhile, heat 1 tablespoon of the oil in a large nonstick skillet over medium-high heat. Add bread crumbs to skillet and cook for 2 minutes, stirring often, or until lightly browned. Add half of the garlic and ⅛ teaspoon of the red pepper flakes to skillet; cook for 1 minute, stirring constantly. Remove from skillet and wipe clean.
3. Reduce heat to low and add remaining 3 tablespoons oil, garlic and ⅛ teaspoon red pepper flakes to skillet. Cook for about 2 minutes, or until garlic is golden. Add spinach to skillet and toss until wilted, about 2 minutes.
4. Stir spinach mixture and Parmesan cheese into pasta. Sprinkle with bread crumbs and toss gently. Serve immediately.

PER SERVING: 307 calories; 12 g fat (2 g sat.); 10 g protein; 38 g carbohydrate; 6 g fiber; 312 mg sodium; 4 mg cholesterol

family favorites

sponge cake

MAKES: 16 servings. **PREP:** 15 minutes.
BAKE: at 350° for 1 hour.

- 9 eggs, separated
- ¾ cup Passover cake meal
- 5 tablespoons potato starch
- ⅛ teaspoon salt
- 1½ cups sugar
  Zest from 1 orange
- ½ cup orange juice
  Strawberries, for serving (optional)

1. Heat oven to 350°.
2. In a clean, large bowl, beat egg whites on medium-high speed to stiff peaks.
3. In a small bowl, whisk together the cake meal, potato starch and salt.
4. In a second large bowl, beat sugar and egg yolks until lemony in color, about 5 minutes. Beat in zest.
5. Beat in the cake meal mixture in two additions, alternating with the orange juice. Gently fold in beaten egg whites.
6. Spoon into an ungreased, 10-inch angel food cake/tube pan with feet. Bake at 350° for 1 hour or until toothpick inserted in cake comes out dry.
7. Remove from oven; immediately invert onto a baking sheet and allow to cool completely.
8. Turn over pan and run a small knife or small spatula around edge of pan, and center tube. Remove cake from pan. Serve with strawberries, if desired.

PER SERVING: 154 calories; 3 g fat (1 g sat.); 4 g protein; 28 g carbohydrate; 0 g fiber; 58 mg sodium; 119 mg cholesterol

"My mom, Ronnie, always makes several of these during Passover. It's a recipe that's been passed down for generations and definitely reminds me of childhood." CAREN OPPENHEIM, EDITORIAL ASSISTANT

PHOTOGRAPHY BY KATE MATHIS

"This tiramisu-like cake is a tribute to my mother's Italian heritage. My family wouldn't celebrate Easter without one." **LISA KELSEY, ART DIRECTOR**

Food styling: Megan Schlow. Prop styling: Lynda White.

zabaglione cake

MAKES: 12 servings. **PREP:** 30 minutes. **COOK:** 9 minutes. **MICROWAVE:** 15 seconds. **REFRIGERATE:** overnight.

- 10 **eggs, separated**
- 10 **tablespoons sugar**
- ½ **cup Marsala wine**
- 1 **envelope unflavored gelatin**
- 28 **soft ladyfingers (2½ packages, 3 ounces each)**
- 2 **cups refrigerated pasteurized egg whites**
- 1 **cup heavy cream**
  Confectioners' sugar and cocoa powder (optional)

1. Whisk egg yolks and sugar in top of double boiler over simmering water, stirring continuously until the mixture is thick and lemony, about 6 minutes. Add Marsala and continue whisking until mixture is thick enough to coat the back of a spoon, about 3 minutes.

2. Sprinkle gelatin over 1 tablespoon water in a small cup. Heat in the microwave for 15 seconds. Stir to dissolve completely. Stir into the egg yolk and wine mixture. Remove to a bowl and cool.

3. Line a 4-quart bowl with plastic wrap, draping extra over the sides. Line the bowl with the ladyfingers, trimming the tops flat if necessary .

4. In a clean, large bowl, whip the egg whites to stiff peaks. Set aside.

5. In another large bowl, beat the cream to soft peaks. Fold whipped egg whites and whipped cream into cooled egg yolk and wine mixture.

6. Pour mixture into the lined bowl. Cover the top with ladyfingers. Cover and refrigerate overnight.

7. To serve, gently invert onto plate and dust top with confectioners' sugar and cocoa, if desired.

PER SERVING: 289 calories; 14 g fat (7 g sat.); 12 g protein; 29 g carbohydrate; 0 g fiber; 245 mg sodium; 260 mg cholesterol

A

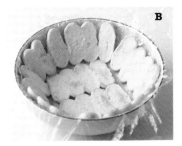

B

food university

I KNOW IT'S FINALLY SPRING WHEN I SEE PENCIL-THIN SPEARS AT MY LOCAL
GREEN MARKET. THE ONLY DOWNSIDE IS DECIDING HOW I'M GOING TO PREPARE
THEM. HERE ARE MY THREE FAVORITE COOKING METHODS—I SUGGEST YOU
TRY THEM ALL. **BY JULIE MILTENBERGER**

**Thick? Thin?
Both are equally good.
Use thick spears for
poaching or steaming,
thin for grilling or
roasting.**

Food styling: Toni Brogan. Prop styling: Christina Lane. Photo (Miltenberger): Karen Pearson. Illustrations: Kate Thomssen.

Look for fresh asparagus bunches with firm, tightly closed tips, and plump—not dry or wrinkly—ends. Store upright in 1 inch of water in a glass or measuring cup. Before cooking rinse thoroughly in water, then prep with steps at bottom.

grilled balsamic asparagus

Heat grill or grill pan to medium-hot. Combine **1 bunch asparagus,** trimmed and peeled, with **¼ cup bottled balsamic vinaigrette** in a plastic bag to coat spears with dressing. Grill asparagus 4 minutes (place spears at a 90˚ angle to grill grate), then carefully flip. Grill 4 more minutes. Transfer to a platter; drizzle with extra dressing.

simmered and sautéed asparagus

Place **1 bunch asparagus,** trimmed, peeled and cut into 2-inch pieces, in a 10-inch skillet. Add enough **water** to cover. Heat until simmering, then simmer 4 minutes. Pour off water, return to heat and add **2 tablespoons butter; 1 shallot,** finely diced; and salt to taste. Cook 3 minutes, then stir in **1 tablespoon fresh lemon juice.**

steamed asparagus with wasabi mayo

Place a steamer insert in a medium saucepan. Add 1 inch of **water** and bring to a boil. Add **1 bunch asparagus,** trimmed, peeled and cut into 2-inch pieces. Cover and steam 5 minutes. Meanwhile, in a small bowl, blend **½ cup light mayonnaise, 2 teaspoons wasabi powder, ½ teaspoon rice vinegar** and **⅛ teaspoon sugar.** Serve steamed asparagus pieces alongside wasabi mayo.

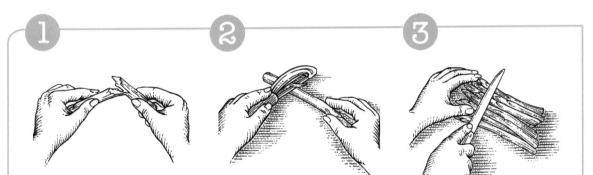

1 Gently bend spear about 2 inches from stem end until it breaks naturally.

2 With a vegetable peeler or small knife, remove tough, stringy skin at stem end.

3 For steaming and simmering, cut into 2-inch lengths, starting at the tips.

food **university**

POUND FOR POUND, DRIED BEANS COST ONE-THIRD THE PRICE OF CANNED BEANS.
BUT WHILE YOU DO NEED TO BUDGET TIME TO CLEAN, SOAK AND COOK THEM
(SEE OPPOSITE PAGE), YOU CAN SAVOR THE SAVINGS. THESE DISHES ARE $2 OR
LESS PER SERVING. **BY JULIE MILTENBERGER**

Black Bean Soup

Cooking soaked beans: Rinse soaked beans. Place **1 pound of beans** in a large pot. Add **6 cups hot water**, **2 tablespoons oil**, **2 teaspoons onion powder**, **¼ teaspoon garlic salt**, **3 small chicken bouillon cubes** and **¼ teaspoon pepper**. Heat to boiling, then simmer 30 minutes or until tender.

white bean spread

Heat broiler. Slice **2 loaves of Italian bread** on the diagonal into 18 slices. Toast 2 to 3 minutes per side. Add **6 cups soaked and cooked white beans** into food processor with **10 kalamata olives**, pitted and chopped, 1 tablespoon **chopped fresh parsley**, **1 tablespoon olive oil**, **1 tablespoon lemon juice**, **¼ teaspoon salt** and **⅛ teaspoon black pepper**. Puree until smooth. Serve on toast.

black bean soup

Heat **2 tablespoons oil** in 5-quart stockpot over medium heat. Add **2 carrots**, peeled and diced; **2 ribs celery**, trimmed and diced; **1 medium diced onion** and **4 cloves minced garlic**. Cook, over medium heat, for 5 minutes. Once fragrant and slightly softened, add two **14-ounce cans vegetable broth**, **1 envelope ham flavoring** (such as Goya), **1 teaspoon dried oregano**, **½ teaspoon cayenne**, **2 cups water** and **6 cups soaked and cooked black beans**. Bring to a simmer. Reduce heat to medium-low and cook, covered, for 20 minutes, stirring occasionally. Puree soup in batches; serve warm, with **sour cream**, if desired.

beef and bean tacos

Cook **½ pound ground beef** in a large nonstick skillet until no longer pink, 5 minutes. Add **1 small onion, chopped**, **3 cups soaked and cooked pinto beans**, **2 teaspoons taco seasoning** (such as Lawry's) and cook 4 more minutes. Spoon in **½ cup bottled salsa** and heat through. Have ready **12 hard or soft taco shells**, warmed as per package directions. Spoon scant ½ cup bean mixture onto taco shells and top with **shredded cheese**, **lettuce** and **sour cream**, if desired. Serve additional **salsa** on the side.

Pick through: Pour dried beans onto a large baking sheet. Spread out and pick through, discarding any rocks, dirt and debris.

Quick soak: Combine 1 pound beans in large pot with 12 cups water and 2 teaspoons salt. Boil 2 minutes, then soak in pot for 1 hour.

Overnight soak: In a large bowl, combine 1 pound beans with 8 cups water and 1 teaspoon salt. Refrigerate overnight.

may

Chicken Rollatini
page 109

WATCH YOUR WAISTLINE AND PROTECT
YOUR POCKETBOOK WITH QUICK TAKES ON
FAMILY FAVORITES, SUCH AS QUESADILLAS,
SLOPPY JOES, AND SPAGHETTI PIE.

**Sweet and Spicy
Chicken Thighs**
page 117

**Fresh Fruit Salad with
Pomegranate Syrup**
page 121

Coffee Cake
page 123

master
CLASS

A FEW LUCKY *FAMILY CIRCLE* EDITORS GOT SCHOOLED IN SOME
ESSENTIAL RECIPES FROM OUR IN-HOUSE PROS. PUT THE LESSONS
THEY LEARNED TO THE TEST IN YOUR OWN KITCHEN.

Editorial assistants Amanda Flores, Caren Oppenheim and Allison Baker worked with Julie, our senior food editor, on how to make a **weeknight dinner** that's also **great for entertaining.** "This impressive dish was easier than I expected," says Allison, "even for a beginner like me."

chicken rollatini

MAKES: 4 servings. **PREP:** 10 minutes. **COOK:** 4 minutes. **BAKE:** at 350° for 25 minutes.

- 4 **thin-sliced chicken breast halves (about 1 pound)**
- 8 **slices deli smoked turkey (about ¼ pound)**
- 4 **slices provolone cheese, folded in half**
- 8 **large fresh basil leaves**
- 4 **toothpicks**
- ¼ **teaspoon salt**
- ⅛ **teaspoon black pepper**
- 1 **tablespoon olive oil**
  Noodles and a vegetable (optional)

1. Heat oven to 350°. Spread chicken cutlets on a cutting board. If you can't find thin-sliced chicken, simply slice 4 thick cutlets in half to form 8 thin cutlets. Save 4 for another use.

2. Place 2 slices smoked turkey on each piece of chicken. Top each with one slice folded provolone cheese and 2 of the basil leaves. Roll up chicken to enclose filling, folding any overlapping edges of turkey over cheese (see tip, at right). Secure closed with toothpicks. Season with salt and pepper.

3. Heat oil in a 10-inch nonstick skillet over medium-high heat. Add chicken rolls and brown on all sides, turning, about 4 minutes. Transfer chicken rolls to a 13 × 9 × 2-inch baking dish and cover with foil. Bake at 350° for 20 to 25 minutes or until chicken is cooked through.

4. To serve: Remove toothpicks and cut chicken rolls crosswise into ½-inch-thick slices. Serve with cooked noodles and a green vegetable, if desired.

PER SERVING: 275 calories; 14 g fat (6 g sat.); 35 g protein; 2 g carbohydrate; 0 g fiber; 752 mg sodium; 92 mg cholesterol

GET SCHOOLED

Amanda, Caren and Allison were such novices at cooking they were even at a loss about buying chicken.

›› Look for well-sealed, odorless packages that have a few days remaining on the sell-by date.

›› Rinse your chicken in cold water when you get home; pat dry with paper towels.

›› If needed, pound thicker part of chicken breast to flatten, so it cooks evenly in the oven.

—Julie Miltenberger, *senior food editor*

TIP
Fold edges of sliced turkey over the cheese before tightly rolling chicken. This will help keep melted cheese from oozing out of the open ends while baking.

FC staffers Susan Hennessey and Meg Ragland wanted Cindy, our assistant food editor, to give them strategies for **cooking for two** and tips for **properly seasoning food.** "Now I know to salt and pepper each part of a dish," says Meg. "No more hot sauce!"

pork chops with roasted vegetables

MAKES: 2 servings. **PREP:** 10 minutes. **ROAST:** at 450° for 25 minutes. **COOK:** 10 minutes.

- 3 cups cauliflower florets
- 1 cup baby carrots
- 2 tablespoons butter, melted
- 1 teaspoon salt
- ¾ teaspoon black pepper
- 2 thin bone-in pork chops (about ¾ pound total)
- ½ cup reduced-sodium chicken broth
- 2 tablespoons heavy cream
- 1½ tablespoons grainy mustard

1. Heat oven to 450°. Place cauliflower and carrots on a rimmed baking sheet and drizzle with 1 tablespoon butter. Sprinkle with ½ teaspoon salt and ¼ teaspoon pepper; stir to coat evenly. Roast for 25 minutes or until browned around edges.
2. Heat remaining 1 tablespoon butter in a large nonstick skillet over high heat. Pat pork chops dry with paper towels and sprinkle both sides with ¼ teaspoon each salt and pepper. Place pork in skillet and cook for 1½ minutes per side. Remove from skillet to a platter and cover with foil.

3. Discard remaining fat and return skillet to medium heat. Add broth to skillet; boil 4 minutes. Return pork and any juices to skillet and stir in heavy cream; cook another 3 minutes or until thickened. Stir in mustard and remaining ¼ teaspoon each salt and pepper and serve with vegetables.

PER SERVING: 408 calories; 24 g fat (13 g sat.); 30 g protein; 18 g carbohydrate; 6 g fiber; 1,140 mg sodium; 121 mg cholesterol

Orange Sauce Variation: Prepare above recipe through step 2. Add 1 tablespoon **olive oil,** 2 minced **garlic cloves,** ½ teaspoon **ground cumin** and a pinch of **red pepper flakes** to pan. Cook over medium heat 1 minute. Stir in ¾ cup **orange juice;** increase heat to medium-high. Cook 5 minutes. Pour over pork chops, roasted **green beans** and **red pepper strips.**

GET SCHOOLED

Meg and Susan were bored with their tried-and-true recipes and wanted to add flavor to their "date nights."

» Buy meat and chicken in multiples of two, and freeze in pairs for future use.

» Use freshly ground spices if possible. You can find spice grinders at most dollar stores.

» Season food when you start cooking, then taste at the end to see if more is needed.

—Cindy Heller, *assistant food editor*

TIP
Remove seared pork from skillet before it's cooked through—it will finish cooking when you add it back into the sauce.

Editors Jonna Gallo Weppler and Robb Riedel are both accomplished home cooks but felt they needed a primer from Michael, our associate food editor, for **sautéing a simple steak.** "I am comfortable in the kitchen but have never been able to nail the perfect steak. It's always too rare or well-done," says Jonna.

GET SCHOOLED

Jonna and Robb used to cut into the middle of their steaks to check for doneness.

» For optimum browning, use a stainless steel skillet (not nonstick).

» Heat pan well over medium-high heat before adding oil.

» Don't move meat around until ready to flip over; check internal temp with an instant-read thermometer.

—Michael Tyrrell, *associate food editor*

TIP
Use tongs—instead of piercing steak with a fork, which releases juices—to turn the steak. At the end, season meat with additional salt and pepper, if needed.

sliced sautéed sirloin with shallot pan sauce

MAKES: 4 servings. **PREP:** 10 minutes. **COOK:** 12 minutes.

- 1 **boneless sirloin steak, about 1 inch thick, 1¼ pounds**
- 2 **tablespoons canola oil**
- ¼ **teaspoon salt**
- ⅛ **teaspoon black pepper**

Shallot Pan Sauce:
- 2 **tablespoons finely chopped shallot (or onion)**
- 1 **tablespoon chopped fresh rosemary**
- 1 **clove garlic, finely chopped**
- ½ **cup dry red wine**
- ½ **cup beef broth**
- 1 **tablespoon butter**
- 1 **tablespoon chopped flat-leaf parsley**

1. Cook Sirloin: Heat a large skillet over medium-high heat. Brush the steak with 1 tablespoon of the oil and season with salt and pepper.

2. Add remaining tablespoon oil to skillet and add steak. Cook the steak 4 minutes per side or until internal temperature registers 125° on an instant-read thermometer for medium-rare. Remove to a warm plate and allow to rest 5 minutes while making sauce.

3. Make Shallot Pan Sauce: Drain off all but 1 tablespoon of skillet drippings. Add shallot to skillet and cook 1 minute, stirring frequently. Add rosemary and garlic and cook 30 seconds to 1 minute, until fragrant. Add wine and boil for 1 minute, scraping up the browned bits on the bottom of the skillet. Add broth and boil 1 minute. Whisk in butter; stir in parsley.

4. Thinly slice steak against the grain. Serve with the pan sauce.

PER SERVING: 290 calories; 16 g fat (4 g sat.); 29 g protein; 2 g carbohydrate; 0 g fiber; 319 mg sodium; 60 mg cholesterol

Executive Editor Darcy Jacobs and her family love fish, but she asked Michael to show her a **healthier—but still quick—alternative** to sautéing. "The cod was moist and delicious—and I can throw it all together after work."

oven-roasted cod with tomato relish

MAKES: 4 servings. **PREP:** 10 minutes. **BAKE:** at 450° for 18 minutes.
BROIL: 1 minute. **COOK:** 1 minute.

- 4 cod fillets, about 1½ pounds total
- 2 tablespoons extra-virgin olive oil
- ¼ teaspoon salt
- ¼ teaspoon black pepper
- 2 cups grape tomatoes, quartered
- ¼ cup pitted kalamata olives, coarsely chopped
- ½ cup fresh basil, chopped
- 1 to 2 teaspoons balsamic vinegar
- 2 cups chicken broth
- 1 cup shredded carrot
- 1 cup uncooked couscous

1. Heat oven to 450°. Spray a 13 × 9 × 2-inch baking dish with nonstick cooking spray.
2. Place cod in prepared baking dish, skin-side down. Brush with 1 tablespoon of the oil and ⅛ teaspoon each of the salt and pepper. Bake at 450° for 15 to 18 minutes or until fish flakes easily with a fork. Run under the broiler for a minute, if desired, to lightly brown.
3. Meanwhile, in a small bowl, mix together the tomatoes, olives, basil, remaining 1 tablespoon olive oil, vinegar, remaining ⅛ teaspoon each salt and pepper. Cover and set aside.
4. While cod is cooking, bring the chicken broth to a simmer and stir in the carrots. Simmer for 1 minute. Stir in the couscous and take off heat. Cover and allow to sit 5 minutes.
5. Serve the cod with the tomato relish and couscous on the side.

PER SERVING: 430 calories; 13 g fat (2 g sat.); 34 g protein; 43 g carbohydrate; 5 g fiber; 976 mg sodium; 65 mg cholesterol

GET SCHOOLED

Darcy's goal was to get a weeknight meal on the table in under 30 minutes.

›› The tomato relish also pairs nicely with chicken or pork.

›› Other fish, such as salmon, tilapia or tuna, can be baked using this simple method.

›› Quick-cooking couscous makes a satisfying side dish.

TIP
To be sure the fish is done, use a thicker piece as a test. Fish is ready when it is opaque and flakes easily with a fork.

Senior editor Gay Norton Edelman looks for **healthy vegetarian dinners** for her family that are filling too. "Regina taught me how to caramelize onions without burning them!"

escarole with caramelized onions and chickpeas

MAKES: 4 servings. **PREP:** 10 minutes. **COOK:** 32 minutes.

- 2 tablespoons olive oil
- 1 large sweet onion (such as Vidalia; about 1 pound), thinly sliced
- 1 large bunch escarole (about 1½ pounds), washed and torn into pieces
- ¼ cup golden raisins
- ¼ teaspoon salt
- ½ pound (2⅓ cups uncooked) multigrain penne pasta (such as Barilla Plus)
- 1 can (15.5 ounces) chickpeas, undrained
- Grated Parmesan cheese (optional)

1. Heat oil in 12-inch skillet over medium heat. Add onion and cook, stirring often, for 15 to 23 minutes or until golden. Lower heat if onion is browning too quickly.

2. Add escarole and raisins to skillet. Cook, turning occasionally, for about 6 minutes, until leaves are tender and stem ends are still crunchy. Sprinkle with salt.

3. Meanwhile, bring a large pot of salted water to a boil. Cook penne according to package directions, about 11 minutes. Drain, reserving ½ cup pasta water, and return pasta to pot.

4. Stir in chickpeas with their liquid. Simmer, stirring occasionally, for 3 minutes or until heated through. Serve over pasta, adding reserved pasta water if needed to thin sauce. Sprinkle with grated cheese, if desired.

PER SERVING: 487 calories; 10 g fat (1 g sat.); 19 g protein; 83 g carbohydrate; 16 g fiber; 540 mg sodium; 0 mg cholesterol

TIP
Cook onions over medium heat—it may take 15 to 23 minutes—to give the sugar in the onions enough time to caramelize.

money-saving meals

YOU CAN STICK TO YOUR DIET AND ENJOY THE SAME DELICIOUS DINNERS AS THE REST OF YOUR FAMILY WITH OUR BUDGET-FRIENDLY RECIPES. **BY MICHAEL TYRRELL**

Spaghetti Pie is a clever way to use leftover pasta—and sure to become a family favorite. (Recipe, page 119)

bean and cheese quesadillas

MAKES: about 6 servings. **PREP:** 15 minutes. **COOK:** 7 minutes for filling, about 3 minutes per quesadilla.

1 tablespoon olive oil
1 small onion, finely chopped
½ small green pepper, seeded and chopped
1 can (15 ounces) black beans, drained and lightly mashed
½ cup lower sodium salsa (such as Muir Glen)
½ teaspoon chili powder
1 package (10 count) fajita-size flour or whole-wheat tortillas
8 ounces reduced-fat pepper Jack cheese, shredded
½ cup cilantro leaves
Extra salsa for serving (optional)

1. Heat oil in a large nonstick skillet over medium-high heat. Add onion and green pepper and cook for 4 minutes, stirring occasionally. Stir in beans, salsa and chili powder. Cook for 3 minutes, stirring occasionally.

2. Spray a large nonstick skillet with cooking spray. Place over medium-high heat. Place one tortilla in the skillet and cook for 1 minute. Spread ⅓ cup of the bean mixture and ⅓ cup of the cheese evenly over the tortilla. Sprinkle some of the cilantro over the top. Place another tortilla on top and cook 1 minute. Press gently with a spatula and turn. Cook for 1 minute or until browned.

3. Place quesadilla on a baking sheet and keep warm in 200° oven. Repeat with the remaining ingredients to make four additional quesadillas. Allow skillet to cool slightly if it becomes too hot.

4. To serve, cut each quesadilla into quarters. Serve 3 quarters to each person (there will be 2 leftover wedges for nondieters to enjoy).

PER SERVING: 312 calories; 13 g fat (6 g sat.); 16 g protein; 34 g carbohydrate; 5 g fiber; 786 mg sodium; 23 mg cholesterol

$1.63 per serving

The creamy filling made with healthful ingredients makes these quesadillas a guilt-free treat.

PHOTOGRAPHY BY YUNHEE KIM

Food styling: Megan Schlow. Prop styling: Megan Hedgpeth.

At 25 cents a serving, versatile potatoes supply a valuable dose of vitamin C and potassium.

$1.89
per serving

eggs florentine casserole

MAKES: 6 servings. **PREP:** 10 minutes. **MICROWAVE:** 5 minutes. **BAKE:** at 375° for 40 minutes.

 1 large potato, about 10 ounces, diced
12 eggs
 1 cup reduced-fat shredded Cheddar cheese
 ½ cup grated Parmesan cheese
 ½ teaspoon salt
 ½ teaspoon ground nutmeg
 ¼ teaspoon black pepper
 2 packages (10 ounces each) frozen chopped spinach, thawed and water squeezed out
 2 ounces Canadian bacon, finely chopped

1. Place potato in a microwave-safe dish. Add ½ cup water and cover with plastic, venting at corner. Microwave 5 minutes on HIGH. Drain and reserve.

2. Heat oven to 375°. Coat a 13 × 9 × 2-inch baking dish with nonstick cooking spray.
3. In a large bowl, whisk together eggs, cheeses, salt, nutmeg and black pepper. Stir in spinach and potato.
4. Pour egg mixture into prepared baking dish. Sprinkle the chopped Canadian bacon over the top. Bake at 375° for 40 minutes or until set in center. Cool slightly before serving.

PER SERVING: 313 calories; 18 g fat (8 g sat.); 26 g protein; 11 g carbohydrate; 2 g fiber; 864 mg sodium; 451 mg cholesterol

spicy sloppy joes

MAKES: 6 sandwiches. **PREP:** 10 minutes. **COOK:** 18 minutes.

 1 pound lean (90%) ground beef
 ½ small onion, finely chopped
 ½ small green pepper, finely chopped
 1 can (8 ounces) no-salt-added tomato sauce
 2 tablespoons ketchup
 1 tablespoon distilled white vinegar
1½ teaspoons Worcestershire sauce
 2 teaspoons sugar
 ¼ teaspoon hot sauce
 6 whole-wheat English muffins, toasted
    Prepared cole slaw and pickles (optional)

1. Spray a large nonstick skillet with nonstick cooking spray. Crumble in ground beef; add onion and green pepper. Cook over medium heat for 8 minutes. Stir occasionally.
2. Add tomato sauce, ketchup, vinegar, Worcestershire, sugar and hot sauce. Mix well, breaking up beef with a wooden spoon. Simmer on medium-low, uncovered, for 10 minutes, stirring occasionally.
3. Spoon equal portions of meat mixture onto English muffins. Serve with cole slaw and pickles on the side, if desired.

PER SANDWICH: 271 calories; 5 g fat (2 g sat.); 22 g protein; 34 g carbohydrate; 5 g fiber; 459 mg sodium; 47 mg cholesterol

$1.87
per serving

sweet and spicy chicken thighs

MAKES: 4 servings (plus leftover chicken for Chicken Alfredo Potatoes, page 119).
PREP: 10 minutes. **BAKE:** at 375° for 30 minutes.

- 2 tablespoons light soy sauce
- 2 teaspoons honey
- 2 teaspoons spicy brown mustard
- 6 skinless bone-in chicken thighs, about 5 ounces each
- ¾ cup barley
- 1 can (14½ ounces) chicken broth with roasted vegetables and herbs
- ½ cup frozen peas
- ¼ teaspoon salt
- ⅛ teaspoon black pepper

1. Heat oven to 375°. Coat a baking dish with nonstick cooking spray.
2. In a small bowl, whisk together the soy sauce, honey and mustard. Place the chicken thighs in the prepared baking dish. Brush the thighs with half of the soy sauce mixture. Bake at 375° for 15 minutes. Brush the chicken with the remaining soy sauce mixture and bake for an additional 15 minutes.
3. While the chicken is baking, prepare the barley following package directions, substituting the chicken broth for water. Stir in the peas, salt and pepper during the last 5 minutes.
4. Serve 4 pieces of chicken with the barley. Shred the meat from the remaining 2 chicken thighs and reserve for the Chicken Alfredo Potatoes, page119.

PER SERVING: 350 calories; 10 g fat (3 g sat.); 28 g protein; 35 g carbohydrate; 7 g fiber; 987 mg sodium; 81 mg cholesterol

$1.49
per serving

By substituting flavorful chicken thighs for pricy chicken breasts, we've cut the cost of this meal by 25%.

Serve this high-fiber, low-fat and meatless take on the New Orleans classic with hot sauce on the side.

$1.99
per serving

red bean vegetable jambalaya

MAKES: 6 servings. **PREP:** 20 minutes.
COOK: 40 minutes.

- 1 tablespoon vegetable oil
- 1 large onion, sliced
- 4 large carrots, peeled and sliced into ½-inch coins
- ½ cauliflower, cut into florets, about 6 cups
- 1 large green pepper, cut into 1-inch pieces
- 2 cloves garlic, peeled and chopped
- 2 cans (14½ ounces each) no-salt-added diced tomatoes (such as Muir Glen)
- 1 tablespoon salt-free Cajun/Creole seasoning (such as the Spice Hunter)
- ½ teaspoon salt
- 1 can (15 ounces) red kidney beans, drained and rinsed
- 1 package (7.6 ounces) whole-grain couscous

1. Heat oil in a stockpot over medium heat. Add the onion and carrots and cook 6 minutes, stirring occasionally. Add cauliflower and pepper and cook an additional 6 minutes, stirring occasionally.
2. Stir in the garlic, tomatoes, Cajun seasoning and salt. Simmer with lid ajar for 25 minutes. Stir occasionally.
3. Add beans and simmer 3 minutes, until beans are heated through and vegetables are fork-tender.
4. While jambalaya is cooking, prepare couscous following package directions.
5. Serve jambalaya over couscous.

PER SERVING: 263 calories; 3 g fat (0 g sat.); 11 g protein; 50 g carbohydrate; 9 g fiber; 418 mg sodium; 0 mg cholesterol

$1.82
per serving

chicken alfredo potatoes

MAKES: 4 servings. **PREP:** 10 minutes.
MICROWAVE: 8 minutes. **COOK:** about 4 minutes.

- 4 small potatoes, about 4 ounces each
- 1 bag (14 ounces) frozen broccoli florets
- 1 cup shredded chicken thighs (left over from Sweet and Spicy Chicken Thighs, page 117)
- 1 cup jarred light Alfredo sauce

1. Pierce potatoes a few times with a fork and place in microwave. Microwave on HIGH for 8 minutes.
2. Cook broccoli following package directions.
3. Place shredded chicken and Alfredo sauce in a small saucepan and heat gently, about 4 minutes.
4. To serve, cut each potato in half lengthwise. Place ¼ of the broccoli over each cut potato. Spoon equal amounts of the chicken and Alfredo sauce mixture over each potato.

PER SERVING: 339 calories; 11 g fat (5 g sat.); 20 g protein; 36 g carbohydrate; 6 g fiber; 437 mg sodium; 55 mg cholesterol

$1.56
per serving

spaghetti pie

MAKES: 6 servings. **PREP:** 10 minutes.
COOK: 8 minutes. **BAKE:** at 350° for 40 minutes.

- ½ pound whole-wheat spaghetti
- 2 cups chunky pasta sauce
- 1 cup reduced-fat shredded mozzarella cheese
- 4 ounces (¼ pound) Canadian bacon, diced
- ¼ cup pitted black olives, coarsely chopped
- 4 eggs, lightly beaten
- ¼ cup unseasoned bread crumbs
- 3 tablespoons grated Parmesan cheese

1. Heat oven to 350°.
2. Break spaghetti into thirds and cook 8 minutes. Drain and add back to pot.
3. Stir in the pasta sauce, mozzarella, Canadian bacon and olives. Add the eggs; stir mixture until combined.
4. Coat a 10-inch cast-iron skillet or oven-proof nonstick skillet with cooking spray. Sprinkle the inside of the skillet with the bread crumbs.
5. Spoon the spaghetti mixture into the skillet. Bake at 350° for 30 minutes. Top with the Parmesan cheese and bake for 10 minutes.
6. Cut into 6 wedges. Serve with a green salad tossed with reduced-fat dressing, if desired.

PER SERVING: 349 calories; 10 g fat (4 g sat.); 21 g protein; 44 g carbohydrate; 7 g fiber; 820 mg sodium; 166 mg cholesterol

healthy snacks

BETWEEN-MEAL HUNGER PANGS ARE INEVITABLE. HAVE A ½ CUP OF THIS FRUIT SALAD AS A MID-MORNING NIBBLE AND ½ CUP OF THE VEGGIES TO WARD OFF THE MUNCHIES AND GET 2 OF YOUR 5 DAILY SERVINGS.

Bottled roasted red peppers and marinara sauce provide the base for a quick-to-fix Red Pepper Sauce.

grilled vegetables with red pepper sauce

MAKES: 6 servings. **PREP:** 20 minutes.
GRILL: 12 minutes per batch.
COOK: 5 minutes.

- 8 plum tomatoes (about 1½ pounds), cored and halved
- 4 medium-size zucchini, sliced in half lengthwise
- 2 sweet red peppers, cored, seeded and quartered
- 2 yellow peppers, cored, seeded and quartered
- 1 pound asparagus, ends trimmed
- 1 pound large mushrooms, stemmed
- 3 tablespoons extra-virgin olive oil
- ½ teaspoon salt
- ½ teaspoon black pepper
- 1 jar (24 ounces) roasted red peppers, drained and chopped
- 1 small onion, chopped
- 1 tablespoon balsamic vinegar
- 1 tablespoon Italian seasoning
- ⅓ cup marinara sauce

1. Heat a gas grill to medium-high or prepare a charcoal grill with medium-hot coals.
2. Place tomatoes, zucchini, red and yellow peppers, asparagus and mushrooms in a large bowl and toss with 2 tablespoons of the olive oil and ¼ teaspoon each of the salt and pepper.
3. Grill (in batches if necessary) for about 5 to 6 minutes per side. Set aside.
4. Meanwhile, place remaining 1 tablespoon olive oil, red peppers, onion, vinegar, Italian seasoning and marinara sauce in a blender. Puree until smooth, then pour into a small saucepan. Stir in remaining ¼ teaspoon each salt and pepper and simmer over medium heat for 5 minutes.
5. Serve vegetables with red pepper sauce.

PER SERVING: 175 calories; 8 g fat (1 g sat.); 8 g protein; 23 g carbs; 7 g fiber; 968 mg sodium; 0 mg cholesterol

fresh fruit salad with pomegranate syrup

MAKES: 8 cups. **PREP:** 15 minutes. **COOK:** 5 minutes.

- ⅓ cup pomegranate juice
- ¼ cup sugar
- 1 teaspoon fresh grated orange zest
- 2 large navel oranges, sectioned
- 2 kiwis, peeled, halved and sliced
- 1 large banana, sliced
- 1 Granny Smith apple, cored and cut into ½-inch slices
- 1 Red Delicious apple, cored and cut into ½-inch slices
- 1 large pear, cored and cut into ½-inch slices
- ½ pineapple, peeled, cored and cubed
- ½ cup pomegranate seeds (optional)

1. Combine pomegranate juice and sugar in a medium saucepan; bring to a boil, stirring until sugar dissolves, about 5 minutes. Remove from heat and stir in orange zest. Let cool to room temperature.
2. Combine oranges, kiwis, banana, apples, pear, pineapple and pomegranate seeds in a bowl; pour syrup over fruit and toss to coat.

PER 1-CUP SERVING: 184 calories; 0 g fat (0 g sat.); 1 g protein; 47 g carbs; 3 g fiber; 5 mg sodium; 0 mg cholesterol

PHOTOS: CHARLES SCHILLER; TINA RUPP.

food **university**

OUR CLASSIC RECIPE BOASTS THE PERFECT ALL-IMPORTANT
RATIO OF CRUMB TO CAKE. **BY JULIE MILTENBERGER**

If you don't own a
powdered sugar
sifter, use a wire-
mesh colander or
strainer to dust
the top of the cake.

PHOTOGRAPHY BY ALEXANDRA GRABLEWSKI

coffee cake

MAKES: 9 servings. **PREP:** 25 minutes. **BAKE:** at 350° for 1 hour.

Topping:
- ½ cup firmly packed light-brown sugar
- ⅔ cup all-purpose flour
- ½ teaspoon cinnamon
- Pinch salt
- ¼ cup (½ stick) cold unsalted butter, cut up

Cake:
- 2 tablespoons white vinegar plus enough milk to equal 1 cup
- 2 cups all-purpose flour
- 1½ teaspoons baking powder
- ½ teaspoon baking soda
- ¼ teaspoon salt
- 6 tablespoons butter, softened
- ⅔ cup firmly packed light-brown sugar
- 1 teaspoon vanilla extract
- 2 large eggs
- 2 teaspoons confectioners' sugar

1. Heat oven to 350°. Coat a 9-inch square baking pan with cooking spray. **Topping:** In medium-size bowl, blend brown sugar (step 1, below), flour, cinnamon and salt. With pastry blender (step 2, below), cut butter into flour mixture until crumbs form. Chill.

2. Cake: Pour vinegar into a measuring cup. Add enough milk to equal 1 cup (step 3, below). Set aside. In a medium-size bowl, whisk together flour, baking powder, baking soda and salt.

3. In large bowl, beat butter, sugar and vanilla until fluffy, 2 minutes. Add eggs, one at a time, beating well after each. Working in batches, beat in milk mixture alternately with flour mixture.

4. Scrape batter into pan. Sprinkle with topping. Bake at 350° for 1 hour, until a toothpick inserted into cake comes out clean. Cool in pan on wire rack. Dust with confectioners' sugar; cut in squares.

PER SERVING: 387 calories; 15 g fat (9 g sat.); 6 g protein; 58 g carbohydrate; 1 g fiber; 240 mg sodium; 83 mg cholesterol

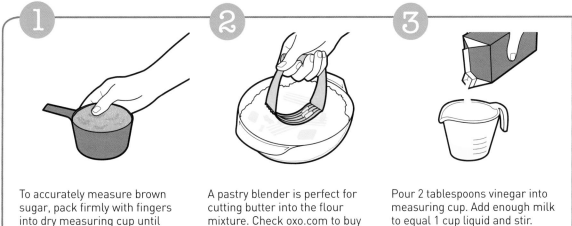

1 To accurately measure brown sugar, pack firmly with fingers into dry measuring cup until smooth and level.

2 A pastry blender is perfect for cutting butter into the flour mixture. Check oxo.com to buy one or to find a local retailer.

3 Pour 2 tablespoons vinegar into measuring cup. Add enough milk to equal 1 cup liquid and stir. Mixture will look curdled.

june

Blueberry Pie
page 151

SUMMER IS IN FULL SWING, AND THE
MARKETS ARE BURSTING WITH
PRODUCE. BAKE A BLUEBERRY PIE—
THEN TOSS A CRISP SALAD FOR SUPPER.

Layered Cobb Salad
page 133

Fish Tacos
page 136

Caesar Pasta Primavera
page 145

STACKED HIGH WITH ICE CREAM AND BERRIES, WAFFLES GO BEYOND BREAKFAST. **BY JULIE MILTENBERGER**

strawberry waffle sundaes

MAKES: 12 servings (½ stack each). **PREP:** 10 minutes. **COOK:** 3 minutes per batch. **KEEP WARM:** in 200° oven.

 1 **container (1 pound) fresh strawberries, hulled and sliced**
 2 **tablespoons orange juice**
1½ **teaspoons sugar**
 2 **cups biscuit mix (such as Bisquick)**
1⅓ **cups milk**
 1 **egg**
 2 **tablespoons oil**
 2 **teaspoons vanilla extract**
 ¼ **teaspoon ground cinnamon**
 9 **cups vanilla ice cream**
 6 **tablespoons whipped topping**
    Chocolate sauce, for drizzling

1. Heat oven to 200°. In a medium-size bowl, toss together strawberries, orange juice and sugar. Refrigerate.

2. Heat a waffle maker following manufacturer's directions. (Either a square or a round waffle maker works well here.) In a large bowl, combine biscuit mix, milk, egg, oil, vanilla and cinnamon.

3. Make waffles, as per manufacturer's directions. Keep waffles warm on rack of 200° oven while cooking next batch. (You will need 12 waffles or waffle sections.)

4. To serve: Place one waffle or waffle section on a plate. Top with 1½ cups ice cream, ½ cup of the strawberry mixture and a second waffle. Add a few more strawberries and dollop with one tablespoon whipped topping. Drizzle with chocolate sauce and serve.

PER ½ STACK: 330 calories; 12 g fat (5 g sat.); 8 g protein; 49 g carbohydrate; 1 g fiber; 348 mg sodium; 47 mg cholesterol

Food styling: Karen Tack. Prop styling: Leslie Siegel.

PHOTOGRAPHY BY RITA MAAS

BOWLED over

IT'S A TOSS-UP AS TO WHICH OF THESE HEARTY MAIN DISH SALADS YOU'LL WANT TO TRY FIRST.

With cucumbers, scallions and peppers, this savory Thai Salad with Pork packs serious crunch. (Recipe page 133)

Layered Cobb Salad (recipe page 133). Who can say no to layers of chicken, veggies, shrimp and bacon? Since the dressing doesn't cover all the greens in this mile-high salad, it's one easy do-ahead dinner that won't get soggy. In fact, the dish gets better if you can resist digging in right away—let it sit in your fridge for an hour or two before serving.

crunchy turkey salad

MAKES: 4 servings. **PREP:** 15 minutes.

⅓ cup olive oil
3 tablespoons white vinegar
3 tablespoons sugar
1 tablespoon poppy seeds
¼ teaspoon black pepper
1 large head Bibb lettuce, washed
2 cups diced cooked turkey (about ¾ pound) or cooked chicken
3 scallions, sliced
1 cup sliced almonds
1 cup chow mein noodles (such as La Choy)

1. In a small bowl, whisk olive oil, vinegar, sugar, poppy seeds and pepper; set aside.
2. Chop lettuce; you should have about 8 cups. Transfer to a medium-size bowl and add turkey, scallions, almonds and noodles. Toss with dressing and serve immediately.

PER SERVING: 506 calories; 34 g fat (4 g sat.); 24 g protein; 28 g carbohydrate; 5 g fiber; 692 mg sodium; 30 mg cholesterol

blt salad

MAKES: 8 servings. **PREP:** 10 minutes. **COOK:** 6 minutes. **REFRIGERATE:** 2 hours.

1 pound thick-sliced bacon
2 large heads romaine lettuce, washed, dried and chopped (about 16 cups)
3 large ripe tomatoes (1½ pounds), cored and cut into bite-size pieces
1 cup whipped salad dressing (such as Miracle Whip)
1 teaspoon salt-free seasoning mix

1. Cook bacon in a large skillet about 6 minutes, until crispy. Drain on paper towels; crumble when cool.
2. Place half of the lettuce in a 14- to 16-cup salad or trifle bowl. Sprinkle half of the tomato pieces and half of the crumbled bacon over the lettuce. Press to compress ingredients.

3. Spread with half of the salad dressing. Sprinkle with half the seasoning mix. Repeat layering with lettuce, tomato (reserving some for garnish), bacon and dressing. Sprinkle with remaining seasoning and tomato. Cover and chill for at least 2 hours.

PER SERVING: 224 calories; 16 g fat (4 g sat); 9 g protein; 11 g carbohydrate; 3 g fiber; 695 mg sodium; 31 mg cholesterol

Photos (from left): Dasha Wright, Ann Stratton, Brian Hagiwara.

mediterranean chicken and orzo

MAKES: 8 servings. **PREP:** 25 minutes. **MICROWAVE:** 6 minutes. **COOK:** 10 minutes.

Dressing:
- 1 tablespoon Dijon mustard
- ¼ cup red-wine vinegar
- ¾ teaspoon salt
- ¼ teaspoon black pepper
- ¾ cup extra-virgin olive oil
- ½ teaspoon dried Italian seasoning

Salad:
- 4 extra-large sweet red peppers, halved lengthwise, cored and seeded
- 1 pound orzo
- 1 cup grape tomatoes, halved
- ½ cup pitted kalamata olives, coarsely chopped
- ¼ pound feta cheese, crumbled
- 2 packages (5 ounces each) precooked Italian-flavored chicken, chopped
  Fresh herbs, to garnish (optional)

1. Dressing: Whisk together mustard, vinegar, salt and black pepper in a small bowl. Add olive oil in a thin stream, whisking constantly. Whisk in Italian seasoning. Cover and refrigerate.

2. Salad: Place peppers in microwave-safe dish. Add cold water to depth of ⅛ inch (cook in batches, if necessary). Cover dish tightly with plastic wrap. Microwave 6 minutes or until peppers have softened slightly. Remove from dish; cool. Pat dry.

3. Cook orzo according to package directions, about 10 minutes. Combine with tomatoes, olives, feta and chicken in a large bowl. Pour ¾ cup of the dressing over top and gently stir until evenly coated. Drizzle with remaining dressing.

4. To serve, fill each pepper half with about 1⅓ cups of the orzo filling. Garnish with fresh herbs, if desired.

PER SERVING: 554 calories; 27 g fat (6 g sat); 23 g protein; 56 g carbohydrate; 5 g fiber; 735 mg sodium; 43 mg cholesterol

Baked Goat Cheese Salad
(Recipe opposite page)

Photos (from left): Dasha Wright, David Prince, James Baigrie.

baked goat cheese salad

MAKES: 6 servings. **PREP:** 15 minutes.
BAKE: at 375° for 10 minutes; at 400° for
8 minutes.

- 4 slices wheat bread
- 2 tablespoons toasted wheat germ
- ½ cup walnut pieces
- ½ teaspoon dried oregano
- ⅛ teaspoon salt
- ⅛ teaspoon black pepper
- 3 tablespoons raspberry vinegar
- ½ teaspoon Dijon mustard
- 1½ teaspoons sugar
- ⅓ cup extra-virgin olive oil
- 1 log (10 ounces) herbed goat cheese
- 2 bags (6 ounces each) spring greens salad mix

1. Heat oven to 375°. Pulse one slice bread in food processor until fine crumbs are formed. Stir in wheat germ. Transfer to a 15 x 10 x 1-inch baking pan (push crumbs to one side).
2. Cut remaining 3 slices of bread into ½-inch pieces. Transfer to pan with bread crumbs. Place the walnuts on a second smaller baking sheet.
3. Spray bread pieces and crumbs with nonstick cooking spray. Season with oregano, salt and pepper. Transfer both baking pans to 375° oven and bake for 10 minutes or until crumbs and nuts are lightly browned, stirring halfway through. Remove pans from oven; increase oven temperature to 400°.
4. In small bowl, whisk vinegar, mustard and sugar. While whisking, add olive oil in a thin stream.
5. Cut goat cheese log into 6 equal pieces. Place one goat cheese slice on a paper towel; fold towel over slice. Gently press down to form a disc approximately 2½ inches in diameter. Repeat.
6. Coat slices with nonstick cooking spray. Dip in crumb mixture. Transfer coated cheese discs to baking sheet. Bake at 400° for 8 minutes or until cheese discs are lightly browned.
7. While the cheese is warming, toss together salad greens, dressing, walnuts and croutons. To serve: Divide salad evenly among 6 plates. Top each with 1 goat cheese disc.

PER SERVING: 385 calories; 32 g fat (12 g sat); 15 g protein; 13 g carbohydrate; 3 g fiber; 385 mg sodium; 37 mg cholesterol

thai salad with pork

MAKES: 6 servings. **PREP:** 20 minutes.
GRILL: 8 minutes.

Dressing:
- ⅓ cup reduced-fat creamy peanut butter
- 3 tablespoons vegetable oil
- 3 tablespoons fresh lemon juice
- 2 tablespoons low-sodium soy sauce
- 2 teaspoons sugar
- ½ tablespoon red pepper flakes
- ¼ teaspoon garlic powder
- ¼ teaspoon ground ginger

Pork and salad:
- 6 boneless, thin-cut pork chops
- 2 tablespoons low-sodium soy sauce
- 8 cups shredded iceberg lettuce, washed
- 1 cup bean sprouts
- 1 cucumber, peeled, seeded and thinly sliced
- 2 large sweet red peppers, cored, seeded and thinly sliced
- 3 large scallions, thinly sliced

1. Heat gas grill to hot or prepare outdoor grill with hot coals.
2. Dressing: Whisk peanut butter, oil, lemon juice, soy sauce, sugar, red pepper flakes, garlic powder and ginger in a bowl until smooth. Slowly whisk in ⅓ cup warm water. Cover and set aside.
3. Pork and salad: Brush chops with soy sauce. Grill 4 minutes. Turn and grill 3 to 4 minutes or until internal temperature registers 160° on an instant-read thermometer. Set aside and keep warm.
4. In a large bowl, toss lettuce, sprouts, cucumber, red pepper and scallions with ¾ cup of the dressing. Place a scant 2 cups of salad on each plate. Thinly slice pork; fan slices over each salad. Drizzle each with about 1 tablespoon dressing.

PER SERVING: 353 calories; 20 g fat (4 g sat.); 28 g protein; 17 g carbohydrate; 4 g fiber; 541 mg sodium; 58 mg cholesterol

layered cobb salad

MAKES: 8 servings. **PREP:** 15 minutes. **REFRIGERATE:** 1 hour

- 6 cups sliced romaine lettuce, washed
- ½ pound grape tomatoes, halved
- 4 cups shredded cooked chicken
- 2 ripe avocados, peeled and diced
- 1 large red onion, peeled and sliced
- 1 pound cooked medium-size shrimp, peeled (¾ pound peeled)
- 1 cup chunky blue cheese dressing
- 6 slices cooked bacon, crumbled

1. Place sliced lettuce in the bottom of a 14-cup glass salad bowl or trifle dish. Pack down slightly.
2. On top of lettuce, neatly layer tomatoes, chicken, avocados, red onion and shrimp. Press down lightly to compress.
3. Spread with dressing. Refrigerate at least 1 hour; sprinkle with bacon just before serving.

PER SERVING: 464 calories; 32 g fat (7 g sat.); 35 g protein; 12 g carbohydrate; 2 g fiber; 691 mg sodium; 155 mg cholesterol

stress-free dinners

NO TIME TO LOSE? A WINNING RECIPE FOR DIET SUCCESS INCLUDES ROTISSERIE CHICKEN, FROZEN VEGGIES AND OTHER HEALTHY STAPLES THAT MAKE IT EASY TO GET DINNER ON THE TABLE IN 25 MINUTES OR LESS. **BY CINDY HELLER**

Tortilla Soup
(Recipe page 139)

PHOTOGRAPHY BY DAVID PRINCE

asian lettuce wraps

MAKES: 4 servings. **PREP:** 10 minutes. **COOK:** 8½ minutes.

1 **head Boston lettuce**
2 **teaspoons vegetable oil**
2 **cloves garlic, chopped**
2 **teaspoons minced ginger**
2½ **cups frozen bell pepper blend (such as Birds Eye Pepper Stir-Fry)**
1 **pound extra-lean beef**
¼ **cup stir-fry sauce**

1. Remove 12 small bowl-shaped leaves from head of lettuce; rinse and set aside.
2. Heat oil in a large nonstick skillet over medium-high heat. Cook garlic and ginger for 30 seconds. Stir in peppers and cook for 2 minutes. Add beef and cook for 5 minutes. Drain off any accumulated fat in the pan.

3. Stir in stir-fry sauce and cook for 1 minute or until thickened. Spoon about ¼ cup beef mixture into each lettuce cup and serve.

PER SERVING: 215 calories; 8 g fat (3 g sat.); 26 g protein; 8 g carbohydrate; 2 g fiber; 609 mg sodium; 70 mg cholesterol

turkey waldorf salad

MAKES: 6 servings. **PREP:** 10 minutes.
REFRIGERATE 1 hour.

- ¾ cup low-fat ranch salad dressing
- 3 tablespoons cider vinegar
- 2 tablespoons sugar
- ¼ teaspoon black pepper
- 1 bag (16 ounces) coleslaw mix
- 1 bag (10 ounces) shredded carrots
- 1 package (9 ounces) precooked carved turkey pieces (such as Perdue Short Cuts), cut into ½-inch chunks
- 1 Fuji apple, cored and cut into ½-inch chunks
- ¾ cup chopped walnuts

1. In a small bowl, stir together ranch dressing, vinegar, sugar and black pepper; set aside.
2. Combine coleslaw mix, carrots, turkey, apple and walnuts in a large bowl. Drizzle salad dressing mixture over top and toss well to combine. Refrigerate at least 1 hour before serving.

PER SERVING: 268 calories; 14 g fat (2 g sat.); 15 g protein; 24 g carbohydrate; 5 g fiber; 615 mg sodium; 38 mg cholesterol

These crunchy, kid-friendly fish tacos rely on frozen breaded fillets to make them a flash in the pan.

fish tacos

MAKES: 5 servings. **PREP:** 10 minutes. **BAKE:** at 425° for 25 minutes. **MICROWAVE:** 1 minute.

- ⅔ cup shredded iceberg lettuce
- ¼ cup light mayonnaise
- 2 tablespoons lime juice
- 6 crunchy fish fillets (such as Gorton's)
- 10 corn tortillas
- 1 cup frozen corn kernels, thawed
- 1 container purchased fresh salsa (optional)

1. Heat oven to 425°. In a small bowl, stir together the lettuce, mayonnaise and lime juice; set aside.

2. Bake fish at 425° according to package directions. Wrap tortillas in aluminum foil and place in oven for final 10 minutes of cook time. Remove fish from oven and cut each fillet into 6 chunks.
3. Microwave corn for 1 minute. Place 3 to 4 pieces of fish in each tortilla and top with about 2 tablespoons lettuce mixture and 1 tablespoon of corn.
4. Serve tacos with salsa, if desired.

PER SERVING: 381 calories; 17 g fat (3 g sat.); 12 g protein; 47 g carbohydrate; 6 g fiber; 526 mg sodium; 25 mg cholesterol

Lightened-up ingredients such as lean ham, low-fat cheese, and light whole wheat bread make this decadent-looking sandwich healthful.

ham and caramelized onion grilled cheese

MAKES: 4 paninis; 1 per serving. **PREP:** 10 minutes. **COOK:** 20 minutes.

1 large onion, very thinly sliced
¼ teaspoon sugar
    Pinch salt
4 teaspoons spicy brown mustard
3 teaspoons horseradish
2 teaspoons honey
8 slices light whole-wheat bread (such as Pepperidge Farm)
12 slices (about 6 ounces) light ham (such as Healthy Ones)
4 slices (about 4 ounces) low-fat Swiss cheese (such as Alpine Lace)
4 cups mixed greens (optional)

1. Coat a medium-size nonstick skillet with nonstick cooking spray and place over medium heat. Add onion, sugar and salt to skillet; cover. Cook for 10 minutes, stirring occasionally, or until lightly browned; remove from heat.
2. Stir together mustard, horseradish and honey; set aside.
3. Spread 4 slices of bread evenly with mustard mixture, then layer 3 slices ham over each piece of bread. Place about 2 tablespoons onions on top of the ham, then place 1 slice cheese on top of the onions. Place 4 remaining bread slices over cheese.

4. Spritz both sides of sandwich with nonstick cooking spray and cook in a nonstick skillet over medium heat for 5 to 8 minutes or until cheese has melted, turning halfway through. Serve with mixed greens on the side, if desired.

PER SERVING: 262 calories; 8 g fat (4 g sat.); 21 g protein; 28 g carbohydrate; 3 g fiber; 616 mg sodium; 39 mg cholesterol

shrimp lo mein

MAKES: 6 servings. **PREP** 10 minutes. **MICROWAVE:** 1 minute. **COOK:** 12 minutes.

- 2 **packages (8 ounces each) tofu spaghetti noodles (such as Shirataki), drained and rinsed thoroughly**
- 1 **pound medium-size frozen raw shrimp (31-40 count), thawed according to package directions**
- 3 **tablespoons light teriyaki sauce**
- 2 **boxes (9 ounces each) frozen Szechuan vegetable blend with sesame sauce (such as Birds Eye)**
- 1 **cup frozen shelled edamame**
- 1 **tablespoon cornstarch**

1. Microwave noodles for 1 minute; set aside. Place shrimp in a small bowl and toss with 2 tablespoons teriyaki sauce; set aside.

2. Place mixed vegetables and edamame in a large nonstick skillet with ¼ cup water. Cover and cook, stirring occasionally, over medium-high heat for 7 minutes or until cooked through.

3. Stir shrimp into vegetable mixture; cover and cook 4 to 5 minutes or until shrimp is pink and cooked through.

4. Stir together remaining 1 tablespoon teriyaki sauce and the cornstarch, then stir into the mixture in the skillet until thickened. Gently stir noodles into skillet and cook until warmed through.

PER SERVING: 174 calories; 4 g fat (1 g sat.); 19 g protein; 14 g carbohydrate; 4 g fiber; 639 mg sodium; 115 mg cholesterol

tortilla soup

MAKES: 6 servings. PREP: 15 minutes.
COOK: 23 minutes.

- 1 tablespoon vegetable oil
- 1 medium-size green pepper, seeded and finely chopped
- 1 small onion, finely chopped
- 1 jalapeño pepper, seeded and finely chopped
- 1 tablespoon chili powder
- 5 cups low-sodium chicken broth
- 3 cups cooked, shredded chicken (from a rotisserie chicken)
- 1 can (14.5 ounces) no-salt-added diced tomatoes
- 1 can (14.5 ounces) black beans, drained and rinsed
- 2 tablespoons lime juice
- ¾ teaspoon salt
- ½ of a firm, ripe avocado, cut into chunks
- 1 cup crumbled baked tortilla chips (optional)

1. Heat oil in a large saucepan over medium-high heat. Add green pepper, onion and jalapeño to saucepan and cook, stirring often, for 7 minutes. Stir chili powder into pot and cook, stirring occasionally, for 1 minute.
2. Pour broth and 1 cup water into saucepan. Bring to a boil and reduce heat to medium; simmer for 10 minutes. Stir in chicken, tomatoes, beans, lime juice and salt; cook for 5 minutes or until warmed through.
3. Ladle 1½ cups soup into bowls; divide avocado chunks among bowls. Serve with chips on top, if desired.

PER SERVING: 165 calories; 4 g fat (0 g sat.); 15 g protein; 16 g carbohydrate; 5 g fiber; 983 mg sodium; 26 mg cholesterol

ravioli with spinach and squash

MAKES: 6 servings PREP: 10 minutes. COOK: 9 minutes.

- 2 packages (9 ounces each) light four-cheese ravioli (such as Buitoni)
- 1 bag (6 ounces) baby spinach
- 2 medium-size (about 7 ounces each) yellow squash, cut into ¼-inch-thick half-moons
- 1 medium-size (about 8 ounces) zucchini, cut into ¼-inch-thick half-moons
- 1 package (4.4 ounces) light spreadable herb cheese (such as Boursin Light Garlic & Herb cheese)
- ½ teaspoon salt
- ½ teaspoon black pepper

1. Cook ravioli according to package directions, about 9 minutes. Add spinach during final minute.
2. Meanwhile, heat a large nonstick skillet over medium-high heat. Coat skillet with nonstick cooking spray; add squash and zucchini to pan. Lightly coat squash mixture with nonstick spray. Cover and cook, stirring occasionally, for 6 to 7 minutes or until tender.
3. Drain pasta, reserving ½ cup pasta water; return pasta mixture to pot. Stir herb cheese into pasta mixture until well blended. Gently stir in squash, salt and pepper. Stir in pasta water by the tablespoonful if mixture becomes too dry.

PER SERVING: 291 calories; 7 g fat (4 g sat.); 15 g protein; 43 g carbohydrate; 5 g fiber; 786 mg sodium; 51 mg cholesterol

grill seekers

GET FIRED UP FOR SUMMER! OUR BARBECUE RECIPES ARE
BETTER THAN EVER, WITH DELICIOUS NEW TAKES ON THE CLASSICS
PLUS A FEW SURPRISES (THINK PIZZA). **BY MICHAEL TYRRELL**

Lemonade
(Recipe on
page143)

NewYork-Style
Hot Dog Topping

Avocado
Salsa

Chicago-Style
Hot Dogs

PHOTOGRAPHY BY TINA RUPP

chicago-style hot dogs

MAKES: 8 hot dogs. **PREP:** 10 minutes.

- ½ cup yellow mustard
- 8 toasted hot dog buns
- 1 large ripe tomato, cut into thin half-moons
- 1 small cucumber, peeled and sliced into thin half-moons
- 8 hot dogs, grilled to taste
  Celery salt, to taste
- ⅓ cup pickle relish
- 4 dill pickle spears, halved lengthwise

For each serving, spread 2 teaspoons mustard over a toasted bun. Arrange tomatoes down one side of the bun and cucumbers down the other side. Add hot dog and sprinkle with celery salt. Top each with 1 teaspoon mustard, 2 teaspoons relish and a piece of pickle.

new york–style hot dog topping

MAKES: 2 cups. **PREP:** 5 minutes.
COOK: 25 minutes.

- 1 pound sweet onions, peeled and sliced
- 1 tablespoon vegetable oil
- ⅓ cup ketchup
- 1 teaspoon sugar
- ¼ teaspoon red pepper flakes
- ⅛ teaspoon salt

1. In a large nonstick skillet, cook onions in the oil over medium-low heat, covered, for 15 minutes. Stir occasionally.
2. Stir in ½ cup water, the ketchup, sugar, red pepper flakes and salt. Cook, covered, for 10 minutes, stirring occasionally. Spoon about ¼ cup topping over each hot dog.

avocado salsa

MAKES: 3 cups. **PREP:** 10 minutes

- 3 ripe avocados, peeled, pits removed
- 1 medium tomato, seeds squeezed out, diced
- ¼ cup diced red onion
- 1 small jalapeño, seeds removed, diced
- 2 tablespoons lemon juice
- 1 tablespoon olive oil
- ½ teaspoon garlic salt

In a medium-size bowl, gently mix the avocados, tomato, red onion, jalapeño, lemon juice, olive oil and garlic salt. Serve as a topping for grilled burgers or hot dogs. Can be refrigerated a few hours with plastic wrap placed directly on surface of salsa.

mustard glazed ribs

MAKES: about 15 ribs. **PREP:** 15 minutes. **BAKE:** at 400° for 1 hour.
COOK: 10 minutes. **GRILL:** 8 minutes.

- 1 rack pork ribs, cut into individual ribs, about 3 pounds
- 1¼ cups ketchup
- ⅓ cup cider vinegar
- 3 tablespoons spicy brown mustard
- 2 tablespoons brown sugar
- 3 tablespoons water
- 1 teaspoon onion powder
- ¼ teaspoon hot sauce

1. Heat oven to 400°. Place ribs in a 13 × 9 × 2-inch baking dish and cover tightly with foil. Bake at 400° for 1 hour. Drain off any accumulated liquid.
2. Meanwhile, in a medium-size saucepan, stir together the ketchup, vinegar, mustard, brown sugar, 3 tablespoons water, the onion powder and hot sauce. Cook over medium-low heat for 10 minutes, stirring. Place half the sauce in a small bowl; set aside.
3. Heat gas grill to medium-high or prepare charcoal grill with medium-hot coals. Lightly coat grill rack with oil or nonstick cooking spray.
4. Baste ribs generously with the remaining sauce and grill for 3 to 4 minutes per side or until nicely browned. Serve ribs with reserved sauce on the side.

PER RIB: 199 calories; 13 g fat (5 g sat.); 12 g protein; 7 g carbohydrate; 0 g fiber; 326 mg sodium; 51 mg cholesterol

Do-Ahead Tip: Bake ribs and make sauce; allow both to cool to room temperature. Cover and refrigerate for up to 2 days. Gently reheat ribs and sauce before grilling.

grilled mango bbq pizza

MAKES: 8 slices. **PREP:** 10 minutes. **GRILL:** 12 minutes.

- 1 **pound frozen pizza dough, thawed**
- ½ **cup bottled barbecue sauce**
- 1 **cup shredded Monterey Jack cheese**
- 3 **ounces Canadian bacon, cut into strips**
- ½ **mango, thinly sliced**

1. Heat gas grill to medium or prepare charcoal grill with medium-hot coals.
2. Coat a 12-inch perforated pizza pan with nonstick cooking spray. Roll dough out to a 12-inch circle. Place on prepared pizza pan. Put on grill rack and close lid of grill. Grill for 5 minutes. Check bottom of pizza. If getting too dark, lower heat to medium-low.

3. Open grill. Spread dough with barbecue sauce and sprinkle evenly with the cheese. Scatter the Canadian bacon and mango slices over the top.
4. Grill for 5 to 7 minutes more, until crust is lightly browned and cheese is melted.
5. Gently slide pizza onto a cutting board.
6. Allow pizza to cool slightly before cutting into slices.

PER SLICE: 227 calories; 7 g fat (3 g sat.); 10 g protein; 35 g carbohydrate; 1 g fiber; 558 mg sodium; 19 mg cholesterol

You can also make pizza directly on grill rack—heat grill and grease rack. Slide rolled-out dough from pan directly onto rack; cover grill. Cook 5 minutes, flip dough, add toppings and cook, covered, 5 more minutes.

potato salad

MAKES: 8 servings. **PREP:** 40 minutes.

- 2 pounds mixed small red and fingerling potatoes, scrubbed
- 1 small red onion, thinly sliced
- 6 tablespoons sherry wine vinegar
- 1 tablespoon grainy mustard
- ½ teaspoon salt
- ¼ teaspoon black pepper
- 6 tablespoons extra-virgin olive oil
- 1 tablespoon chopped fresh oregano
- 1 tablespoon chopped fresh parsley

1. Bring a large pot of lightly salted water to boiling. Add potatoes. Cover and bring back to a boil, then uncover and cook for 20 minutes or until fork-tender. Drain.
2. Cut warm potatoes into bite-size pieces and place in a bowl. Stir in onion.
3. In a small bowl, blend vinegar, mustard, salt, and pepper. Drizzle in olive oil, whisking continuously. Stir in herbs. Pour dressing over potatoes and onions. Stir gently and cover. Refrigerate up to a day.
Note: This can be served warm or at room temperature.

PER SERVING: 175 calories; 10 g fat (1 g sat.); 2 g protein; 19 g carbohydrate; 2 g fiber; 198 mg sodium; 0 mg cholesterol

lemonade

MAKES: 12 cups. **PREP:** 5 minutes.
MICROWAVE: 10 seconds. **CHILL:** 1 hour.

- 12 large lemons
- 1¼ cups superfine sugar
- 1 lemon, sliced, for garnish

1. Microwave lemons for 10 seconds. Cut in half and juice enough for 3 cups. In large pitcher combine juice, 8 cups cold water and sugar. Chill at least 1 hour. Stir and garnish with lemon slices.

PER (1-CUP) SERVING: 98 calories; 0 g fat (0 g sat.); 0 g protein; 27 g carbohydrate; 1 g fiber; 6 mg sodium; 0 mg cholesterol

grilled teriyaki swordfish

MAKES: 4 servings. **PREP:** 10 minutes. **MARINATE:** 1 hour **GRILL:** 10 minutes.

- 2 tablespoons reduced-sodium teriyaki sauce
- 1 tablespoon honey
- 1 tablespoon rice vinegar
- 1 tablespoon chopped fresh ginger
- 1 tablespoon canola oil
- 2 cloves garlic, chopped
- 4 swordfish steaks, ¾ inch thick, about 6 ounces each
- 6 scallions, ends trimmed
- 1 lemon, sliced, for garnish

1. In large resealable plastic bag, combine teriyaki sauce, honey, vinegar, ginger, canola oil and garlic. Add swordfish, close bag and shake to coat fish completely. Place on a plate and refrigerate for 1 hour.

2. Heat gas grill to medium-high or prepare charcoal grill with medium-hot coals. Lightly coat grill rack with oil or nonstick cooking spray. Grill swordfish for 5 minutes. Baste with some of the remaining marinade, turn and grill for an additional 4 to 5 minutes or until cooked through. Brush scallions with marinade and place on the grill for the last 4 minutes of cooking time. Remove fish and scallions to a platter and cover with foil to keep warm.

3. To serve, boil remaining marinade in a small saucepan. Drizzle over the fish. Garnish with lemon slices.

PER SERVING: 273 calories; 10 g fat (2 g sat.); 35 g protein; 9 g carbohydrate; 1 g fiber; 317 mg sodium; 66 mg cholesterol

Often relegated to a side dish, grilled veggies are the main event in Caesar Pasta Primavera.

Fire-roasting vegetables brings out their natural sweetness. Brush your favorites with oil or a marinade before grilling to seal moisture in and keep them from sticking to the rack. Place veggies over medium heat and cook 5 to 10 minutes, turning once, until fork-tender.

caesar pasta primavera

MAKES: 4 servings. **PREP :**20 minutes.
GRILL: 10 minutes. **COOK:** 10 minutes.

- 2 **packages (10 ounces each) white mushrooms**
- 1 **package (12 ounces) firm cherry tomatoes**
- 1 **sweet onion (about 10 ounces), cut into 1-inch pieces**
- 2 **summer squash (1 pound total), cut into ¼-inch slices**
- 2 **red sweet peppers (1 pound), cut into 1-inch pieces**
- ½ **cup reduced-calorie Caesar dressing, (such as Ken's Lite)**
- 12 **ounces whole-wheat spaghetti**
- ½ **cup shaved Parmesan cheese and fresh basil, for garnish**

1. Heat gas grill to medium-high or prepare charcoal grill with medium-hot coals. Lightly coat grill rack with oil or nonstick cooking spray.
2. Evenly divide vegetables and thread alternately onto 8 metal skewers.
3. Generously brush veggies with ¼ cup of the dressing. Grill for 4 to 5 minutes, until lightly charred. Carefully turn and grill covered for an additional 4 to 5 minutes or until vegetables soften and are lightly charred. Remove to a large serving platter and keep warm.
4. Cook pasta following package directions, about 10 minutes. Drain and toss with remaining ¼ cup dressing.
5. Serve the vegetables on a bed of pasta. Garnish with shaved Parmesan and basil.

PER SERVING: 476 calories; 5 g fat (1 g sat.); 21 g protein; 96 g carbohydrate; 14 g fiber; 434 mg sodium; 4 mg cholesterol

Do-Ahead Tip: Assemble skewers; place on a platter and cover with plastic wrap. Refrigerate. Brush with dressing just before grilling.

sunday dinner on the grill

MAKES: 6 servings. **PREP:** 20 minutes. **MARINATE:** 4 hours. **GRILL:** 70 minutes.

- 4 **tablespoons olive oil**
- 2 **tablespoons balsamic or sherry wine vinegar**
- 3 **cloves garlic, peeled and chopped**
- 1 **teaspoon dried oregano**
- 1 **teaspoon dried thyme**
- 1½ **teaspoons Montreal steak seasoning**
- 1 **eye round roast, about 2½ pounds**
- 1½ **pounds small white potatoes, halved**
- 1 **pound peeled baby carrots**
- 1 **container (10 ounces) Brussels sprouts, trimmed and halved**
- ½ **teaspoon salt**

1. In a large resealable plastic bag, mix together olive oil, vinegar, garlic, oregano, thyme and steak seasoning. Add eye round and close bag. Shake to completely coat meat. Place on a plate and refrigerate for at least 4 hours.
2. Heat gas grill to medium-high. Lightly coat grill rack with oil.

3. Remove roast from bag, reserving marinade. Brown eye round on grill on all sides, about 10 minutes. Transfer eye round to a 15¾ × 11¼ × 3-inch disposable roasting pan. Place potatoes and carrots around meat and toss with marinade reserved from meat.
4. Reduce heat to medium-low. Place pan on grill, and cook, covered, for 30 minutes. Stir twice. Stir in Brussels sprouts and salt. Continue to grill, covered, for 15 minutes. Check internal temperature of meat. Take meat out of pan when internal temperature reaches 135° on an instant-read thermometer (meat will contine to cook and should reach 145°). Keep warm. Stir vegetables and continue to cook for 15 more minutes or until all vegetables are tender.

PER SERVING: 454 calories; 15 g fat (3 g sat.); 48 g protein; 28 g carbohydrate; 5 g fiber; 533 mg sodium; 77 mg cholesterol

berry sweet

HERE'S A BUMPER CROP OF DELICIOUS DESSERTS FEATURING SUMMER'S FRESHEST FRUIT—TAKE YOUR PICK, OR BETTER YET, TRY THEM ALL.

Food styling: Liza Jernow. Prop styling: Alistair Turnbull.

strawberry swirl shortcakes

MAKES: 8 servings. **PREP:** 10 minutes. **BAKE:** at 450° for 10 minutes.

- 1½ **pounds strawberries, hulled and sliced**
- 7 **tablespoons sugar**
- 2 **teaspoons grated lemon peel**
- 2½ **cups biscuit mix (such as Bisquick)**
- ⅔ **cup plus 1 tablespoon milk**
- 1 **cup heavy cream**

1. Heat oven to 450°. Stir strawberries and 2 tablespoons of the sugar in a small bowl; set aside.

2. In a second small bowl, combine lemon peel and 3 tablespoons of the sugar and stir until blended; set aside.

3. In large bowl, stir together biscuit mix and ⅔ cup of the milk until a soft dough forms. Turn out onto a well-floured surface. Roll into an 18 × 8-inch rectangle, about ¼ inch thick. Brush with remaining 1 tablespoon milk, then sprinkle with lemon-sugar mixture. Roll up, starting at a short end. Cut into 8 slices, each about 1 inch thick.

4. Place slices on baking sheet, reshaping to flatten slightly. Bake at 450° for 9 to 10 minutes or until golden.

5. While biscuits cool, beat heavy cream and remaining 2 tablespoons sugar in a medium-size bowl until stiff peaks form.

6. Split biscuits in half horizontally. For each serving, place one biscuit bottom on plate and dollop 2 tablespoons whipped cream over top; spoon a scant ¼ cup strawberries over whipped cream. Cover with biscuit top and finish with a little more whipped cream and strawberries.

PER SERVING: 334 calories; 17 g fat (9 g sat.); 5 g protein; 43 g carbohydrate; 3 g fiber; 495 mg sodium; 44 mg cholesterol

PHOTOGRAPH BY TINA RUPP

raspberry tiramisu

MAKES: 9 servings. **PREP:** 20 minutes.
COOK: 2 minutes. **REFRIGERATE:** 4 hours or overnight.

- ½ cup granulated sugar
- 1 tablespoon cornstarch
- 4 cups raspberries
- 2 packages (8 ounces each) low-fat cream cheese, softened
- 1 cup confectioners' sugar
- ¼ cup coffee liqueur or strong coffee
- ½ cup sour cream
- 2 packages (3 ounces each) soft ladyfingers
- 2 tablespoons unsweetened cocoa powder
  Mint, raspberries for garnish (optional)

1. In medium-size saucepan, mix granulated sugar and cornstarch until blended; stir in 3 cups of the raspberries. Bring to a boil over medium-high heat; boil 2 minutes or until thickened. Cool to room temp; add remaining 1 cup berries.
2. In large bowl, beat with electric mixer cream cheese, confectioners' sugar and liqueur until smooth. Stir in sour cream.
3. Separate and arrange half the ladyfingers on bottom of 9-inch square glass baking dish, overlapping slightly. Spoon half of the raspberry mixture (1 cup) on top, then half the cream cheese mixture (1½ cups). Sift half the cocoa powder on top; repeat layering as above, ending with cocoa powder.
4. Cover with plastic wrap; refrigerate at least 4 hours or overnight. Garnish with mint and raspberries, if desired.

PER SERVING: 387 calories; 16 g fat (10 g sat.); 9 g protein; 49 g carbohydrate; 3 g fiber; 252 mg sodium; 111 mg cholesterol

mixed berry fools

MAKES: 4 servings. **PREP:** 10 minutes. **COOK:** 10 minutes. **FREEZE:** 50 minutes.

- 2 cups raspberries
- 1 cup blackberries
- 1 cup blueberries
- ⅓ cup orange juice
- ½ cup sugar
- 3 cups reduced-fat frozen whipped topping (such as Cool Whip Lite), thawed
- 1 container (6 ounces) mixed berry yogurt
  Additional berries for garnish (optional)

1. In a small saucepan, combine raspberries, blackberries, blueberries, orange juice and sugar. Bring to a boil over high heat, then reduce heat to medium-high and simmer for 10 minutes. Carefully add fruit mixture to food processor and puree until smooth. Strain through a fine mesh strainer and place in the freezer for about 50 minutes or until very cold.
2. Place thawed whipped topping in a medium-size bowl; fold in yogurt and cooled fruit puree until just combined. Serve immediately. Garnish with additional berries, if desired.

PER SERVING: 300 calories; 6 g fat (4 g sat.); 3 g protein; 60 g carbohydrate; 7 g fiber; 27 mg sodium; 4 mg cholesterol

PHOTOS (FROM TOP): DAVID PRINCE; ALAN RICHARDSON.

slow-cooker solutions

GREAT-TASTING RECIPES FOR EFFORTLESS MEALS. **BY CINDY HELLER**

summer fruit compote

MAKES: 6 cups. **PREP:** 15 minutes. **SLOW-COOK:** 3¾ hours on HIGH or 5¾ hours on LOW.

- 3 cups fresh pineapple chunks
- 2 medium-size pears, peeled, cored and cut into ½-inch chunks (about 2 cups)
- 2 cups frozen sliced peaches
- 1 cup frozen pitted cherries
- ¾ cup dried apricots, quartered
- ⅔ cup frozen orange juice concentrate, thawed
- 1 tablespoon packed dark-brown sugar

- 1 teaspoon vanilla extract
- 2 tablespoons cornstarch
- ½ cup sliced almonds, toasted vanilla ice cream (optional)

1. Combine pineapple, pears, peaches, cherries, apricots, orange juice, brown sugar and vanilla in a slow cooker insert. Cover and cook on HIGH for 3½ hours or LOW for 5½ hours.
2. Uncover and remove 2 tablespoons liquid. In a small bowl, stir together

liquid and cornstarch. Stir cornstarch mixture back into slow cooker; cook 15 minutes more or until thickened. Sprinkle with almonds. Serve warm with ice cream, if desired.

PER ½ CUP: 139 calories; 2 g fat (0 g sat.); 2 g protein; 29 g carbohydrate; 3 g fiber; 3 mg sodium; 0 mg cholesterol

PHOTOGRAPHY BY TINA RUPP

molasses baked beans

MAKES: 10, ½ cup servings.
PREP: 10 minutes. **COOK:** 15 minutes.
SLOW-COOK: 5 hours on HIGH or 6½ hours on LOW.

- 1 **pound navy beans, picked over, rinsed and soaked overnight**
- ½ **teaspoon baking soda**
- 4 **slices bacon, finely chopped**
- 1 **medium-size onion, finely chopped**
- ¼ **cup molasses**
- ¼ **cup dark-brown sugar, packed**
- 2 **cups boiling water**
- 2 **teaspoons dry mustard**
- 1 **teaspoon cider vinegar**
- ½ **teaspoon salt**
- ½ **teaspoon black pepper**

1. Drain beans; place in a large saucepan. Cover with water by 2 inches; stir in baking soda. Bring to a boil over medium-high heat; boil for 15 minutes, skimming off any foam that accumulates.
2. Meanwhile, heat a 10-inch nonstick skillet over medium-high heat. Add bacon to skillet; cook 4 minutes, stirring occasionally. Add onion to pan; cook 5 more minutes, stirring almost constantly.
3. Drain beans and transfer to slow cooker insert. Top with bacon mixture. Stir in molasses, sugar, boiling water and 1 teaspoon of the dry mustard. Cover; cook on HIGH for 5 hours or LOW for 6½ hours.
4. Remove cover; stir in remaining 1 teaspoon dry mustard, the cider vinegar and salt and pepper; serve immediately.

PER ½ CUP: 261 calories; 6 g fat (2 g sat.); 11 g protein; 42 g carbohydrate; 7 g fiber; 283 mg sodium; 8 mg cholesterol

country-style barbecue ribs

MAKES: 6 ribs. **PREP:** 15 minutes. **SLOW-COOK:** 6 hours on HIGH or 9 hours on LOW.

- 1 **cup ketchup**
- 3 **tablespoons molasses**
- 1 **tablespoon cider vinegar**
- 1 **tablespoon Worcestershire sauce**
- 1 **tablespoon dark-brown sugar**
- 1½ **teaspoons Dijon mustard**
- ½ **teaspoon hot pepper sauce (such as Tabasco)**
- ¼ **teaspoon liquid smoke**
- 4 **pounds country-style pork ribs**

1. In a small bowl, stir together ketchup, molasses, vinegar, Worcestershire sauce, sugar, mustard, hot sauce and liquid smoke.

2. Place pork ribs in the slow cooker insert and pour 1 cup sauce over top, reserving the rest for later. Cover and cook on HIGH for 6 hours or LOW for 9 hours or until very tender.
3. Remove ribs from slow cooker and brush with reserved sauce.

PER RIB: 393 calories; 16 g fat (6 g sat.); 38 g protein; 21 g carbohydrate; 0 g fiber; 705 mg sodium; 127 mg cholesterol

food **university**

SWEET, JUICY BERRIES BAKED IN A FLAKY CRUST IS A SURE SIGN OF SUMMER. A LATTICE TOP MAY LOOK LIKE A LOT OF WORK, BUT A LITTLE TIME YIELDS A BIG PAYOFF. CAN'T GET THE WEAVE DOWN? FOR A VARIATION THAT'S AS EASY AS PIE, JUST PLACE STRIPS VERTICALLY AND HORIZONTALLY ACROSS THE TOP. **BY JULIE MILTENBERGER**

The best blueberries are firm with a gray bloom on the skin—any visible redness means fruit is underripe.

PHOTOGRAPHY BY TINA RUPP

blueberry pie

MAKES: 12 servings. **PREP:** 15 minutes. **BAKE:** at 400° for 15 minutes; at 350° for 50 minutes.

1 **package refrigerated rolled-out piecrusts (15-ounce package; 2 crusts)**
2 **packages (1 pint each) blueberries**
⅔ **cup plus 1 teaspoon sugar**
¼ **cup cornstarch**
1 **teaspoon fresh lemon zest**
2 **tablespoons fresh lemon juice**
1 **egg white, lightly beaten**
   Vanilla ice cream (optional)

1. Heat oven to 400°. Roll crusts out slightly. Fit one crust into a 9-inch deep-dish pie plate. Set aside second crust.
2. In a large bowl, toss blueberries, ⅔ cup of the sugar, the cornstarch, lemon zest and juice. Let stand 5 minutes.
3. Meanwhile, with a pastry cutter or pizza cutter, cut remaining crust into ½-inch-wide strips (see step A, below).

4. Transfer blueberry mixture to crust-lined pie plate. Weave a lattice top, alternating strips of crust (see steps B and C, below). Crimp edges to seal. Brush crust with egg white; sprinkle with remaining teaspoon sugar.
5. Bake pie at 400° for 15 minutes. Reduce heat to 350° and continue to bake for an additional 45 to 50 minutes or until center is bubbly and crust is golden (tent with foil if browning too quickly). Serve slightly warm with vanilla ice cream, if desired.

PER SERVING: 242 calories; 9 g fat (4 g sat.); 2 g protein; 38 g carbohydrate; 1 g fiber; 137 mg sodium; 7 mg cholesterol

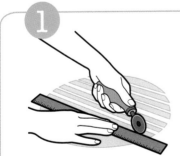

With a straight edge and a pie or pizza cutter, cut pie crust into ½-inch- wide strips (about 16 to 18 strips).

Lay down two strips at a 90° angle. Add a third on top of the cross strip about 1 inch away; the fourth goes under. Repeat across the pie.

Fold back every other strip and lay a new one in the opposite direction. Return folded strips to create weave. Continue until filling is covered.

july

Perfect Corn on the Cob
page 169

CELEBRATE THE FOURTH OF JULY WITH A
PATRIOTIC CAKE THAT LOOKS AS GOOD
AS IT TASTES AND SMOKY-SWEET
GRILLED CORN WITH CHILI-LIME BUTTER.

Flag Cake
page 155

**Greek-Style Steak
and Tomato Salad**
page 159

Chicken and Apple Salad
page 164

FAMILY AND FRIENDS WILL SALUTE YOU—AND THIS GORGEOUS
LEMON-FLAVORED CAKE THAT STARTS WITH A MIX.

flag cake

MAKES: 35 servings. **PREP:** 10 minutes. **BAKE:** at 350° for 20 minutes. **DECORATE:** 45 minutes.

Cake:
- Zest and juice of 2 lemons
- 2 boxes (18.25 ounces each) white cake mix
- 6 large egg whites
- 1 teaspoon lemon extract

Frosting:
- ½ cup (1 stick) unsalted butter, at room temperature
- ½ cup solid vegetable shortening, at room temperature
- 2 boxes (1 pound each) confectioners' sugar
- 4 tablespoons milk
- 2 tablespoons lemon juice

Decoration:
- ¾ cup fresh blueberries, washed and dried
- 3 cups fresh large raspberries, washed and dried

1. Cake: Heat oven to 350°. Coat two 15 × 10-inch jelly-roll pans with nonstick cooking spray. Pour lemon juice into 4-cup measuring cup; add enough water to equal 2⅔ cups.

2. In large bowl, beat cake mixes, egg whites, lemon zest, juice-water mixture and lemon extract to blend, about 3 minutes. Divide evenly between two prepared pans; smooth tops.

3. Bake at 350° until cake springs back when lightly touched, about 20 minutes. Let cool on wire racks 10 minutes. Place rack over each cake. Carefully invert cakes and racks and remove pans from cakes. Let cool to room temperature. If making ahead, wrap cooled layers in plastic wrap; refrigerate for several days. Bring to room temperature before proceeding.

4. Frosting: Beat butter and shortening in large bowl 1 to 2 minutes, until fluffy. Add confectioners' sugar, milk and lemon juice. Continue beating on low until well blended and good spreading consistency, adding more milk a teaspoon at a time.

5. Decoration: Place one layer on serving tray. Reserve 1 cup frosting for piping. Frost layer with 1 cup frosting; top with second layer; frost top and sides. Place reserved frosting in pastry bag with a star tip.

6. Mark off a field for "stars" with toothpicks— 6 inches across and 5 inches down. Fill in with blueberries.

7. Place seven red "stripes" of raspberries on cake as shown, leaving equal spacing for 6 white "stripes" between them. Carefully pipe white frosting stripes between the rows of raspberries. Refrigerate uncovered to set frosting, then loosely cover with nonstick aluminum foil. Refrigerate until ready to serve. Let stand at room temperature for about 20 minutes before serving.

PER SERVING: 289 calories; 9 g fat (3 g sat.); 2 g protein; 51 g carbohydrate; 1 g fiber; 210 mg sodium; 7 mg cholesterol

Food styling: Karen Tack. Prop styling: Leslie Siegel.

PHOTOGRAPHY BY RITA MAAS

stay-slim dinners

WHAT KIND OF DIET INCLUDES PASTA, PIZZA, SUBS AND STEAK? THE KIND YOU STICK TO FOR GOOD. BY MICHAEL TYRRELL

Scallop and Broccoli Toss (recipe page 161) is a deliciously convenient way to add seafood, whole grains and vegetables to your diet.

grilled shrimp caesar salad

MAKES: 4 servings. **PREP:** 15 minutes. **REFRIGERATE:** 15 minutes. **GRILL:** 4 minutes.

- 6 tablespoons olive oil
- 3 tablespoons lemon juice
- 2 teaspoons Worcestershire sauce
- 1 teaspoon Dijon mustard
- 1 clove garlic, finely chopped
- ¼ teaspoon salt
- ¼ teaspoon black pepper
- 4 tablespoons grated Parmesan cheese
- 1 pound large shrimp, shelled and deveined
- 1 large head romaine lettuce, sliced (about 8 cups)
- ½ medium red onion, thinly sliced
- 6 garlic-flavored bagel chips, crushed (such as New York Style)

1. In a medium bowl, stir together olive oil, lemon juice, Worcestershire sauce, mustard, garlic, salt and pepper. Whisk in 2 tablespoons of the Parmesan.

2. Place shrimp in a large resealable plastic bag and add 2 tablespoons of the olive oil–lemon mixture. Seal bag and shake to coat shrimp. Refrigerate for 15 minutes.

3. Heat grill pan on stovetop or heat gas grill to medium-high heat. Coat cooking surface with nonstick cooking spray. Grill shrimp for about 2 minutes per side. Remove from grill.

4. In a large bowl, mix together the lettuce and onion. Toss with the remaining olive oil–lemon mixture.

5. To serve, place equal amounts of salad on 4 plates. Top each with ¼ of the remaining Parmesan. Divide shrimp and bagel chip pieces evenly over salads. Serve immediately.

PER SERVING: 348 calories; 24 g fat (5 g sat.); 22 g protein; 11 g carbohydrate; 3 g fiber; 526 mg sodium; 172 mg cholesterol

Homemade pizza can be quicker than takeout, costs less and is rich in fiber.

sausage and pepper hero

MAKES: 4 servings. **PREP:** 15 minutes. **ROAST:** at 400° for 1 hour.

- ½ pound hot Italian turkey sausage, cut into ½-inch coins
- 2 green bell peppers, seeded, cored and cut into ½-inch strips
- 2 sweet red peppers, seeded, cored and cut into ½-inch strips
- 1 large sweet onion, peeled and cut into ½-inch slices
- 1 large baking potato, peeled and cut into ½-inch pieces
- 4 teaspoons olive oil
- 1 teaspoon dried Italian seasoning
- ½ teaspoon salt
- ¼ teaspoon black pepper
- 2 tablespoons balsamic vinegar
- 4 hot dog buns, toasted

1. Heat oven to 400°. Spray a large roasting pan with nonstick cooking spray. Place sausage in the pan and roast for 15 minutes.
2. Place peppers, onion and potato in a large bowl. Toss with olive oil, Italian seasoning, salt and pepper. Add vegetables to the roasting pan and stir to combine with sausage. Roast for an additional 45 minutes, stirring twice, until vegetables are tender. Remove from oven and stir in vinegar.
3. To serve, spoon 1 generous cup of sausage and peppers over each toasted bun.

PER SERVING: 350 calories; 11 g fat (3 g sat.); 18 g protein; 46 g carbohydrate; 5 g fiber; 683 mg sodium; 40 mg cholesterol

veggie pizza

MAKES: 4 servings. **PREP:** 15 minutes. **BAKE:** at 450° for 30 minutes. **BROIL:** 2 minutes.

- 1 pound zucchini, cut lengthwise into ¼-inch slices
- 1 pound summer squash, cut lengthwise into ¼-inch slices
- ½ pound Japanese eggplant, cut lengthwise into ¼-inch slices
- ¼ pound sliced portobello mushrooms
- 4 tablespoons fat-free Italian dressing (such as Wish-Bone)
- 4 whole-wheat pitas, cut in half horizontally
- ¾ cup jarred marinara sauce
- 4 ounces sliced provolone cheese, cut into thin ribbons
  Fresh basil, for garnish

1. Heat oven to 450°. Spray 3 large baking sheets with nonstick cooking spray. Place the zucchini, summer squash, eggplant and portobello mushrooms on the baking sheets in a single layer. Brush both sides of the vegetables with the Italian dressing.
2. Bake at 450° for 25 to 30 minutes or until vegetables are tender, turning them after 15 minutes. Remove from oven and set oven to broil.
3. Place the pita halves, cut-side up, on a baking sheet and broil for 30 seconds. Spoon about 1½ tablespoons of marinara sauce over each. Arrange an equal amount of roasted vegetables and cheese ribbons over each pizza. Broil for 1 to 2 minutes, until heated through and cheese melts.
4. Garnish with basil.

PER SERVING: 371 calories; 12 g fat (6 g sat.); 18 g protein; 53 g carbohydrate; 12 g fiber; 967 mg sodium; 20 mg cholesterol

greek-style steak and tomato salad

MAKES: 4 servings. **PREP:** 15 minutes. **GRILL:** 10 minutes.

- 6 teaspoons sherry vinegar
- 1 teaspoon spicy brown mustard
- ½ teaspoon salt
- 4 tablespoons olive oil
- 1 pound flank steak
- 2 teaspoons Spice Hunter Greek Seasoning
- 1 pound ripe tomatoes, sliced
- 1 cucumber, peeled and sliced into thin half-moons
- 12 large radishes, quartered
- 2 ounces herb-and-garlic-seasoned feta cheese, crumbled

1. In a small bowl, whisk together vinegar, mustard and salt. Gradually whisk in olive oil.

2. Heat grill pan on the stovetop or set grill to medium-high heat. Coat cooking surface with nonstick cooking spray. Season steak with Greek seasoning. Grill for 4 minutes. Turn and grill 4 to 6 minutes more or until internal temperature reaches 135° on an instant-read thermometer, for medium-rare. Allow to rest for 5 minutes. Thinly slice against the grain.

3. On a large serving platter, fan out tomatoes. Scatter cucumber, radishes and feta over the top. Drizzle the dressing over the salad and serve with the sliced steak.

PER SERVING: 357 calories; 24 g fat (7 g sat.); 28 g protein; 6 g carbohydrate; 2 g fiber; 548 mg sodium; 58 mg cholesterol

caribbean chicken strips and rice

MAKES: 4 servings. **PREP:** 15 minutes. **COOK:** 45 minutes. **BROIL:** 5 minutes.

- 2 **cups low-sodium beef broth**
- 2 **teaspoons Mrs. Dash Caribbean Citrus seasoning**
- ¾ **teaspoon salt**
- 1 **cup uncooked brown rice**
- 1 **cup frozen peas, thawed**
- 1 **small yellow pepper, cored, seeded and chopped**
- 4 **scallions, thinly sliced**
- 1 **pound chicken tenders**

1. Place broth and **¾ cup water** in a medium-size saucepan and bring to a boil. Stir in 1 teaspoon of the citrus seasoning, ½ teaspoon of the salt and the rice. Reduce heat to low. Cook, covered, for 30 minutes. Stir in peas, yellow pepper and half the scallions. Cook for 15 minutes more or until rice is tender and liquid is absorbed.

2. Heat broiler. Coat broiler pan with nonstick cooking spray. Season the chicken with the remaining teaspoon citrus seasoning and remaining ¼ teaspoon salt. Broil for 5 minutes, turning halfway through cooking time, or until internal temperature reaches 160° on an instant-read thermometer.

3. Garnish with remaining scallions and serve alongside rice.

PER SERVING: 347 calories; 5 g fat (1 g sat.); 31 g protein; 43 g carbohydrate; 5 g fiber; 561 mg sodium; 63 mg cholesterol

A squeeze of fresh lemon or lime perks up almost any dish without adding fat or sodium.

Spices like cinnamon can boost the taste of a dish and are good for you too.

scallop and broccoli toss

MAKES: 4 servings. **PREP:** 15 minutes.
COOK: 13 minutes.

- ⅓ **pound whole-wheat thin linguine**
- 1 **head broccoli, cut into florets (about 6 cups)**
- ½ **cup vegetable broth**
- 2 **tablespoons reduced-sodium soy sauce**
- 2 **tablespoons ketchup**
- 1 **tablespoon sugar**
- ¼ **teaspoon hot sauce**
- 1¼ **pounds sea scallops, cut in half horizontally**
- 1 **can (5 ounces) water chestnuts, drained and quartered**
- 1 **teaspoon sesame oil**

1. Cook linguine following package instructions, about 9 minutes. Add broccoli during last 5 minutes of cooking; drain.
2. In a small bowl, whisk together the broth, soy sauce, ketchup, sugar and hot sauce.
3. Place the broth mixture in a large skillet and bring to a simmer. Add scallops and water chestnuts and simmer for 4 minutes, turning halfway through, or until cooked through. Remove from heat and stir in sesame oil.
4. Place cooked pasta and broccoli in the skillet and toss with the scallops. Serve immediately.

PER SERVING: 345 calories; 3 g fat (0 g sat.);
33 g protein; 49 g carbohydrate; 9 g fiber;
793 mg sodium; 47 mg cholesterol

chicken couscous with cherry tomatoes

MAKES: 4 servings. **PREP:** 15 minutes. **COOK:** 17 minutes. **STAND:** 5 minutes.

- 1 **tablespoon olive oil**
- 1 **pound boneless, skinless chicken breasts, cut into 1-inch pieces**
- 2 **cups reduced-sodium chicken broth**
- ½ **teaspoon salt**
- ½ **teaspoon black pepper**
- ½ **teaspoon cumin**
- ½ **teaspoon ground cinnamon**
- 2 **carrots, sliced and cut into ¼-inch pieces**
- ½ **small onion, peeled and chopped**
- 2 **cups cherry tomatoes, halved**
- 1 **cup plain couscous**

1. Heat oil in a large skillet over medium-high heat. Add chicken and sauté for 6 to 7 minutes, turning halfway through, or until internal temperature registers 160° on an instant-read thermometer. Remove to a plate and keep warm.
2. Add the broth to the skillet and stir in salt, pepper, cumin and cinnamon. Add carrots and onion. Simmer, covered, for 10 minutes or until tender.
3. Remove from heat and stir in tomatoes, couscous and chicken. Cover and let stand 5 minutes.
4. Fluff gently with a fork and serve.

PER SERVING: 361 calories; 7 g fat (1 g sat.);
31 g protein; 43 g carbohydrate; 5 g fiber;
685 mg sodium; 65 mg cholesterol

think fast

7 DINNERS. 20 MINUTES. ENOUGH SAID. BY JULIE MILTENBERGER

Shrimp Fried Rice
(Recipe opposite)

PHOTOGRAPHY BY RICK LEW

shrimp fried rice

MAKES: 4 servings. **PREP:** 5 minutes.
COOK: 13 minutes

- 5 teaspoons olive oil
- 2 eggs, lightly beaten
- 1 pound frozen, raw, shelled and deveined medium-size shrimp, thawed
- 1 package (8.8 ounces) fully cooked rice pilaf (such as Uncle Ben's Ready Rice)
- ½ teaspoon ground ginger
- 1 package (10 ounces) frozen peas and onions, thawed
- 1 tablespoon reduced-sodium soy sauce
- 1 tablespoon oyster sauce
- 1 can (5 ounces) sliced water chestnuts, drained

1. Heat 2 teaspoons of the olive oil in a large nonstick skillet over medium heat. Add eggs; cook until set, about 2 minutes. Remove eggs; slice into thin strips.
2. Heat remaining 3 teaspoons olive oil over medium-high heat. Add shrimp. Cook, turning, for 3 minutes. Remove and keep warm.
3. Reduce heat to medium. Add rice pilaf, **3 tablespoons water** and ground ginger. Cover and reheat 2 minutes. Uncover and stir in peas, soy and oyster sauces and water chestnuts. Cook 4 minutes. Add **⅓ cup water** if mixture is dry.
4. Stir in shrimp and egg strips and raise heat to medium-high. Cook, covered, for 2 minutes or until heated through. Serve warm.

PER SERVING: 362 calories; 12 g fat (2 g sat.); 32 g protein; 32 g carbohydrate; 5 g fiber; 935 mg sodium; 278 mg cholesterol

Food styling: Toni Brogan. Prop styling: Loren Simons.

A smart combination of fresh ingredients and high-quality prepared ingredients—along with quick cooking methods—makes a delicious 20-minute dinner possible.

penne rapini

MAKES: 6 servings. **PREP:** 5 minutes. **MICROWAVE:** 30 seconds. **COOK:** 11 minutes.

- 5 slices precooked bacon
- 1 pound rapini (broccoli rabe), cut into 2-inch pieces
- 1 pound whole-wheat penne pasta
- 3 tablespoons extra-virgin olive oil
- 4 garlic cloves, peeled and sliced
- ¼ cup sliced, pitted black olives
- ¼ teaspoon crushed red pepper
- ¼ pound sliced mushrooms
- 2 tablespoons grated Parmesan cheese

1. Microwave bacon on paper towel–lined microwave-safe plate for 30 seconds. Crumble.
2. Blanch rapini in a large pot of lightly salted boiling water for 1 minute. Remove with a slotted spoon; scoop out ¼ cup water. Return remaining water to boiling; add pasta. Cook 10 minutes, as per package instructions. Drain.
3. While pasta cooks, heat olive oil over medium heat. Add garlic, olives, red pepper and mushrooms to pan. Cook 3 minutes, until garlic is softened. Add reserved water and rapini. Cook 2 minutes. Toss with pasta, bacon and Parmesan.

PER SERVING: 410 calories; 12 g fat (2 g sat.); 15 g protein; 62 g carbohydrate; 7 g fiber; 196 mg sodium; 6 mg cholesterol

chicken and apple salad

MAKES: 4 servings. **PREP:** 5 minutes. **BAKE:** at 425° for 12 minutes.

- 1 package (12 ounces) chicken cutlet patties
- 7 ounces mixed salad greens (about 8 cups)
- 2 Gala apples, cored and cut into 1-inch pieces
- ⅔ cup glazed walnuts
- ½ cup bottled balsamic vinaigrette
- 8 teaspoons shredded Asiago cheese

1. Heat oven to 425°. Line a baking sheet with foil. Place chicken patties on prepared baking sheet. Bake at 425° for 12 minutes, turning once.

2. Meanwhile, divide salad greens, apples and nuts among four dinner plates. Drizzle each with 2 tablespoons vinaigrette.

3. Remove cutlets from oven and transfer to a cutting board. Slice cutlets into strips. Fan over salad and sprinkle each with 2 teaspoons Asiago.

PER SERVING 411 calories; 26 g fat (4 g sat.); 14 g protein; 33 g carbohydrate; 3 g fiber; 900 mg sodium; 4 mg cholesterol

This main-dish salad starts with fully cooked breaded chicken cutlets.

tuna melts

MAKES: 6 servings. **PREP:** 10 minutes.
COOK: 6 minutes.

- 6 slices rye bread
- 3 cans (6 ounces each) solid albacore tuna in water, drained
- ⅔ cup light mayonnaise
- 2 celery ribs, trimmed and diced
- ½ cup shredded carrots, chopped
- 2 tablespoons sweet pickle relish
- ½ teaspoon hot sauce
     Pinch of salt and pepper
- 12 thin slices Alpine Lace American cheese (a generous ¼ pound)
- 2 large ripe tomatoes, cored and sliced

1. Heat broiler. Line a large baking sheet with aluminum foil. Toast rye bread under broiler for 3 minutes, turning once. Set aside.
2. In medium-size bowl, combine tuna, mayonnaise, celery, carrots, pickle relish, hot sauce, salt and pepper. Stir until blended, then taste and adjust seasonings, if needed.
3. Spread a scant ½ cup tuna salad onto each slice of rye toast. Top each with two slices of cheese. Return to broiler; heat 3 minutes, until cheese is melted and lightly browned. Serve one open-face melt with sliced tomato on the side.

PER SERVING: 361 calories; 17 g fat (5 g sat.);
28 g protein; 24 g carbohydrate; 3 g fiber;
994 mg sodium; 59 mg cholesterol

peanut turkey noodles

MAKES: 4 servings. **PREP:** 10 minutes. **COOK:** 10 minutes.

- 8 ounces (½ box) linguine
- 8 ounces snow peas, trimmed and halved lengthwise
- 1 cup shredded carrots (from an 8-ounce bag)
- 1 package (9 ounces) fully cooked carved turkey breast (such as Purdue Short Cuts)
- 3 scallions, trimmed and sliced
- 1 jar (7 ounces) Thai peanut sauce (such as Asian Gourmet)
- 1 tablespoon white vinegar

1. Bring a large pot of lightly salted water to boiling. Add linguine and cook 9 minutes. Stir in snow peas and carrots and cook another minute. Drain and rinse under cold running water until cool to the touch.
2. Transfer linguine mixture to a large bowl. Add turkey and scallions. Pour the peanut sauce over the top, then add vinegar to peanut sauce jar. Screw cap back on and shake jar. Pour contents over linguine mixture, toss to coat completely with sauce and serve.

PER SERVING: 458 calories; 10 g fat (3 g sat.);
28 g protein; 62 g carbohydrate; 4 g fiber;
934 mg sodium; 36 mg cholesterol

**Grilled Pork
Tenderloin with
Black Bean Salsa**

Make the fresh salsa while the pork tenderloin grills so it's done when the meat is done—and you're ready to sit down and dig in!

grilled pork tenderloin with black bean salsa

MAKES: 4 servings. **PREP:** 5 minutes. **GRILL:** 18 minutes.

- 1 pork tenderloin, about 1¼ pounds
- ¾ cup light lime vinaigrette dressing (such as Newman's Own)
- ½ teaspoon ground cumin
- 1 cup black beans, drained and rinsed
- 1 can (10 ounces) pineapple tidbits, drained
- ½ sweet red pepper, finely chopped
- ⅛ teaspoon salt
- ⅛ teaspoon pepper

1. Place tenderloin in a large resealable plastic bag. Whisk together the vinaigrette and cumin in a measuring cup. Pour ½ cup of the dressing into bag with pork. Let marinate at room temperature while heating grill.

2. Heat grill to medium-high or medium-hot coals. Once hot, remove pork from marinade and grill for 18 minutes, turning frequently, until it registers 140° on an instant-read thermometer. Remove to a cutting board, tent with foil and let rest 5 minutes.

3. Meanwhile, in a small bowl, stir together the black beans, pineapple, red pepper, salt, pepper and remaining ¼ cup cumin-dressing mixture. Slice pork on a slight diagonal into ¼-inch-thick slices. Serve with salsa alongside.

PER SERVING: 290 calories; 10 g fat (3 g sat.); 32 g protein; 25 g carbohydrate; 4 g fiber; 763 mg sodium; 94 mg cholesterol

bbq pork tacos

MAKES: 4 servings. **PREP:** 10 minutes. **BAKE:** at 350° for 7 minutes. **MICROWAVE:** 8 minutes.

- 1 bag (16 ounces) coleslaw mix
- ⅓ cup Miracle Whip
- ⅛ teaspoon celery seed
- ⅛ teaspoon salt
- ⅛ teaspoon black pepper
- 1 tub (18 ounces) prepared shredded barbecue pork or chicken (such as Lloyd's)
- 8 hard taco shells
  Cherry tomatoes (optional)

1. Heat oven to 350°. In a medium-size bowl, stir together ½ bag coleslaw mix (save remainder for another use), the Miracle Whip, celery seeds, salt and pepper. Set aside for flavors to blend.

2. Place taco shells on a baking sheet. Heat at 350° for 7 minutes, until warmed. Meanwhile, heat shredded barbecue pork in microwave following package directions for 8 minutes.

3. Assemble tacos: Spoon about ¼ cup pork into each taco shell. Top each with about 2 tablespoons cole slaw. Serve with cherry tomatoes, if desired.

PER TACO: 191 calories; 7 g fat (2 g sat.); 8 g protein; 22 g carbohydrate; 1 g fiber; 605 mg sodium; 21 mg cholesterol

food university

COME JULY AND AUGUST, I CAN'T GET ENOUGH OF SUMMER'S SWEETEST VEGETABLE. YELLOW, WHITE, BICOLOR—I LOVE THEM ALL. ANY OF THESE THREE METHODS ARE A GREAT WAY TO COOK CORN. I LOVE EATING IT WITH THE DELICIOUS CHILI-LIME BUTTER, OPPOSITE. **BY JULIE MILTENBERGER**

Ears should have bright green husks, golden-brown silks and kernels that reach the tip. Corn loses its sweetness from the moment it's picked, so whether you're buying from a farm stand or a market, try to eat it the same day. If you need to store, leave husks on and keep in coldest part of the fridge up to 3 days.

Food styling: Michael Pederson. Prop styling: Christina Lane. Illustrations: Brown Bird Design.

perfect corn on the cob

PICK A METHOD

A Stovetop Bring a large pot of water to boiling. Remove husks from 4 to 6 ears of corn. Add to boiling water, cover pot and turn off heat. Let corn sit in water for 10 minutes; remove with tongs to platter.

B Microwave Leave husks on 6 ears of corn. Place on paper towels in microwave and cook on HIGH for 6 to 9 minutes. Let rest 5 minutes, then using dishcloth or oven mitts, remove husks from corn and serve.

C Grill Heat gas grill to medium-high or coals on a charcoal grill to medium-hot. Remove husks from 6 ears of corn. Place one ear of corn on a sheet of foil and spread with 2 teaspoons of the Chili-Lime Butter. Wrap tightly in foil and repeat with remaining ears. Place foil-wrapped corn on grill and cook 15 to 20 minutes, turning every so often. Carefully remove from grill and unwrap foil; transfer to platter and serve.

chili-lime butter

MAKES: ½ cup   **PREP:** 5 minutes

- ½ cup (1 stick) unsalted butter, softened
- 1 teaspoon grated fresh lime zest
- 2 teaspoons freshly squeezed lime juice
- 1 teaspoon chili powder
- ¼ teaspoon salt
   Pinch black pepper

Combine butter, lime zest, lime juice, chili powder, salt and pepper in a mini chopper. Pulse until well blended, then transfer to a ramekin or crock. Keep at room temperature until serving. Refrigerate any extra for up to 1 week (or freeze for up to 6 months).

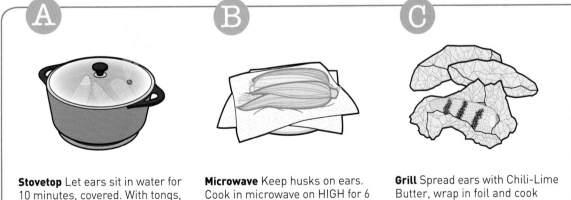

Stovetop Let ears sit in water for 10 minutes, covered. With tongs, remove to a platter.

Microwave Keep husks on ears. Cook in microwave on HIGH for 6 to 9 minutes, then remove husks.

Grill Spread ears with Chili-Lime Butter, wrap in foil and cook on grill for 15 minutes. Unwrap and serve.

august

Nectarine Shortcake
page 175

CELEBRATE THE PEAK OF SUMMER WITH A
FRESH-FRUIT DESSERT AND SIMPLE BUT
LIVELY RECIPES FOR GRILLING
EVERYONE'S FAVORITE BIRD.

**Asian BBQ Chicken Thighs
and Broccoli Slaw**
page 183

**Southwestern
Ham and Cheese
Salad Cup**
page 187

Coleslaw 3 Ways
page 193

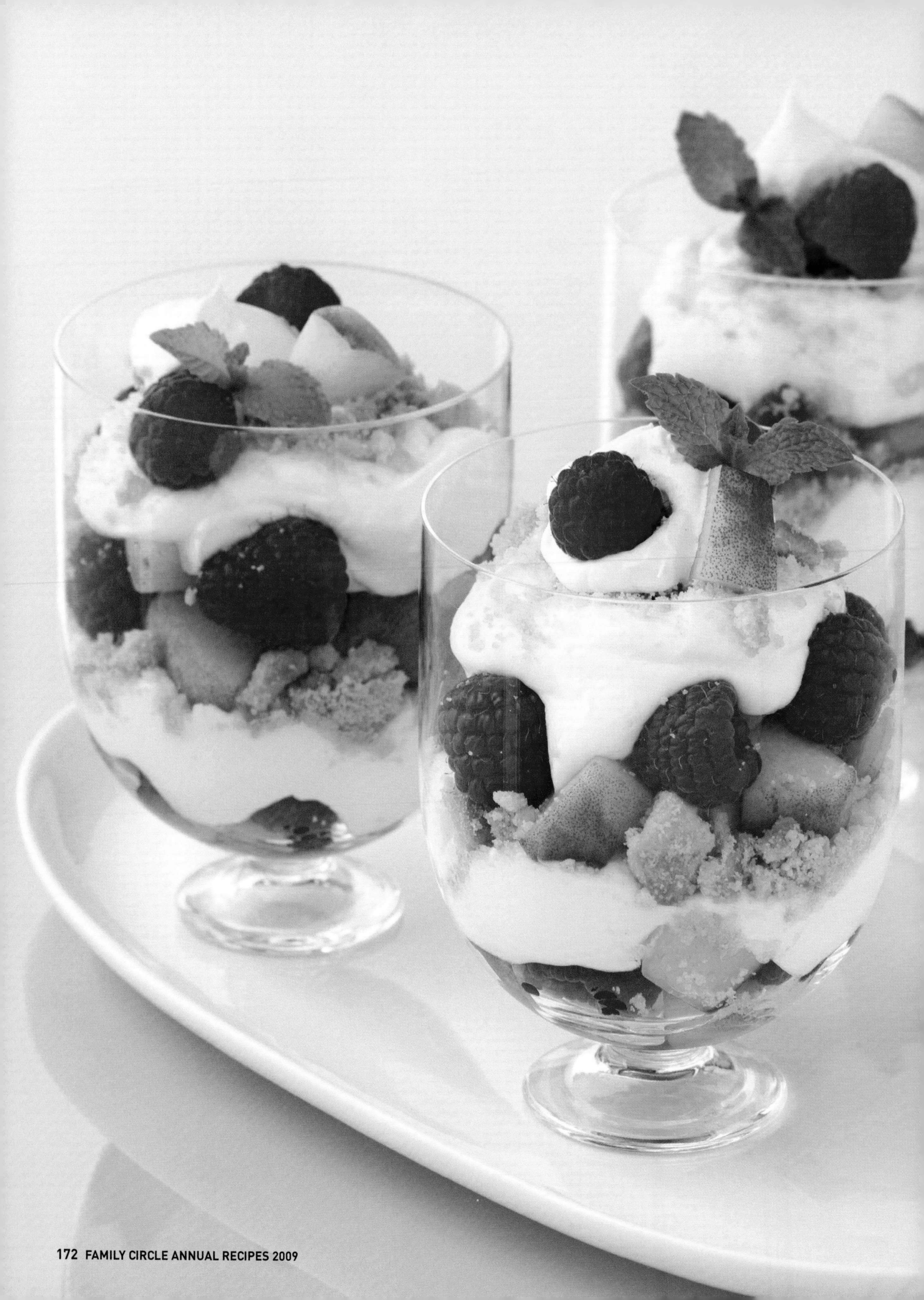

A VERY PRETTY DESSERT FEATURING THE PERFECTLY RIPE PEACHES NOW PERFUMING THE PRODUCE SECTION. **BY JULIE MILTENBERGER**

peach and raspberry parfaits

MAKES: 4 servings. **PREP:** 5 minutes.

- 2 medium-size peaches, rinsed and pitted
- 1 container raspberries, rinsed and gently patted dry
- 2 teaspoons sugar
- ½ teaspoon vanilla extract
- 1 envelope dry whipped topping mix (such as Dream Whip)
- ½ cup 2% milk
- 1 container (6 ounces) vanilla yogurt
- 8 shortbread cookies (such as Lorna Doone) Mint, to garnish (optional)

1. Cut 1½ peaches into ½-inch pieces; reserve remaining half for snacking. Set aside 4 peach pieces and 4 raspberries for garnish. In a medium-size bowl, gently stir together remaining peach pieces, remaining raspberries, sugar and vanilla. Let stand 5 minutes.

2. In a large bowl, combine whipped topping mix and milk. Beat on low speed for 1 minute, then increase speed to high and beat 4 minutes, until fluffy and stiff (makes about 2 cups). Fold 1½ cups of the whipped topping into yogurt in a small bowl (reserve remaining ½ cup topping).

3. Begin layering: Place about ¼ cup fruit in the bottom of 4 glasses. Top each with ¼ cup yogurt mixture. Crumble one cookie into each glass. Repeat layering, ending with cookies. Dollop reserved whipped topping over parfaits, about 2 tablespoons for each. Garnish with reserved fruit and mint, if desired.

PER SERVING: 222 calories; 5 g fat (1 g sat.); 4 g protein; 40 g carbohydrate; 3 g fiber; 106 mg sodium; 8 mg cholesterol

PHOTOGRAPHY BY RITA MAAS

bumper crop

FRUIT DESSERTS WITH ALL THE RIPE STUFF
BY JULIE MILTENBERGER

Lattice-Topped Peach
Pie (Recipe opposite)

nectarine shortcake

MAKES 6 servings. **PREP:** 20 minutes. **BAKE:** at 425° for 12 minutes.

- **4 nectarines**
- **¼ cup plus 2 tablespoons sugar**
- **½ teaspoon vanilla extract**
- **2⅓ cups reduced-calorie biscuit mix**
- **½ cup milk**
- **3 tablespoons unsalted butter, melted**
- **2 cups whipped topping**

1. Heat oven to 425°. Pit and slice 3 of the nectarines and toss together with ¼ cup of the sugar and the vanilla. Set aside. Peel, pit and dice remaining nectarine.
2. In a large bowl, combine biscuit mix, remaining 2 tablespoons sugar, milk and butter. Stir in diced nectarine.

Drop ½-cup mounds onto a heavy-duty nonstick baking sheet.
3. Bake at 425° for 12 minutes. Cool biscuits on a wire rack. Split one in half horizontally and place bottom on a plate. Top with ⅓ cup of the sliced nectarines and ¼ cup whipped topping. Place top half of biscuit on whipped topping, and dollop with 1 tablespoon additional topping. Repeat with remaining biscuits, nectarines and whipped topping and serve immediately.

PER SERVING 397 calories; 14 g fat (9 g sat.); 5 g protein; 62 g carbohydrate; 2 g fiber; 550 mg sodium; 17 mg cholesterol

lattice-topped peach pie

MAKES: 12 servings. **PREP:** 20 minutes.
BAKE: at 375° for 45 minutes, 350° for 20 minutes.

- **1 package refrigerated rolled piecrusts (15 ounces, 2 per package)**
- **½ cup plus 1 teaspoon sugar**
- **3 tablespoons cornstarch**
  Pinch salt
  Pinch ground allspice
- **3 pounds peaches, peeled, pitted and sliced (about 8 peaches)**
- **1 egg white**

1. Heat oven to 375°. Fit one piecrust into a 9-inch pie dish. Refrigerate while preparing filling. In a small bowl, blend ½ cup of the sugar, the cornstarch, salt and allspice.
2. Place peaches in a large bowl. Add sugar mixture and stir to combine. Pour peach mixture, scraping bowl, into bottom crust.
3. Unroll the second crust. Place a lattice cutter (visit confectionery house.com for options) on a cutting board. Drape crust over cutter and roll with rolling pin until piecrust is cut. Carefully lift crust from cutter and drape over pie filling. Fold top crust edges together and crimp decoratively. Brush with the egg white; sprinkle with remaining teaspoon sugar.
4. Bake pie at 375° for 45 minutes. Lower oven temperature to 350° and continue to bake for an additional 20 minutes, until fruit is bubbly and crust is nicely browned (tent with foil if browning too quickly). Cool on a wire rack for 20 minutes before slicing and serving.

PER SERVING: 241 calories; 10 g fat (4 g sat.); 3 g protein; 37 g carbohydrate; 1 g fiber; 138 mg sodium; 7 mg cholesterol

peach smoothie

MAKES: 6 cups. **PREP:** 5 minutes.

- 2 **cups ice**
- 2 **peaches, pitted and cut into pieces**
- ¾ **cup skim milk**
- 1 **container (7 ounces) plain 2% Greek yogurt**
- ½ **cup tangerine or orange juice**
- 3 **tablespoons honey**

In a blender, combine ice, peaches, milk, yogurt and juice. Place lid on blender and select mix or crush setting. Blend until smooth; while machine is on, pour in honey and blend an additional 30 seconds. Pour into glasses and serve.

PER CUP: 89 calories; 1 g fat (0 g sat.); 4 g protein; 18 g carbohydrate; 1 g fiber; 30 mg sodium; 2 mg cholesterol

plum and blueberry galette

MAKES: 12 servings. **PREP:** 15 minutes. **BAKE:** at 375° for 35 minutes.

Filling:
- 1¼ **pounds red or black plums, pitted and cut into ½-inch wedges**
- ½ **cup blueberries**
- ½ **cup granulated sugar**
- 4 **teaspoons cornstarch**

Crust:
- 1 **box (11 ounces) piecrust mix**
- 3 **tablespoons granulated sugar**
   Pinch of ground ginger
- 1 **egg, lightly beaten**
- ½ **cup confectioners' sugar**

1. Heat oven to 375°. Line a large baking sheet with nonstick foil. Prepare **Filling:** In a medium-size bowl, toss together the plums, blueberries, granulated sugar and cornstarch. Set aside.

2. Prepare **Crust:** In a large bowl, combine piecrust mix, granulated sugar, ginger and ⅓ cup *water*. Stir until mixture begins to come together, then roll out to a 13-inch circle on a lightly floured surface. Carefully roll up onto rolling pin and transfer to prepared baking sheet.

3. Spoon filling onto center of crust, leaving a 3-inch border all around. Fold edge of crust partway over plum mixture. Brush with beaten egg.

4. Bake galette at 375° for 35 minutes, until crust is browned and center bubbly (some juices may leak out of the crust). Run a thin spatula under galette, then carefully transfer to a serving platter, using 2 spatulas to balance.

5. In a small bowl, mix together the confectioners' sugar and 1 tablespoon water. Drizzle over galette and serve.

PER SERVING: 232 calories; 9 g fat (2 g sat.); 3 g protein; 37 g carbohydrate; 1 g fiber; 202 mg sodium; 18 mg cholesterol

nectarine cobbler

MAKES: 8 servings. **PREP:** 15 minutes. **BAKE:** at 375° for 35 minutes.

- 6 nectarines, peeled, pitted and diced
- ½ cup sugar
- 2 tablespoons cornstarch
  Pinch nutmeg

Biscuits:
- 1½ cups all-purpose flour
- ½ teaspoon baking soda
- ¼ teaspoon salt
- ¾ cup reduced-fat sour cream
- 1 large egg
- 2 tablespoons unsalted butter, melted
- 2 tablespoons sugar
- 1 tablespoon milk

1. Heat oven to 375°. Coat a 2-quart baking dish with nonstick cooking spray. In bowl, combine nectarines, sugar, cornstarch and nutmeg. Pour into dish.

2. Prepare **Biscuits:** In a large bowl, stir together the flour, baking soda and salt. In a small bowl, whisk together the sour cream, egg, butter and 1 tablespoon of the sugar. Stir sour cream mixture into the flour mixture until a dough is formed.

3. On a lightly floured surface, pat or roll out dough to ⅓-inch thickness. Using a 1¾-inch round biscuit cutter, cut out 6 biscuits. Gather dough together and repeat for a total of 12 biscuits.

4. Place biscuits on top of fruit mixture, spacing evenly over fruit filling, and brush with milk. Sprinkle with remaining 1 tablespoon sugar. Bake at 375° for 35 minutes, until biscuits are browned and fruit is bubbly. Cool at least 15 minutes before serving.

PER SERVING: 246 calories; 4 g fat (2 g sat.); 5 g protein; 48 g carbohydrate; 2 g fiber; 175 mg sodium; 38 mg cholesterol

TO PEEL FRUIT THE TRADITIONAL WAY, FOLLOW THESE EASY STEPS.

For peaches, plums and nectarines, cut a shallow "X" in the end opposite stem.

Plunge into boiling water; remove after a minute or two when skin pulls away.

Immediately transfer to a bowl of cold water and ice cubes to stop the cooking.

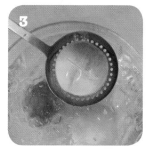

When cool enough to handle, peel back skin, starting at the "X."

best bbq chicken

SEASONING, SPICES AND SAUCES GIVE EVERYONE'S FAVORITE EXTRA SIZZLE. BY CINDY HELLER

Stirring in ¾ cup chow mein noodles into the slaw adds a bunch more crunch to the side dish for Asian BBQ Chicken Thighs and Broccoli Slaw. (Recipe page 183)

Turn main-dish Chicken Satay Skewers with Mango Relish into appetizers by cutting each chicken tender in half. (Recipe page 183)

PHOTOGRAPHY BY TINA RUPP

tandoori chicken with raita

MAKES: 4 servings. **PREP:** 10 minutes.
REFRIGERATE: 30 minutes. **GRILL:** 25 minutes.

- 1¼ **cups plain yogurt**
- 1 **kirby cucumber, peeled, seeded and finely chopped**
- 2 **teaspoons fresh lemon juice**
- ¾ **teaspoon salt**
- 1 **tablespoon grated fresh ginger**
- 1 **tablespoon garam masala spice blend (such as McCormick)**
- ⅛ **teaspoon cayenne pepper**
- 4 **bone-in, skinless chicken breasts (about 3 pounds), cut in half diagonally**

1. For raita, stir together ¾ cup yogurt, cucumber, lemon juice and ¼ teaspoon salt in a small bowl; set aside.
2. In another small bowl, stir together remaining ½ cup yogurt, remaining ½ teaspoon salt, ginger, garam masala and cayenne. Place chicken in a baking dish and spread yogurt mixture over top. Cover with plastic wrap and refrigerate 30 minutes.
3. Heat gas grill to medium-high or prepare charcoal grill with medium-hot coals. Lightly coat grill with nonstick cooking spray or oil. Grill chicken, covered, about 20 minutes over direct heat, turning every 5 minutes. Then move chicken to indirect heat for 5 minutes or until internal temperature measures 160° on an instant-read thermometer. Serve with raita.
Broiler Method: Heat broiler. Coat a broiler pan with nonstick cooking spray. Brush chicken with sauce and broil for about 20 minutes. Proceed from Step 3 above.

PER SERVING: 359 calories; 6 g fat (3 g sat.); 66 g protein; 6 g carbohydrate; 1 g fiber; 649 mg sodium; 168 mg cholesterol

chicken burgers

MAKES: 4 servings. **PREP:** 10 minutes. **GRILL:** 12 minutes.

- ¼ **cup low-fat mayonnaise**
- 1 **tablespoon chopped parsley**
- 1 **tablespoon chopped basil, plus 4 large, whole basil leaves**
- 1 **teaspoon lemon juice**
- 16 **ounces ground chicken**
- 1 **small onion, finely chopped**
- 3 **tablespoons part-skim ricotta cheese**
- 3 **tablespoons seasoned bread crumbs**
- 4 **hamburger buns**
- 1 **small tomato, sliced**

1. Stir together mayonnaise, ½ tablespoon parsley, ½ tablespoon chopped basil and lemon juice in a small bowl; set aside.
2. Heat gas grill to medium-high or prepare charcoal grill with medium-hot coals.

3. In a large bowl, stir together remaining ½ tablespoon each parsley and basil, chicken, onion, ricotta and bread crumbs until combined. Form into four 4-inch patties. Grill for 6 minutes per side or until internal temperature registers 160° on an instant-read thermometer.
4. Remove burgers from grill and place on buns. Top with a basil leaf, a slice of tomato and 1 tablespoon mayonnaise mixture.
Broiler Method: Heat broiler. Coat a broiler pan with nonstick cooking spray. Broil burgers 5 to 6 minutes per side. Proceed from Step 4 above.

PER SERVING: 409 calories; 20 g fat (6 g sat.); 26 g protein; 31 g carbohydrate; 2 g fiber; 519 mg sodium; 146 mg cholesterol

Crispy, hearty vegetables like endive and radicchio hold up well on the grill; they take on a nice smoky flavor and soften slightly but don't fall apart.

apricot chicken with endive and radicchio salad

MAKES: 4 servings. **PREP:** 15 minutes. **GRILL:** 30 minutes.

- ⅔ cup apricot preserves
- 3 tablespoons Dijon mustard
- 3 tablespoons cider vinegar
- ½ teaspoon salt
- ½ teaspoon black pepper
- 1 package chicken pieces, skin removed, wings discarded and breasts cut in half diagonally
- 2 heads endive, stem and outer leaves removed, cut in half lengthwise
- 1 small head radicchio, outer leaves removed, cut into quarters

1. Heat gas grill to medium-high or prepare charcoal grill with medium-hot coals.

2. Stir together apricot preserves, mustard, vinegar and ¼ teaspoon each salt and pepper. Remove 2 tablespoons mixture and set aside.

3. Place chicken on grill over direct heat; brush with apricot sauce. Close cover; cook for about 20 minutes, turning pieces and brushing with additional sauce every 5 minutes. Transfer chicken to indirect heat. Continue to cook, turning once, for about 10 minutes or until internal temperature registers 160° on an instant-read thermometer.

4. Brush endive and radicchio with 1 tablespoon reserved sauce; place on grill for the last 12 minutes of cook time.

Remove from grill and cut into 1-inch pieces. Place pieces in a large bowl and toss with remaining sauce and ¼ teaspoon each salt and pepper.

Oven Method: Heat oven to 400°. Coat a roasting pan with cooking spray. Place chicken in pan; brush with sauce. Bake for 35 minutes, brushing often with sauce. Coat a baking sheet with cooking spray. Place endive and radicchio on sheet; bake for last 15 minutes cook time, until browned. Proceed from Step 4.

PER SERVING: 694 calories; 13 g fat (3 g sat.); 95 g protein; 46 g carbohydrate; 8 g fiber; 958 mg sodium; 295 mg cholesterol

The sweet mustard sauce for Mustard-Basil Chicken with Grilled Corn isn't just for chicken—it's terrific with pork, fish and veggies too.

mustard-basil chicken with grilled corn

MAKES: 4 servings. **PREP:** 10 minutes.
GRILL: 23 minutes.

- 3 tablespoons grainy Dijon mustard
- 4 tablespoons basil-infused olive oil
- 1 tablespoon honey
- ½ teaspoon salt
- ½ teaspoon black pepper
- 4 boneless, skinless chicken breasts (about 1½ pounds)
- 4 ears corn

1. Heat a gas grill to medium-high or prepare a charcoal grill with medium-hot coals.

2. Stir together mustard, 3 tablespoons oil, honey and ¼ teaspoon each salt and pepper.

3. Lightly coat grill with nonstick cooking spray or oil. Place chicken on the grill and brush generously with mustard mixture; cover and grill for 5 minutes. Remove cover and flip breasts, baste generously with sauce and cover.

4. Continue flipping chicken every 5 minutes, basting each time, for about 18 minutes or until internal temperature registers 160° on an instant-read thermometer.

5. Meanwhile, brush corn with remaining tablespoon oil; sprinkle with remaining ¼ teaspoon each salt and pepper. Wrap corn in aluminum foil. Grill corn, turning once, about 18 minutes or until tender. Serve alongside chicken.

Broiler method: Heat broiler. Coat a broiler pan with nonstick cooking spray. Coat chicken with sauce and broil for about 20 minutes, brushing occasionally with sauce. Meanwhile, broil corn for about 18 minutes or until tender.

PER SERVING: 412 calories; 17 g fat (3 g sat.); 42 g protein; 24 g carbohydrate; 3 g fiber; 685 mg sodium; 98 mg cholesterol

asian bbq chicken thighs and broccoli slaw

MAKES: 4 servings. **PREP:** 10 minutes.
COOK: 5 minutes. **GRILL:** 25 minutes.

- ¼ cup ketchup
- 2 tablespoons hoisin sauce
- 2 tablespoons low-sodium soy sauce
- 1 teaspoon sesame oil
- 2¼ pounds bone-in, skinless chicken thighs
- 1 bag (12 ounces) broccoli slaw
- 2 tablespoons rice wine vinegar
- ¼ teaspoon salt
- ¼ teaspoon black pepper

1. Heat gas grill to medium-high or prepare charcoal grill with medium-hot coals.

2. In a small saucepan, stir together ketchup, hoisin, soy sauce and sesame oil. Cook over medium-high heat until bubbling, about 5 minutes. Remove 3 tablespoons sauce from pot and set aside.

3. Lightly coat grill with nonstick cooking spray or oil. Place chicken thighs on grill bottom-side up and baste with sauce. Close grill cover and cook 5 minutes. Remove cover and flip thighs, basting generously with sauce. Continue brushing with sauce every 5 minutes for about 20 minutes or until internal temperature reaches 160° on an instant-read thermometer.

4. While chicken is cooking, stir together reserved sauce, broccoli slaw, vinegar and salt and pepper. Refrigerate until ready to serve.

Broiler method: Heat broiler. Coat a broiler pan with nonstick cooking spray. Broil chicken about 20 minutes, basting often and generously with sauce. Proceed from Step 4 above.

PER SERVING: 361 calories; 16 g fat (4 g sat.); 38 g protein; 16 g carbohydrate; 3 g fiber; 992 mg sodium; 129 mg cholesterol

chicken satay skewers with mango relish

MAKES: 6 servings. **PREP:** 10 minutes.
GRILL: 10 minutes.

- ⅓ cup satay sauce (such as Thai Kitchen)
- 4 tablespoons lime juice
- ½ teaspoon salt
- ½ teaspoon black pepper
- 2 pounds chicken tenders
- 1 bunch scallions
- 3 large ripe mangoes, peeled and flesh cut into ¼-inch cubes
- ⅓ cup finely chopped red onion
- 1 tablespoon vegetable oil

1. Heat gas grill to medium-high or prepare charcoal grill with medium-hot coals.

2. Combine satay sauce, 2 tablespoons lime juice and ¼ teaspoon each salt and pepper.

3. Thread tenders onto skewers; brush each with satay sauce. Grill skewers for 5 minutes per side or until chicken is cooked through. Grill scallions for last 3 minutes of cook time.

4. Meanwhile, stir together remaining 2 tablespoons lime juice, ¼ teaspoon each salt and pepper, mangoes, red onion and vegetable oil in a bowl.

5. Remove chicken and scallions from grill and thinly slice scallions. Stir half of scallions into mango relish and sprinkle remaining half over meat. Serve skewers with relish.

Broiler Method: Heat broiler. Coat a broiler pan with cooking spray. Brush chicken with sauce; broil 5 minutes per side. Broil scallions for final 3 minutes of cook time. Proceed from Step 4 above.

PER SERVING: 264 calories; 5 g fat (1 g sat.); 36 g protein; 20 g carbohydrate; 2 fiber; 296 mg sodium; 88 mg cholesterol

no-cook suppers

SEVEN DELICIOUS DINNERS—KEEP YOUR OVEN OFF.

BY **MICHAEL TYRRELL**

Cape Cod Turkey Pitas
burst with almonds
and cranberries.
(Recipe page 189)

PHOTOGRAPHY BY ALEXANDRA GRABLEWSKI

chutney shrimp

MAKES: 4 servings. **PREP:** 10 minutes. **MICROWAVE:** 2 minutes.

1 package (8½ ounces) Uncle Ben's Whole Grain Medley Ready Rice
1 cup frozen peas, thawed
1 jar (10 ounces) mango chutney (such as Major Grey's)
¼ cup warm water
¾ pound cooked large shrimp
Tandoori naan (such as Fabulous Flats) or pita (optional)

1. In a large microwave-safe bowl, mix together rice and peas. Cover with plastic wrap and microwave for 90 seconds.
2. In another bowl, combine chutney and warm water. Microwave for 30 seconds. Stir half of the chutney into rice and peas.
3. To serve, spoon the rice mixture onto a large serving platter. Arrange the shrimp and remaining chutney mixture around the rice. If desired, serve with purchased naan bread or pita.

PER SERVING: 385 calories; 9 g fat (0 g sat.); 18 g protein; 61 g carbohydrate; 4 g fiber; 943 mg sodium; 126 mg cholesterol

Food styling: Michael Pederson. Prop styling: Lynda White.

asian chicken wraps

MAKES: 4 wraps. **PREP:** 15 minutes.

- ½ cup creamy peanut butter
- ½ cup warm water
- 2 tablespoons reduced-sodium soy sauce
- 2 tablespoons rice wine vinegar
- 1 clove garlic, finely chopped
- 1 scallion, chopped
- ½ rotisserie chicken, shredded (about 2½ cups), from a 3-pound chicken
- 4 large rectangular wraps or large tortillas
- ½ sweet red pepper, cored, seeds removed and thinly sliced
- ½ large cucumber, peeled, halved lengthwise and thinly sliced
- 1 cup mung bean sprouts

1. In large bowl, whisk together the peanut butter, warm water, soy sauce and vinegar until smooth. Stir in the garlic and scallion. Add chicken and stir until coated.

2. Place one wrap or tortilla on a flat work surface. Scatter one-fourth each of chicken, red pepper, cucumber and bean sprouts over the top. Tightly roll up from one narrow end. Cut in half on the bias. Repeat with the remaining ingredients to make 4 wraps.

PER WRAP: 322 calories; 19 g fat (4 g sat.); 15 g protein; 27 g carbohydrate; 4 g fiber; 767 mg sodium; 4 mg cholesterol

italian tomato and antipasto salad

MAKES: 4 servings. **PREP:** 20 minutes. **REFRIGERATE:** 1 hour.

- 1½ pounds ripe plum tomatoes (about 6), cored and cut into bite-size pieces
- 4 tablespoons Italian dressing (such as Wish-Bone)
- 3 hot cherry peppers, seeds removed, chopped
- 3 cloves garlic, thinly sliced
- ¼ teaspoon salt
- ¼ teaspoon black pepper
- 1 head red leafy lettuce, rinsed and patted dry
- 2 ounces Genoa salami, cut into ribbons
- 2 ounces spicy Italian ham (capicola) cut into thin ribbons
- ¼ pound fresh mozzarella, cut into bite-size pieces, or bocconcini, halved
- 8 pitted kalamata olives, coarsely chopped
  Additional Italian dressing (optional)

1. In a large bowl, mix together the tomatoes, Italian dressing, cherry peppers, garlic, salt and pepper. Cover and refrigerate for 1 hour.

2. Arrange the lettuce leaves on a large serving platter. Spoon the tomato salad and any accumulated liquid over the lettuce. Scatter the salami, ham, mozzarella and olives over the tomatoes.

3. Serve immediately with additional Italian dressing on the side, if desired.

PER SERVING: 263 calories; 18 g fat (7 g sat.); 14 g protein; 13 g carbohydrate; 2 g fiber; 1,193 mg sodium; 44 mg cholesterol

southwestern ham and cheese salad cup

MAKES: 4 servings. **PREP:** 10 minutes. **REFRIGERATE:** 1 hour.

1 can (15 ounces) black beans, drained and rinsed

6 ounces ham steak, cut into ½-inch cubes

4 ounces cheese cubes (such as Kraft Snackables 2% Cheddar and Jack cheese)

¼ cup Miracle Whip

¼ cup medium or hot salsa

2 scallions, chopped

1 tablespoon chopped cilantro

1 large head Bibb lettuce, washed and dried thoroughly

1. In a large bowl, mix together the beans, ham, cheese cubes, Miracle Whip, salsa, scallions and cilantro. Cover and refrigerate for 1 hour.

2. Divide and arrange Bibb lettuce onto four plates, and spoon about ¾ cup of bean and ham mixture onto each.

PER SERVING: 331 calories; 10 g fat (1 g sat.); 19 g protein; 40 g carbohydrate; 7 g fiber; 1,123 mg sodium; 24 mg cholesterol

Spinach Salad
with Chicken
(recipe opposite)

spinach salad with chicken

MAKES: 4 servings. PREP: 15 minutes.
MICROWAVE: 30 seconds.

- 2 tablespoons red-wine vinegar
- 1 teaspoon brown mustard
- ½ teaspoon lemon-pepper seasoning
- 5 tablespoons extra-virgin olive oil
- 2 bags (6 ounces each) baby spinach
- 1 cup (4 ounces) sliced mushrooms
- ½ medium red onion, halved and thinly sliced
- ½ rotisserie chicken, shredded (about 2½ cups), from a 3-pound chicken
- 10 slices fully cooked microwavable bacon

1. In a small bowl, whisk together the vinegar, mustard and lemon-pepper. Slowly drizzle in the olive oil, whisking continuously. Set aside.
2. In a large bowl, mix together the spinach, mushrooms and onion. Toss with the dressing. Add in the shredded chicken.
3. Microwave the bacon following package directions, about 30 seconds. Crumble and sprinkle over salad. Serve immediately.

PER SERVING: 410 calories; 26 g fat (5 g sat.); 34 g protein; 13 g carbohydrate; 5 g fiber; 864 mg sodium; 84 mg cholesterol

cape cod turkey pitas

MAKES: 8 pitas. PREP: 10 minutes.
REFRIGERATE: 1 hour.

- 1 slice deli smoked turkey, cut ¾ inch thick (about 1 pound)
- ½ cup light ranch dressing
- ⅓ cup sliced, blanched almonds
- ⅓ cup Craisins, coarsely chopped
- 2 scallions, chopped
- 8 small pitas, about 1 ounce each (such as Toufayan Bakeries Pitettes)

1. Cut the turkey into ¼-inch cubes.
2. In a large bowl, mix together the turkey, dressing, almonds, Craisins and scallions. Cover and refrigerate for 1 hour.
3. To serve, cut open each pita about 1 inch from the top. Spoon a scant ½ cup of turkey mixture into each.

PER PITA: 216 calories; 8 g fat (1 g sat.); 14 g protein; 25 g carbohydrate; 3 g fiber; 794 mg sodium; 30 mg cholesterol

surimi rolls

MAKES: 8 rolls. PREP: 10 minutes. REFRIGERATE: at least 1 hour.

- 1 pound imitation crabmeat (surimi), chopped
- ¾ cup light mayonnaise
- ¾ cup chopped celery (about 2 large ribs)
- 4 teaspoons fresh chopped tarragon
- 1 tablespoon Dijon mustard
- 1 tablespoon olive oil
- 8 hot dog buns, top-sliced variety Curly parsley (optional)

1. In a large bowl, mix together the imitation crab, mayonnaise, celery, tarragon, mustard and olive oil until well combined. Cover and refrigerate for at least 1 hour.
2. To serve, spoon a generous ⅓ cup of the crab mixture into each bun. Garnish with parsley, if desired.

PER ROLL: 268 calories; 11 g fat (2 g sat.); 9 g protein; 32 g carbohydrate; 1 g fiber; 916 mg sodium; 19 mg cholesterol

slow-cooker solutions

CLASSIC DISHES WITH A HEALTHIER TWIST. **BY CINDY HELLER**

Food styling: Liza Jernow. Prop styling: Deborah Williams.

lemon and caper chicken

MAKES: 4 servings. **PREP:** 15 minutes. **SLOW-COOK:** 3 hours on HIGH or 5 hours on LOW. **COOK:** 3 minutes.

  1 **large lemon**
  ¼ **cup low-sodium chicken broth**
1½ **tablespoons capers, chopped**
2½ **teaspoons dried oregano**
  ¼ **teaspoon garlic salt**
  ¼ **teaspoon black pepper**
  5 **boneless, skinless chicken thighs**
  4 **cups broccoli florets**
  ¼ **cup low-fat cream cheese, softened**

1. Grate zest from lemon. Cut lemon in half; juice one half; thinly slice the other.

2. Combine 3 tablespoons juice, 1 tablespoon zest, the broth, capers, oregano, garlic salt and pepper.

3. Place thighs in slow cooker; drizzle with 4 tablespoons juice mixture. Place lemon slices on top of each thigh. Cover; cook 3 hours on HIGH or 5 hours on LOW.

4. Add broccoli to center of slow cooker for last 15 minutes on HIGH or 30 minutes on LOW. Whisk together remaining juice and cream cheese.

5. Remove chicken and broccoli to a platter; keep warm. Discard lemon. Pour liquid from slow cooker, juice mixture and cheese into a saucepan. Cook, stirring, over medium heat for 3 minutes. Drizzle over chicken and broccoli and serve.

PER SERVING: 309 calories; 14 g fat (5 g sat.); 43 g protein; 6 g carbohydrate; 3 g fiber; 414 mg sodium; 203 mg cholesterol

PHOTOGRAPHY BY TINA RUPP

rich squash casserole

MAKES: 6 servings. **PREP:** 15 minutes.
COOK: 6 minutes. **SLOW-COOK:** 2 hours on
HIGH or 4 hours on LOW.

- 1 **cup grated Gruyère cheese**
- 1 **cup ricotta cheese**
- ½ **cup plain bread crumbs**
- 1 **tablespoon cornstarch**
- 1¼ **teaspoons dried basil**
- 1½ **teaspoons dried thyme**
- ¾ **teaspoon each salt and black pepper**
- 1 **tablespoon olive oil**
- 1 **package (8 ounces) sliced
  mushrooms**
- 1 **large onion, chopped**
- 3 **large summer squash, sliced
  ¼ inch thick**
- 2 **large zucchini, sliced ¼ inch thick**

1. Stir together Gruyère, ricotta, bread
crumbs, cornstarch, basil, ¾ teaspoon of
the thyme and ½ teaspoon each of the
salt and pepper; set aside.
2. Heat olive oil in a large skillet over
medium-high heat. Add mushrooms
and onion; sprinkle with remaining
¾ teaspoon thyme and ¼ teaspoon each
salt and pepper. Cover; cook 6 minutes,
stirring occasionally.
3. Coat slow cooker with cooking spray.
Layer ⅓ of the squash in bottom. Add
1 cup mushroom mixture over squash;
sprinkle ⅔ cup ricotta mixture on top.
Layer with another ⅓ of squash, the rest
of the mushrooms and another ⅔ cup of
ricotta mixture. Place remaining squash
and ricotta mixture on top.
4. Cover; cook for 2 hours on HIGH or
4 hours on LOW. Serve immediately.

PER SERVING: 262 calories; 14 g fat (7 g sat.);
15 g protein; 20 g carbohydrate; 5 g fiber;
465 mg sodium; 41 mg cholesterol

poached salmon with swiss chard

MAKES: 4 servings. **PREP:** 15 minutes. **SLOW-COOK:** 1½ hours on HIGH or 3 hours on LOW.

- 1½ **pounds salmon, patted dry**
- 2 **cloves garlic, minced**
- 3 **tablespoons Dijon mustard**
- 2 **tablespoons honey**
- 1 **tablespoon white wine vinegar**
- 1 **tablespoon dried dill**
- 1 **small onion, chopped**
- ¼ **cup low-sodium chicken broth**
- 2 **bunches (about 1½ pounds) Swiss
  chard, washed, trimmed of stems
  and cut into 1-inch pieces**

1. Coat slow cooker bowl with nonstick
cooking spray; arrange salmon in it,
tucking the thin ends of fillets
underneath. Sprinkle with garlic.
2. Stir together mustard, honey, vinegar
and dill. Place 2 tablespoons in a small
bowl and stir in onion and broth.

Reserve remaining mustard mixture for
later. Drizzle broth mixture over salmon.
Cover; cook on HIGH for 1½ hours or
LOW for 3 hours.
3. Add the Swiss chard around or on top
of salmon for final 15 minutes of
cooking on HIGH or final 30 minutes on
LOW; stir halfway through.
4. Carefully remove salmon from slow
cooker; set aside and keep warm. Stir
1 tablespoon mustard mixture into
Swiss chard. Serve with remaining
mustard sauce.

PER SERVING: 340 calories; 11 g fat (2 g sat.);
38 g protein; 22 g carbohydrate; 4 g fiber;
808 mg sodium; 94 mg cholesterol

food **university**

COLESLAW 3 WAYS CABBAGE IS SUPERCHEAP—WE'RE TALKING ABOUT A DOLLAR A HEAD— AND SO EASY TO TURN INTO ONE OF SUMMER'S MOST BELOVED DISHES. NAPA, GREEN OR RED, EACH TYPE HAS ITS OWN UNIQUE TEXTURE. **BY JULIE MILTENBERGER**

Asian Slaw

Tangy Red Slaw

Classic Coleslaw

PHOTOGRAPHY BY TINA RUPP

classic coleslaw
MAKES: 8 servings. **PREP:** 10 minutes
REFRIGERATE: at least 1 hour.

- ½ green cabbage (about 1½ pounds)
- 1 cup shredded carrots
- ½ cup light mayonnaise
- ½ cup sour cream
- ¼ cup sugar
- 2 tablespoons fresh lemon juice (½ lemon)
- ½ teaspoon celery seeds
- ¼ teaspoon salt

1. Cut cabbage in quarters and cut out tough stem (see steps A and B, below). Thinly slice into shreds (step C, below). Combine with carrots in large bowl.
2. In a small bowl, whisk the mayo, sour cream, sugar, lemon juice, celery seeds and salt until blended. Toss with cabbage mixture in bowl. Cover bowl with plastic; refrigerate at least an hour.

PER SERVING: 137 calories; 8 g fat (3 g sat.); 2 g protein; 15 g carbohydrate; 2 g fiber; 228 mg sodium; 15 mg cholesterol

tangy red slaw
MAKES: 8 servings. **PREP:** 10 minutes
REFRIGERATE: 30 minutes.

- 1 small head red cabbage (1½ pounds)
- 1 small red onion, peeled and sliced
- 1 small sweet red pepper, cored and sliced into thin strips
- ⅓ cup cider vinegar
- 3 tablespoons honey
- 1 tablespoon spicy brown or Dijon mustard
- ½ teaspoon caraway seeds
- ¼ teaspoon salt
- ¼ teaspoon ground black pepper
- ⅓ cup olive oil

1. Cut cabbage in quarters and cut out tough stem. Thinly slice into shreds (see steps, below). Combine with onion and sweet red pepper in large bowl.
2. In small bowl, whisk vinegar, honey, mustard, caraway, salt and pepper. While whisking, add oil in a thin stream. Toss with cabbage mixture to coat. Cover with plastic; refrigerate 30 minutes to soften.

PER SERVING: 143 calories; 9 g fat (1 g sat.); 2 g protein; 15 g carbohydrate; 3 g fiber; 136 mg sodium; 0 mg cholesterol

asian slaw
MAKES: 8 servings. **PREP:** 15 minutes.
COOK: 4 minutes.

- ½ cup sliced almonds
- 1 small head napa cabbage (about 2 pounds), rinsed, loose leaves discarded
- 1 cup shredded carrots
- 1 cup loosely packed basil leaves, rinsed and sliced into thin ribbons
- 8 ounces sugar snap peas, trimmed
- ⅓ cup rice vinegar
- 2 tablespoons reduced-sodium soy sauce
- 1 tablespoon sugar
- 2 teaspoons sesame oil
- ¼ teaspoon salt
- ¼ cup vegetable oil

1. Place almonds in a small nonstick skillet. Toast over medium-high heat for 4 minutes, shaking pan, until lightly browned. Remove from heat; set aside.
2. Trim cabbage. Cut lengthwise into quarters, then crosswise into thin shreds; put in a large bowl. Add carrots, basil and peas. Toss to combine.
3. In small bowl, whisk together rice vinegar, soy sauce, sugar, sesame oil and salt. While whisking, add vegetable oil in a thin stream, until blended. Sprinkle almonds over cabbage mixture; drizzle slaw with dressing. Toss to combine and serve.

PER SERVING: 158 calories; 11 g fat (1 g sat.); 4 g protein; 9 g carbohydrate; 3 g fiber; 123 mg sodium; 0 mg cholesterol

Look for heads of cabbage that are compact and firm with fresh, crisp, blemish-free leaves. Choose dark purple, deep green or green tips, respectively, for red, green or napa varieties. Store uncut heads one to two weeks in crisper. Wrap cut pieces in plastic and store for a few days.

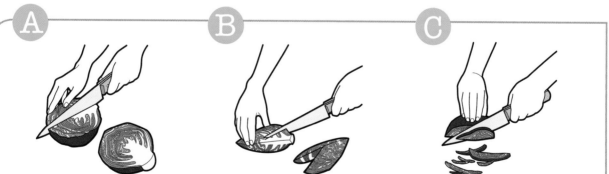

A Remove loose outer leaves. Then cut cabbage in half through stem end. Next, cut into quarters.

B With each cabbage quarter, cut out tough stem end by first separating one side and then the other. Discard stem.

C Turn one quarter on one cut edge. Slice to desired thickness, repeating with all cabbage pieces.

For napa cabbage, rinse, then trim tough bottom stem. Slice in half lengthwise. Keeping leaves and stem intact, shred crosswise into thin slices.

september

Oven-Fried Chili Chicken
page 201

INVITE THE NEIGHBORS OVER FOR A
FINAL SUMMER CELEBRATION FEATURING
EASY OVEN-FRIED CHICKEN AND
KID-FRIENDLY FAVORITES.

Mint Ice Cream Chocolate Sandwiches page 207

Ginger-Teriyaki Sliders page 209

Meatball Stew page 224

neighborhood dish

DELICIOUS IDEAS FOR BLOCK PARTIES AND BACKYARD BARBECUES—EACH FOR LESS THAN A BUCK A SERVING. **BY MICHAEL TYRRELL**

Layered Taco Dip
(Recipe page 201)

99¢
per serving

69¢
per thigh

Oven-Fried Chili Chicken
(Recipe page 201)

Food styling: Michael Pederson. Prop styling: Lynda White.

PHOTOGRAPHY BY ALEXANDRA GRABLEWSKI

55¢
per serving

dilled salmon potato salad

MAKES: 12 servings. **PREP:** 15 minutes.
COOK: 50 minutes. **BAKE:** at 450° for
20 minutes. **REFRIGERATE:** at least 2 hours.

- 3 **pounds red-skinned potatoes**
- ½ **pound salmon fillet**
- ⅛ **teaspoon plus ½ teaspoon salt**
- ⅛ **teaspoon plus ¼ teaspoon black pepper**
- ½ **medium-size onion, thinly sliced**
- 1 **cup light mayonnaise**
- 2 **tablespoons cider vinegar**
- 2 **tablespoons chopped fresh dill**
- ¼ **teaspoon ground nutmeg**

1. Place potatoes in a large saucepan.
Cover with **cold water** and **salt** lightly.
Bring to a boil over high heat. Reduce
heat to medium and simmer for 45 to 50
minutes or until fork- tender. Drain and
allow to cool slightly.
2. Meanwhile, heat oven to 450°. Place
salmon in a baking dish skin-side down
and season with ⅛ teaspoon each of
the salt and pepper. Bake at 450° for
20 minutes.
3. Peel potatoes, slice into ½-inch slices
and place in large bowl. Stir in onion.
In a small bowl, whisk together
mayonnaise, vinegar, dill, remaining
½ teaspoon salt, remaining ¼ teaspoon
pepper and the nutmeg. Gently stir into
potatoes. Remove skin from salmon and
flake with a fork. Fold into the potatoes.
4. Cover and refrigerate for at least
2 hours.

PER SERVING: 176 calories; 8 g fat (2 g sat.);
6 g protein; 21 g carbohydrate; 2 g fiber;
302 mg sodium; 17 mg cholesterol

sweet and spicy deviled eggs

MAKES: 24 halves. **PREP:** 20 minutes.
COOK: 12 minutes. **REFRIGERATE:** at least
1 hour.

- 12 **large eggs**
- ½ **cup light mayonnaise**
- 3 **tablespoons apricot preserves**
- 1 **teaspoon curry powder**
- ½ **teaspoon salt**
- ⅛ **teaspoon cayenne pepper**

1. Place eggs in large saucepan; add **cold
water** to cover. Bring to a boil over
medium-high heat. Reduce heat to
medium; simmer 12 minutes. Drain and
run under cold water. Peel and cool.
2. Cut eggs in half lengthwise and gently
squeeze yolks into a medium-size bowl,
reserving the white halves. With a fork,
mash the yolks with the mayonnaise,
preserves, curry, salt and cayenne
pepper until smooth.
3. Pipe or spoon the yolk and mayonnaise
mixture into the white halves. Refrigerate
for at least 1 hour, until chilled.

PER HALF: 59 calories; 4 g fat (1 g sat.);
3 g protein; 2 g carbohydrate; 0 g fiber;
123 mg sodium; 107 mg cholesterol

12¢
per half

77¢
per serving

hot dog and bean casserole

MAKES: 12 servings. **PREP:** 10 minutes.
COOK: 6 minutes. **BAKE:** at 350° for
45 minutes.

- 1 package (16 ounces) all-meat hot dogs
- 3 cans (15½ ounces each) pork and beans, drained
- ⅓ cup bottled barbecue sauce
- 2 tablespoons light-brown sugar
- 1 package (8.5 ounces) corn bread mix (such as Jiffy)
- ⅓ cup milk
- 1 egg

1. Heat oven to 350°. Coat a 13 × 9 × 2-inch baking dish with nonstick cooking spray.
2. Heat a large nonstick skillet over medium-high heat. Add the hot dogs and cook about 3 minutes per side until hot dogs are nicely browned. Remove to a cutting board and cut into ½-inch pieces on the bias.
3. In large bowl, mix together hot dogs, beans, barbecue sauce and brown sugar. Spoon mixture into the prepared baking dish.
4. Prepare corn bread following package directions, using milk and egg. Spread evenly over the top of the casserole.
5. Bake at 350° for 45 minutes, until bubbly. Allow to cool slightly before serving. Dish may be served hot or slightly warm.

PER SERVING: 342 calories; 13 g fat (5 g sat.); 13 g protein; 45 g carbohydrate; 7 g fiber; 902 mg sodium; 46 mg cholesterol

99¢
per serving

white cheddar mac and cheese

MAKES: 12 servings. **PREP:** 15 minutes. **COOK:** 12 minutes. **BAKE:** at 350° for 30 minutes.

- 1 pound farfalle pasta
- 2 tablespoons unsalted butter
- 2 tablespoons all-purpose flour
- 2 cups milk
- ½ teaspoon salt
- ¼ teaspoon black pepper
- ¼ teaspoon ground nutmeg
- 1 pound white cheddar cheese, shredded (about 4 cups)
- 1 package (10 ounces) frozen peas, thawed
- ½ pound finely diced smoked ham (such as Cumberland Gap)

1. Heat oven to 350°. Coat 13 × 9 × 2-inch baking dish with nonstick cooking spray. Cook pasta in **lightly salted water** following package directions, about 12 minutes. Drain.
2. While pasta is cooking, melt butter in a medium-size, heavy-bottomed saucepan (not nonstick) over medium heat. Stir in flour until well blended; cook 1 minute. Whisk in 1 cup of milk and cook, whisking continuously, until smooth. Whisk in remaining 1 cup milk and continue to cook, whisking until thickened and smooth, about 5 minutes. Remove from heat; stir in salt, pepper and nutmeg. Whisk in 2 cups of the cheese until smooth.
3. In a large bowl, mix together the pasta, cheese sauce and 1 cup of the remaining cheese. Stir in the peas and ham. Pour into prepared baking dish. Scatter remaining 1 cup cheese evenly over the top.
4. Bake at 350° for 30 minutes or until bubbly. Remove from oven; allow to cool 10 minutes. May be served warm or at room temperature.

PER SERVING: 372 calories; 17 g fat (10 g sat.); 21 g protein; 34 g carbohydrate; 3 g fiber; 625 mg sodium; 58 mg cholesterol

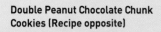

**Double Peanut Chocolate Chunk
Cookies (Recipe opposite)**

36¢
per cookie

double peanut chocolate chunk cookies

MAKES: 16 large cookies. **PREP:** 20 minutes.
BAKE: at 325° for 22 minutes.

2⅓ cups all-purpose flour
1 teaspoon baking soda
½ teaspoon salt
1 cup (2 sticks) unsalted butter, softened
1 cup light brown sugar
¾ cup granulated sugar
2 eggs
1 teaspoon vanilla extract
1 cup unsalted peanuts, chopped
½ of a 12-ounce bag Reese's Dark Chocolate Peanut Butter Cups Miniatures, coarsely chopped

1. Heat oven to 325°.
2. In a large bowl, whisk together the flour, baking soda and salt. Set aside.
3. In another large bowl, beat butter, brown sugar and granulated sugar on medium-high speed until light and fluffy, about 3 minutes. Beat in the eggs and vanilla until blended. On low speed beat in the flour mixture until just blended and a dough forms. Stir in the peanuts and chopped chocolate cups.
4. Using a ¼-cup ice cream scoop or measuring cup, drop dough in slightly rounded mounds onto ungreased cookie sheets, about 3 inches apart.
5. Bake at 325° for 22 minutes or until crispy around the edges and slightly golden. Place baking sheet on cooling rack for 3 minutes. Remove cookies to rack to cool completely.

PER COOKIE: 374 calories; 20 g fat (9 g sat.); 6 g protein; 45 g carbohydrate; 2 g fiber; 196 mg sodium; 57 mg cholesterol

layered taco dip

MAKES: 12 servings. **PREP:** 15 minutes.
COOK: 10 minutes.

1 pound ground beef chuck
1 package (1.25 ounces) reduced-sodium taco seasoning
1 can (16 ounces) refried beans
1 pound ripe tomatoes, chopped
6 scallions, trimmed and chopped (about ¾ cup)
1 teaspoon sugar
½ teaspoon garlic salt
¼ teaspoon black pepper
1 package (8 ounces) shredded taco cheese blend
1 cup sour cream
Baked tortilla chips, for dipping

1. Cook ground beef in a large nonstick skillet over medium-high heat for 5 minutes, until browned, stirring occasionally. Stir in ¾ cup water and taco seasoning. Reduce heat to medium-low and simmer 5 minutes, stirring occasionally. Stir in refried beans until well combined and heated through. Set aside.
2. In a medium-size bowl, mix together tomatoes, ½ cup of the scallions, the sugar, garlic salt and black pepper. In a second medium-size bowl, mix together 1½ cups of the shredded cheese and the sour cream.
3. In an 8-cup clear bowl, layer half each of the beef mixture, tomatoes and sour cream mixture. Repeat layering. Scatter remaining ¼ cup scallions and ½ cup cheese over the top. Serve at room temperature.

PER SERVING: 216 calories; 12 g fat (7 g sat.); 15 g protein; 10 g carbohydrate; 3 g fiber; 537 mg sodium; 54 mg cholesterol

oven-fried chili chicken

MAKES: 12 pieces. **PREP:** 15 minutes.
BAKE: at 375° for 55 minutes.

1¼ cups cornflake crumbs
2 to 3 teaspoons chipotle chili powder
1 teaspoon ground cumin
¾ teaspoon garlic salt
½ cup evaporated milk
12 bone-in chicken thighs, about 4 pounds total

1. Heat oven to 375°. Line 2 baking sheets with aluminum foil.
2. In a pie dish or shallow bowl, whisk together the cornflake crumbs, chili powder, cumin and garlic salt. Pour evaporated milk into a second pie dish.
3. Dip a chicken thigh into the milk and shake off excess. Roll it around in the cornflake crumbs until completely coated. Shake off excess. Place on a prepared baking sheet. Repeat with remaining chicken.
4. Bake chicken at 375° for 50 to 55 minutes or until golden and crispy and internal temperature registers 160° on an instant-read thermometer. May be served warm or at room temperature.

PER THIGH: 285 calories; 18 g fat (5 g sat.); 21 g protein; 9 g carbohydrate; 0 g fiber; 227 mg sodium; 97 mg cholesterol

freeze!

I SCREAM, YOU SCREAM, WE ALL SCREAM . . . !

Mint Ice Cream
Chocolate Sandwiches
(Recipe page 207)

Fresh raspberries infuse this rich frozen custard with loads of flavor. Dress it up by serving it with chocolate wafer cookies.

raspberry custard ice cream

MAKES: 8 servings. **PREP:** 10 minutes. **COOK:** 20 minutes. **REFRIGERATE:** 4 hours. **PROCESS:** 30 minutes. **FREEZE:** 2 hours.

1 container (6 ounces) fresh
    raspberries
1¼ cups sugar
1½ teaspoons lemon zest (2 lemons)
1¾ cups milk
4 egg yolks
    Pinch salt
6 drops red liquid food coloring
1½ cups heavy cream

1. If using a gel-canister ice cream maker, freeze canister overnight.
2. In a food processor, combine raspberries and 2 tablespoons of the sugar. Puree until smooth, then force through a strainer (you should have ½ to ⅔ cup). Discard solids. Stir together another 2 tablespoons of the sugar and the lemon zest in small bowl. Stir in raspberry puree and set aside.
3. Place a large bowl and strainer on heat-proof surface near stove. Combine milk and yolks in a nonstick medium-size saucepan. Stir in remaining 1 cup sugar. Cook over medium-low heat, stirring constantly, until instant-read thermometer just reaches 190°, about 15 to 20 minutes (do not let boil) or until slightly thickened. Strain immediately into bowl; stir in salt.
4. Add raspberry mixture and food coloring to bowl, stirring well. Place waxed paper on custard; refrigerate until chilled, about 4 hours.
5. Add cream to custard, stirring just until combined. Pour into ice cream maker; process 30 minutes as per manufacturer's directions.
6. Scrape into a 1½-quart container; freeze to firm completely, about 2 hours, then scoop and serve.

PER SERVING: 342 calories; 20 g fat (12 g sat.); 4 g protein; 38 g carbohydrate; 1 g fiber; 62 mg sodium; 171 mg cholesterol

chocolate cups

MAKES: 12 filled chocolate cups. **PREP:** 5 minutes. **MICROWAVE:** 2 minutes. **REFRIGERATE:** 30 minutes.

8 **ounces semisweet chocolate, broken up (see Note)**
1 **tablespoon solid vegetable shortening**
12 **paper or silicone cupcake liners**
12 **scoops assorted ice cream and sherbet flavors**
Chocolate curls, to garnish (optional)

1. Melt chocolate and shortening in a medium-size microwave-safe bowl on HIGH in microwave for 2 minutes, stirring halfway; after melted, stir until smooth.
2. Using a small clean brush, spread about 2 teaspoons melted chocolate into bottom and up sides of each cupcake liner. Chill cups until firm, about 10 minutes, reserving any extra chocolate.
3. Remove cups from refrigerator. Re-melt remaining chocolate in microwave for 20 seconds, if necessary. Reinforce any weak spots inside cups (especially near the rims) with melted chocolate. Return to refrigerator to set, about 20 minutes.
4. To remove chocolate cups from paper liners: Loosen a top edge and peel paper away (it will rip apart, but still come off cleanly). For silicone liners: Pop out of liners by gently pressing on bottom of cups and pulling away side of liner from chocolate shell.
5. To serve: Place 1 generous scoop ice cream or sherbet into each chocolate cup (cups can be filled several hours ahead and frozen, covered). Just before serving, garnish with chocolate curls, if desired.
Note: You may substitute milk or white chocolate for semisweet, depending on flavor preferences.

PER FILLED CUP: 174 calories; 11 g fat (6 g sat.); 2 g protein; 20 g carbohydrate; 1 g fiber; 31 mg sodium; 16 mg cholesterol

layered ice cream cake

MAKES: 12 servings. **PREP:** 25 minutes.
FREEZE: 1 hour, plus overnight.

- 15 chocolate-and-cream sandwich cookies (such as Oreo)
- 1 tablespoon milk
- 8 to 9 ice cream sandwiches
- 1 pint mint chocolate chip ice cream
- 1 pint vanilla frozen yogurt
- 1 pint strawberry ice cream or frozen yogurt
- 1 container (8 ounces) frozen whipped topping, thawed

1. Coat bottom and sides of a 9-inch round springform pan with nonstick cooking spray. Line side with waxed paper, using spray to help adhere to pan. Trim paper to height of pan.

2. Finely crush 12 of the cookies in a food processor. Add milk; pulse just until mixture holds together. Set aside.

3. Unwrap 4 ice cream sandwiches. Working quickly, cut each in quarters (photos A and B). Stack strips of sandwiches on end, packing them snugly together around waxed-paper-lined pan (photo C) to form cake's edge. Spoon cookie crumbs into center of pan; press firmly over bottom. Freeze 1 hour.

4. Remove all 3 flavors of ice cream and frozen yogurt from freezer; let soften for 15 minutes at room temperature. Transfer mint ice cream to a small bowl and stir until firm spreading consistency. Repeat with vanilla and strawberry. Remove pan from freezer. Spread mint ice cream on bottom, then top with vanilla, then strawberry, spreading all layers level. Add thawed whipped topping, swirling decoratively. Break up remaining 3 sandwich cookies and use to decorate cake. Return to freezer; freeze overnight.

5. To serve, remove side of pan, then waxed paper. Let cake stand at room temperature for 10 minutes for easier cutting. Slice into wedges and serve.

PER SERVING: 353 calories; 16 g fat (10 g sat.); 5 g protein; 47 g carbohydrate; 1 g fiber; 153 mg sodium; 29 mg cholesterol

Photos: (left page) James Baigrie, (right page) Tina Rupp

A Cut the ice cream sandwiches in half lengthwise.

B Cut sandwiches in half crosswise (these will be the cake edge).

C Working quickly, stack cut strips on end against side of prepared pan.

toasted-almond triangles

MAKES: 16 servings. **PREP:** 20 minutes. **FREEZE:** 4 hours or overnight.

- **4 cups toasted rice cereal (such as Rice Krispies), slightly crushed**
- **1 cup sliced, toasted almonds**
- **1 cup toasted, sweetened flake coconut**
- **1 cup packed light-brown sugar**
- **⅔ cup unsalted butter, melted**
- **2 quarts vanilla ice cream, softened**
  Prepared caramel sauce (optiona)

1. In a large bowl, mix together cereal, toasted almonds, toasted coconut, brown sugar and butter. Press half of mixture into the bottom of a 13 × 9 × 2-inch baking dish and chill slightly. Spoon softened ice cream over chilled crust and press evenly, using waxed paper and your hands. Top with remaining crumb mixture. Cover and freeze for at least 4 hours or overnight.

2. To serve, cut into 8 equal squares. Cut each square diagonally into triangles. Drizzle with caramel sauce, if desired.

PER SERVING: 369 calories; 21 g fat (12 g sat.); 5 g protein; 42 g carbohydrate; 2 g fiber; 157 mg sodium; 52 mg cholesterol

mint ice cream chocolate sandwiches

MAKES: 12 sandwich cookies. **PREP:** 15 minutes. **BAKE:** at 350° for 14 minutes.
FREEZE: 3 hours.

2 cups all-purpose flour
¾ cup unsweetened cocoa powder
1 teaspoon baking soda
½ teaspoon salt
1 cup (2 sticks) unsalted butter, softened
1 cup firmly packed light-brown sugar
½ cup granulated sugar
2 large eggs
1 tablespoon vanilla extract
1 bag (11.5 ounces) milk chocolate chips
  Drizzle and Filling:
½ cup confectioners' sugar
2¼ teaspoons water
1 container (1¾ quarts) reduced-fat mint chocolate chip ice cream

1. Heat oven to 350°.
2. Sift flour, cocoa powder, baking soda and salt into medium-size bowl.
3. In large bowl, beat butter on medium-high speed until creamy, about 1 minute. Add both kinds of sugar; beat until smooth, about 2 minutes. Beat in eggs, one at a time, beating well after each. Beat in vanilla until well blended.
4. On low speed, beat in flour mixture until smooth. Stir in chocolate chips.
5. For each cookie, drop level ¼ cup of dough onto an ungreased baking sheet, spacing each 2 inches apart.

6. Bake at 350° for about 14 minutes or until slightly puffed and dry on top. Cool cookies on sheets on wire racks for 1 minute. Remove cookies to rack; cool completely.
7. Drizzle: In small bowl, whisk together confectioners' sugar and water. Make sandwich tops by drizzling over 12 of the cookies. Let dry 15 minutes.
8. Filling: Remove the paper carton from the ice cream, and slice ice cream into eight ½-inch-thick slices. Working quickly, place one slice onto a sheet of waxed paper. Using a 3-inch cookie cutter, cut out a circle of ice cream. Transfer slice to a waxed-paper-lined baking sheet. Gather up ice cream scraps and press into cookie cutter to form a second 3-inch circle. Transfer this circle to baking sheet. Repeat with remaining ice cream slices, transferring baking sheet to freezer when 12 circles are formed (save excess ice cream for snacking). Freeze circles 1 hour.
9. Sandwich an ice cream circle with 2 cookies, moving sandwich to freezer for an additional 2 hours. Repeat with remaining cookies and ice cream. Store airtight in freezer for up to 2 weeks.

PER SANDWICH COOKIE: 661 calories; 31 g fat (18 g sat.); 10 g protein; 89 g carbohydrate; 4 g fiber; 297 mg sodium; 94 mg cholesterol

mango granita

MAKES: 6 servings. **PREP:** 10 minutes.
COOK: 3 minutes. **FREEZE:** 3 to 4 hours.

⅓ cup sugar
  Juice of 1 lime
3 mangoes, peeled and cut into 1-inch pieces
½ cup mango-lime juice (such as Dole Mango Lime Fiesta)
  Lime slices for garnish (optional)

1. Place ½ cup cold water and the sugar in a small saucepan and bring to a simmer over medium heat. Stir until sugar dissolves, about 3 minutes. Remove from heat and pour into a large bowl and allow to cool. Stir in lime juice.
2. Place mangoes and mango juice into a blender and puree. Add to sugar syrup and stir. Pour into a shallow metal pan and freeze for 3 to 4 hours. Stir mixture every hour, spooning ice crystals from side of pan into middle.
3. When mixture is frozen, place in food processor and pulse for about 5 seconds until you get a snow-like consistency.
4. To serve, spoon into dessert dishes and garnish with lime slices, if desired.

PER SERVING: 123 calories; 0 g fat (0 g sat.); 1 g protein; 32 g carbohydrate; 2 g fiber; 5 mg sodium; 0 mg cholesterol

burger deluxe

CREATIVE TAKES THAT GO ABOVE AND BEYOND THE CLASSIC—
WITH MORE FLAVOR AND FEWER CALORIES. **BY JULIE MILTENBERGER**

Our All-American Burgers are loaded with taste—not fat. (Recipe page 213)

PHOTOGRAPHY BY DAVID PRINCE

ginger-teriyaki sliders

MAKES: 12 sliders. **PREP:** 10 minutes. **BROIL:** 6 minutes.

- 1 package (12 per package) mini soft dinner rolls (such as King's Hawaiian)
- 4 ounces (1½ cups) sliced mushrooms
- 2 scallions, trimmed and cut up, plus more chopped scallion, for garnish
- 2 teaspoons peeled and coarsely chopped fresh ginger (1-inch piece)
- 1 pound ground pork
- ¼ cup plus 1 teaspoon teriyaki stir-fry sauce (such as House of Tsang)
- ¼ cup panko bread crumbs
- ¼ cup light mayonnaise
- ¼ teaspoon sugar

1. Heat broiler. Line a baking pan with foil; coat foil with nonstick cooking spray. Wrap rolls in separate foil; place in lower part of oven.

2. In a mini chopper, combine mushrooms, 2 of the scallions and the ginger. Pulse until finely chopped. Transfer to a medium-size bowl and add pork, ¼ cup of the stir-fry sauce and the bread crumbs. Stir to blend.

3. Shape mixture into 12 equal-size patties, a scant ¼ cup for each. Place patties on prepared baking pan; broil 4 inches from heat for 6 minutes, turning once, until instant-read thermometer registers 160° when inserted into center of burgers.

4. Meanwhile, stir together mayonnaise, remaining 1 teaspoon teriyaki stir-fry sauce and the sugar in a small bowl. Split rolls and top each with a burger. Spread 1 teaspoon teriyaki mayonnaise on each roll; sprinkle with scallion.

PER SLIDER: 194 calories; 10 g fat (4 g sat.); 9 g protein; 17 g carbohydrate; 1 g fiber; 307 mg sodium; 42 mg cholesterol

Use your oven to toast a batch of buns, muffins or bread. Heat broiler to high and broil, 3 inches from heat, for 3 minutes, turning buns once.

bbq bacon burgers

MAKES: 6 servings. **PREP:** 10 minutes. **COOK:** 7 minutes. **GRILL:** 11 minutes. **BROIL:** 3 minutes.

8 **slices turkey bacon**
1 **package ground turkey (20 ounces)**
½ **cup (1 ounce) French's fried onions**
8 **tablespoons bottled barbecue sauce**
1 **tablespoon Worcestershire sauce**
¼ **teaspoon ground black pepper**
6 **100-calorie English muffins**

1. Heat grill or grill pan to medium-high heat. Heat broiler.
2. Cook 6 slices of the bacon in a medium-size nonstick skillet over medium heat, 7 minutes. Set aside. Chop remaining 2 slices uncooked turkey bacon and place in large bowl.
3. Add ground turkey, fried onions, 2 tablespoons of the barbecue sauce, the Worcestershire and the black pepper to bacon in bowl. Stir to evenly blend. Divide mixture into 6 patties.
4. Grill hamburger patties for 6 minutes. Flip over; continue to grill an additional 5 minutes or until an instant-read thermometer inserted into the center of the burgers registers 160°. Meanwhile, broil English muffins for 3 minutes, turning once.
5. To serve: Place a burger on each muffin bottom. Top each with 1 tablespoon of the remaining barbecue sauce and 1 slice cooked bacon, broken in half. Add muffin top and serve.

PER SERVING 360 calories; 15 g fat (4 g sat.); 24 g protein; 37 g carbohydrate; 5 g fiber; 822 mg sodium; 95 mg cholesterol

black bean chili burgers

MAKES: 6 servings. **PREP:** 10 minutes. **COOK:** 2 minutes. **GRILL:** 8 minutes. **BROIL:** 3 minutes.

- 1 tablespoon chili powder
- 1 teaspoon garlic powder
- ½ teaspoon ground cumin
- 1 pound ground sirloin
- 1 can (15.5 ounces) black beans, drained and rinsed
- ½ cup minced red onion
- ⅓ cup plus 3 tablespoons medium salsa
- ½ teaspoon salt
- ½ teaspoon black pepper
- 6 multigrain seeded hamburger buns
- ½ cup light mayonnaise
- 1 avocado, peeled, pitted and sliced

1. Heat grill or grill pan to medium-high. Heat broiler. Combine chili powder, garlic powder and cumin in a small nonstick skillet. Cook over medium-high heat for 2 minutes, until fragrant. Remove from heat.

2. In a large bowl, stir together the sirloin, black beans, spice mixture, red onion, ⅓ cup of the salsa, the salt and pepper. Transfer to a food processor and pulse until texture is slightly smooth and about half of the beans have been mashed. Return to bowl and divide into 6 hamburger patties.

3. Coat burgers with nonstick cooking spray. Grill 4 minutes, then flip over and grill another 4 minutes or until instant-read thermometer inserted into thickest part of burger registers 140°.

4. Meanwhile, toast buns under broiler for 3 minutes, turning once. In a small bowl, stir together remaining 3 tablespoons salsa and the mayonnaise. Spread each bun with some of the salsa mayo. Add a burger and a few avocado slices and serve.

PER SERVING: 363 calories; 15 g fat (3 g sat.); 23 g protein; 38 g carbohydrate; 7 g fiber; 801 mg sodium; 44 mg cholesterol

To prevent burgers from shrinking while on the grill, form a small indent with your thumb in the center of each when forming them.

spinach-feta chicken burgers

MAKES: 4 servings. **PREP:** 10 minutes. **BAKE:** at 400° for 8 minutes. **GRILL:** 12 minutes.

Tzatziki:
- 1 **English cucumber, peeled and thinly sliced**
- 2 **plum tomatoes, cored and sliced**
- 1 **container (7 ounces) plain 2% Greek yogurt (such as Fage)**
- ¼ **teaspoon salt**

Burgers:
- 1 **pound ground chicken**
- 1 **package (9 ounces) frozen chopped spinach, thawed and squeezed dry**
- ⅔ **cup reduced-fat feta cheese crumbles**
- 1 **tablespoon fresh oregano, chopped**
- 1 **tablespoon plain, dry bread crumbs**
- 1 **teaspoon onion powder**
- ½ **teaspoon salt**
- ½ **teaspoon ground black pepper**
- 1 **package small pitas (8 per package)**

1. Heat oven to 400°. Heat grill or grill pan to medium heat.

2. Tzatziki: In a medium-size bowl, stir together the cucumber slices, tomato, yogurt and salt. Set aside.

3. Burgers: In a large bowl, combine ground chicken, spinach, feta cheese, oregano, bread crumbs, onion powder, salt and pepper. Stir together until blended. Shape into 4 equal-size patties.

Coat patties with nonstick cooking spray.

4. Grill burgers for 12 minutes, flipping once, or until instant-read thermometer inserted into burger registers 160°. Meanwhile, bake pitas at 400° for 8 minutes. Place one burger on a pita round. Top burger with about ¼ cup tzatziki, if desired, and a second pita. Repeat with remaining ingredients; serve extra tzatziki on the side.

PER SERVING: 472 calories; 20 g fat (9 g sat.); 36 g protein; 42 g carbohydrate; 8 g fiber; 968 mg sodium; 161 mg cholesterol

Before heating the grill, clean grate with a wire brush, then coat with a thin layer of vegetable oil.

brown rice veggie burgers

MAKES: 6 servings. **PREP:** 15 minutes. **COOK:** 7 minutes.
MICROWAVE: 90 seconds. **BROIL:** 16 minutes.

- 1 small onion, chopped
- 2 portobello mushroom caps (8 ounces), halved and sliced crosswise
- 2 tablespoons reduced-sodium soy sauce
- 1 pouch (8.8 ounces) fully cooked brown rice (such as Uncle Ben's Ready Rice)
- 1 can (15.5 ounces) chickpeas, drained and rinsed
- 1 medium-size zucchini, shredded
- 1 cup (4 ounces) shredded 50% reduced-fat cheddar cheese (such as Cabot)
- ⅓ cup seasoned bread crumbs
- 1 large egg
- ½ teaspoon salt
- ¼ teaspoon ground black pepper
  Green salad

1. Heat broiler. Line a large baking sheet with foil. Coat foil with nonstick cooking spray. Coat a 10-inch nonstick skillet with nonstick cooking spray. Add onion and cook over medium heat 2 minutes. Add mushrooms and continue to cook for 4 minutes. Add soy sauce; cook 1 minute. Remove from heat.

2. Heat rice in microwave following package directions, 90 seconds. Transfer rice and skillet contents to a food processor. Add chickpeas. Cover and pulse until mixture resembles ground beef (the chickpeas should be chopped up). Transfer to a large bowl.

3. Add shredded zucchini, cheese and bread crumbs to bowl with rice mixture. Stir to combine. Stir in egg, salt and pepper until all ingredients are moistened. Let mixture rest 5 minutes.

4. With wet hands, shape mixture into six 3½-inch patties, a scant cup for each. Place on foil-lined pan. Broil, 3 inches from heat, for 8 minutes. Carefully flip over and continue to broil an additional 8 minutes, until browned and crispy. Serve with green salad alongside.

PER SERVING: 245 calories; 6 g fat (2 g sat.); 14 g protein; 32 g carbohydrate; 5 g fiber; 835 mg sodium; 45 mg cholesterol

all-american burgers

MAKES: 6 servings. **PREP:** 10 minutes.
BAKE: at 400° for 10 minutes.
GRILL: 6 minutes.

- 6 whole-wheat hamburger buns
- 1½ pounds ground sirloin or ground round
- 1 tablespoon Worcestershire sauce
- ½ teaspoon garlic powder
- ½ teaspoon salt
- ½ teaspoon dried Italian seasoning
- ¼ teaspoon ground black pepper
- 6 reduced-fat 2% American cheese slices
- 1 medium-size red onion, thinly sliced
- 2 medium-size tomatoes, cored and sliced
  Ketchup and mustard (optional)

1. Heat grill or grill pan to medium-high heat. Heat oven to 400°. Wrap hamburger buns in foil and place in lower part of oven. Bake 10 minutes.

2. Meanwhile, in a large bowl mix together the ground beef, Worcestershire, garlic powder, salt, Italian seasoning and pepper. Shape into 6 patties and grill 3 minutes. Flip burgers over and grill another 2 minutes. Top with cheese slices and cook 1 minute more for medium.

3. Transfer cheese-topped patties to warmed hamburger buns and add sliced red onion and tomato. Serve with ketchup and mustard, if desired.

PER SERVING: 308 calories; 10 g fat (4 g sat.); 30 g protein; 28 g carbohydrate; 4 g fiber; 755 mg sodium; 60 mg cholesterol

after-school specials

POP QUIZ: WHICH OF THESE SNACKS WILL EARN YOU TOP MARKS
FROM YOUR KIDS? ANSWER: ALL OF THEM. **BY CINDY HELLER**

Sweet and Salty Crunchy
Munch (Recipe opposite)

cheesy chicken quesadillas

MAKES: 4 servings. **PREP:** 10 minutes. **BAKE:** at 450° for 8 minutes.

- 2 **cups chopped cooked chicken**
- ½ **cup shredded reduced-fat cheddar cheese**
- 2 **tablespoons chopped red onion**
- 1¾ **teaspoons taco seasoning**
- 1½ **tablespoons chopped cilantro (optional)**
- 4 **6-inch whole-wheat tortillas**
- ½ **cup salsa (optional)**

1. Heat oven to 450°. In a medium-size bowl, stir together chicken, cheese, onion and taco seasoning. Stir in cilantro, if desired.

2. Place 2 tortillas on baking rack over a baking sheet. Spread 1 heaping cup of chicken mixture over each tortilla. Top each with another tortilla and press down gently. Bake quesadillas at 450° for 8 minutes or until cheese has melted. Cut into quarters and serve with salsa, if desired.

PER SERVING: 264 calories; 8 g fat (2 g sat.); 22 g protein; 25 g carbohydrate; 2 g fiber; 854 mg sodium; 45 mg cholesterol

---

sweet and salty crunchy munch

MAKES: 8 cups. **PREP:** 10 minutes.
BAKE: at 250° for 40 minutes.

- 4 **cups rice Chex cereal**
- 2 **cups popped popcorn**
- 1 **cup cheddar Goldfish crackers**
- 1 **cup pretzel Goldfish crackers**
- 1 **cup lightly crushed plain bagel chips**
- 6 **tablespoons unsalted butter, melted**
- 4 **tablespoons maple syrup**
- 2 **tablespoons reduced-sodium soy sauce**
- 1 **tablespoon cinnamon**

1. Heat oven to 250°. Stir together Chex, popcorn, both kinds of Goldfish and the bagel chips. Whisk together butter, syrup, soy sauce and cinnamon. Drizzle over Chex mixture; stir well.

2. Spread mixture onto a rimmed baking sheet. Bake at 250° for 40 minutes, stirring every 15 minutes, or until golden. Cool completely.

PER ½ CUP: 142 calories; 6 g fat (3 g sat.); 2 g protein; 19 g carbohydrate; 1 g fiber; 245 mg sodium; 12 mg cholesterol

Food styling: Megan Schlow. Prop styling: Megan Hedgpeth.

While Sweet and Salty Crunchy Munch is just the thing to tide over empty stomachs until dinnertime, Cheesy Chicken Quesadillas can be a light and easy-to-make pre-soccer supper.

These sweet and savory snacks fill the bill for an after-school nibble, but they also make great fork-free fare for Friday movie night with the family—or kid-pleasing party food.

buffalo chicken pinwheels

MAKES: 10 pinwheels. **PREP:** 10 minutes.

- 2 tablespoons reduced-fat blue cheese salad dressing
- 2 teaspoons buffalo wing hot sauce (such as Frank's)
- 2 whole-wheat wraps
- 2 large leaves iceberg lettuce
- 8 ounces thick-sliced chicken breast (from the deli)

1. Stir together blue cheese dressing and hot sauce. Spread each wrap with half the blue cheese mixture. Layer 1 lettuce leaf and 4 ounces chicken onto each wrap. Roll up and trim off the ends. Slice into 1-inch-thick pinwheels and serve.

PER PINWHEEL: 72 calories; 2 g fat (0 g sat.); 6 g protein; 8 g carbohydrate; 1 g fiber; 451 mg sodium; 8 mg cholesterol

chili-cheese taco chips

MAKES: 6 servings. **PREP:** 10 minutes. **MICROWAVE:** 2 minutes.

- 6 cups baked scoop-shaped tortilla chips (such as Tostito's Baked Scoops)
- ¾ cup freshly shredded cheddar cheese
- ¼ cup shredded pepper Jack cheese
- ⅔ cup vegetarian chili, warmed
- ¼ cup shredded iceberg lettuce

1. Place 3 cups chips on a microwave-safe plate. Sprinkle with half the cheddar and half the pepper Jack cheese. Drop half the chili by tablespoonfuls over chips; microwave 1 minute.

2. Top with a second layer of chips, cheeses and chili and microwave for 1 minute. Sprinkle with lettuce and serve immediately.

PER SERVING: 167 calories; 7 g fat (4 g sat.); 7 g protein; 19 g carbohydrate; 2 g fiber; 325 mg sodium; 19 mg cholesterol

choco-berry bars

MAKES: 25 bars. **PREP:** 10 minutes. **BAKE:** at 350° for 18 minutes; 300° for 30 minutes. **COOK:** 5 minutes.

 5 cups old-fashioned oats
 1 cup chopped walnuts
 2 tablespoons canola oil
 ½ teaspoon salt
 1 cup light-brown sugar
 ½ cup honey
 2 tablespoons vanilla extract
 1 cup dried cranberries
 ½ cup chocolate chips

1. Heat oven to 350°. Stir together the oats, walnuts, canola oil and salt. Spread evenly into a 15 x 10-inch rimmed baking sheet. Bake at 350° for 18 minutes, stirring occasionally. Remove mixture to a large bowl. Line same baking sheet with nonstick foil and set aside; lower oven temperature to 300°.

2. Combine brown sugar and honey in a small saucepan and cook, stirring often, over medium heat for about 5 minutes or until sugar dissolves. Stir in vanilla extract.

3. Add cranberries and chocolate chips to oat mixture; stir well. Pour brown sugar mixture over top and stir until blended.

4. Spread oat mixture into prepared baking sheet and press into an even layer. Bake at 300° for 30 minutes or until golden. Cool completely in pan on a wire rack, then, using a chef's knife, cut into 2 x 3-inch bars.

PER BAR: 186 calories; 6 g fat (1 g sat.); 4 g protein; 32 g carbohydrate; 2 g fiber; 51 mg sodium; 0 mg cholesterol

raising **the bar**

BROWNIES AND BLONDIES THAT ARE A CUT ABOVE—POUR THE MILK
(OR A CUP OF FRESHLY BREWED COFFEE).

These Kitchen Sink Crunchers are loaded with chocolate chips, pecans, coconut and toffee bits. (Recipe page 223)

Caramel Brownies
(Recipe page 223)
are textured and gooey.

Bars and brownies offer the best of both worlds—a delectable dessert that is simple to make and incredibly versatile. These pages offer sweets from fudgy and decadent brownies to light and lovely lemon bars.

grape-granola blondies

MAKES: 32 bars. **PREP:** 5 minutes.
BAKE: at 375° for 28 minutes.

- 2¼ cups granola (without raisins)
- 3 cups all-purpose flour
- ¾ teaspoon salt
- 1 cup (2 sticks) unsalted butter, softened
- 1 cup confectioners' sugar
- 1 large egg plus 1 large egg yolk
- 1 jar (12 ounces) grape jelly

1. Heat oven to 375°. Coat a 13 × 9 × 2-inch baking pan with nonstick cooking spray. Finely crush 1½ cups of the granola.
2. Whisk 2½ cups of the flour, the salt and the crushed granola. In large bowl, beat together the butter and sugar. Add egg, then yolk, beating well. Stir in flour mixture (dough will be stiff). Set aside ¾ cup. Press remaining dough into bottom and ½ inch up sides of prepared pan.
3. Bake crust at 375° for 10 minutes or until dry. Meanwhile, stir jelly. Remove crust from oven; spread with jelly. Combine remaining ¾ cup granola and ½ cup flour with reserved dough, breaking apart into crumbs. Sprinkle over jelly.
4. Bake cookie bar another 18 minutes or until jelly is bubbly. Let cool in pan on wire rack. Cut into 32 bars.

PER BAR: 170 calories; 7 g fat (4 g sat.); 2 g protein; 26 g carbohydrate; 1 g fiber; 78 mg sodium; 28 mg cholesterol

lemon-blueberry diamonds

MAKES: 20 diamonds. **PREP:** 15 minutes. **BAKE:** at 350° for 50 minutes.

Crust:
- ¾ cup (1½ sticks) unsalted butter, melted
- ½ cup confectioners' sugar
- 2 teaspoons vanilla extract
- ¼ teaspoon salt
- 2¼ cups all-purpose flour

Lemon Filling:
- 2 cups granulated sugar
- ⅓ cup all-purpose flour
- 6 large eggs
- 2 teaspoons grated lemon rind
- ½ cup lemon juice
- 1 cup blueberries, rinsed
- ¼ cup confectioners' sugar

1. Heat oven to 350°. Line 13 × 9 × 2-inch pan with nonstick foil.
2. Crust: In a medium-size bowl, stir together butter, confectioners' sugar, vanilla and salt. Gradually stir in flour until smooth. Press dough evenly over bottom of prepared pan.
3. Bake crust at 350° for 20 minutes or until edges are lightly browned.
4. Lemon Filling: In large bowl, mix granulated sugar and flour. Whisk in eggs until smooth. Stir in lemon rind and juice. Fold in berries. Pour filling over crust.
5. Bake at 350° for 30 minutes or until set. Let cool in pan on wire rack. Dust with the confectioners' sugar. Cut into diamonds.

PER BAR: 244 calories; 9 g fat (5 g sat.); 4 g protein; 39 g carbohydrate; 1 g fiber; 52 mg sodium; 82 mg cholesterol

s'more bars

MAKES: 24 bars. **PREP:** 25 minutes. **CHILL:** 1 hour. **MICROWAVE:** 1 minute. **BAKE:** at 350° for 33 minutes.

Crust:
- 14 whole graham cracker boards, crushed (2¼ cups crumbs)
- 3 tablespoons sugar
- ¼ teaspoon salt
- 6 tablespoons (¾ stick) unsalted butter, melted

Brownie:
- 6 ounces bittersweet chocolate, chopped
- ¾ cup (1½ sticks) butter
- 3 eggs
- 1¼ cups sugar
- 1 cup all-purpose flour
- 1 teaspoon salt
- 2 teaspoons vanilla

Topping:
- 1 jar (7.5 ounces) marshmallow creme (about 1½ cups)
- 2 tablespoons milk
- 1 cup Hershey's mini chocolate Kisses
- 3 whole graham cracker boards, broken up

1. Heat oven to 350°.

2. Crust: Combine cracker crumbs, sugar, salt and butter in a bowl until evenly moistened. Transfer to a 13 × 9 × 2-inch baking pan; press evenly into bottom. Refrigerate 1 hour or until set.

3. Brownie: Combine chocolate and butter in a glass bowl. Heat in microwave on HIGH until chocolate and butter are melted, about 1 minute. Stir mixture until smooth.

4. Beat eggs and sugar in a large bowl until blended. While beating, gradually add chocolate mixture to egg mixture; beat until smooth.

5. Stir in flour and salt. Stir in vanilla. Pour evenly over crust.

6. Bake at 350° for 30 minutes or until center is set.

7. Topping: While brownie layer is baking, whisk marshmallow creme and milk in a small bowl until well blended and smooth. Remove brownie from oven; cover with marshmallow topping. Spread or tilt the pan to level topping and completely cover brownie layer.

8. Sprinkle mini Kisses evenly over marshmallow. Scatter crumbled graham crackers over the top.

9. Bake at 350° for 3 more minutes or until chocolate Kisses are glossy and marshmallow topping is set. Let cool in pan on a wire rack. Cut into 24 bars; remove from pan.

PER BAR: 297 calories; 15 g fat (9 g sat.); 3 g protein; 39 g carbohydrate; 1 g fiber; 239 mg sodium; 50 mg cholesterol

These cheesecake-topped brownies are simple enough to make as an everyday dessert—yet elegant enough for a special occasion.

black and white brownies

MAKES: 16 brownies. **PREP:** 25 minutes.
MICROWAVE: 1 minute. **BAKE:** at 350° for
30 minutes. **COOL:** 15 minutes + 2 hours.

Brownie:
- 1¾ cups all-purpose flour
- ¾ teaspoon baking powder
- ¾ teaspoon salt
- ½ cup (1 stick) unsalted butter
- 4 ounces unsweetened chocolate, chopped
- 1½ cups sugar
- 4 eggs
- 1 teaspoon vanilla

Cheesecake Batter:
- 6 ounces cream cheese, softened
- ⅓ cup all-purpose flour
- ½ cup sugar
- ½ teaspoon vanilla extract
- 2 tablespoons milk

1. Heat oven to 350°. Line a 13 × 9 × 2-inch baking pan with nonstick aluminum foil; set aside.
2. Brownie: In medium-size bowl, blend flour, baking powder and salt.
3. In large glass bowl, combine butter and chocolate. Microwave on HIGH for 1 minute; stir until smooth. If necessary, continue to microwave in 15-second increments to melt chocolate.
4. Add sugar to chocolate mixture; stir to combine. Add eggs and vanilla; stir until smooth. Stir in flour mixture. Spoon into prepared pan; spread evenly.
5. Cheesecake Batter: In medium-size bowl, beat cream cheese until smooth. On low speed, beat in flour, sugar and vanilla. Add milk; beat until smooth.
6. With a spoon, make an indent in top of brownie batter. Fill indent with a dollop of the cream cheese mixture. Continue to make and fill indents over the top in an uneven pattern. (Don't worry about neatness—the cheesecake mounds will flatten during baking.)
7. Bake at 350° for 30 minutes or until firm to the touch and set. Cool in pan on wire rack for 15 minutes. Using foil, lift brownie from pan directly to rack. Cool 2 hours before cutting. Store airtight up to 1 week.

PER BROWNIE: 299 calories; 15 g fat (8 g sat.); 5 g protein; 40 g carbohydrate; 2 g fiber; 176 mg sodium; 80 mg cholesterol

caramel brownies

MAKES: 32 brownies. **PREP:** 30 minutes.
MICROWAVE: 2 minutes. **COOK:** 5 minutes.
BAKE: at 350° for 35 minutes.

- ¾ cup (1½ sticks) unsalted butter
- 4 ounces unsweetened chocolate
- 4 eggs
- 2 cups sugar
- 1¼ cups all-purpose flour
- 2 teaspoons vanilla extract
- 1 cup chopped pecans
- 1 bag (12 ounces) chocolate chunks
- 1 package (14 ounces) soft caramels, unwrapped
- ¼ cup heavy cream

1. Heat oven to 350°. Line 13 × 9 × 2-inch baking pan with nonstick foil.
2. In large microwave-safe bowl, melt together butter and chocolate in microwave oven for 2 minutes; stir until smooth. Whisk in eggs, sugar, flour and vanilla. Stir in pecans. Spread half the batter into prepared pan. Sprinkle with 1 cup chocolate chunks.
3. In medium-size saucepan, melt together caramels and heavy cream over medium-low heat until smooth, about 5 minutes. Evenly pour over batter in pan. Spread with remaining batter. Sprinkle with remaining 1 cup chocolate chunks.
4. Bake at 350° for about 35 minutes or until top is dry to the touch. Let cool completely in pan on wire rack. Grab foil and lift brownie from pan. Cut into squares and serve.

PER BROWNIE: 255 calories; 14 g fat (7 g sat.); 3 g protein; 34 g carbohydrate; 2 g fiber; 41 mg sodium; 41 mg cholesterol

kitchen sink crunchers

MAKES: 24 servings. **PREP:** 5 minutes.
BAKE: at 350° for 30 minutes.

- 1 cup all-purpose flour
- ½ cup unsweetened cocoa powder
- 1 teaspoon baking powder
- ½ teaspoon salt
- ½ teaspoon cinnamon
- ½ cup (1 stick) unsalted butter
- 1 cup packed dark-brown sugar
- 1 large egg
- 2 teaspoons vanilla extract
- ½ cup toffee bits (such as Heath Bits o' Brickle)
- ¾ cup sweetened flake coconut
- ¾ cup chopped pecans
- 1 cup semisweet chocolate chips

1. Heat oven to 350°. Line 13 × 9 × 2-inch baking pan with nonstick foil. Whisk together flour, cocoa powder, baking powder, salt and cinnamon; set aside.
2. Melt butter and sugar in a saucepan. Cool slightly. Whisk in egg and vanilla extract, then whisk in flour mixture. Stir in toffee bits, ½ cup each flake coconut and pecans and all of the chocolate chips. Spread into prepared pan.
3. Press remaining coconut and nuts into batter.
4. Bake at 350° 25 to 30 minutes or until set in center. Let cool in pan on wire rack for 15 minutes. Grab foil and lift bar from pan to rack; let cool completely. Cut into 24 bars.

PER BAR: 195 calories; 12 g fat (6 g sat.); 2 g protein; 23 g carbohydrate; 2 g fiber; 101 mg sodium; 22 mg cholesterol

slow-cooker solutions

GREAT-TASTING RECIPES FOR EFFORTLESS MEALS. **BY CINDY HELLER**

Food styling: Sara Neumeier. Prop styling: Christina Lane.

meatball stew

MAKES: 4 servings. **PREP:** 15 minutes. **SLOW-COOK:** 3 hours, 35 minutes on HIGH or 5 hours, 5 minutes on LOW.

- 1 egg, lightly beaten
- ¾ pound lean ground beef
- ½ cup finely chopped onion
- 3 tablespoons plain bread crumbs
- 2 tablespoons chopped fresh parsley
- 1 tablespoon grated Parmesan cheese
- ½ teaspoon salt
- ½ teaspoon black pepper
- ½ cup ketchup
- ¼ cup plus 1 tablespoon low-sodium beef broth
- 1½ teaspoons balsamic vinegar
- 1 bag (16 ounces) baby carrots

- 3 large parsnips, cut into 2-inch-long pieces
- 1 medium-size onion, chopped
- 1 tablespoon cornstarch

1. Stir together egg, beef, onion, bread crumbs, 1 tablespoon of the parsley, the Parmesan and ¼ teaspoon each of the salt and pepper. Form into 1-inch meatballs (about 20) and set aside.
2. Stir together ¼ cup ketchup, ¼ cup broth and the vinegar. Place carrots, parsnips and onion in slow cooker and

put meatballs on top. Drizzle with ketchup mixture. Cook on HIGH for 3½ hours or LOW for 5 hours.
3. Stir together remaining tablespoon parsley, ¼ teaspoon each salt and pepper, ¼ cup ketchup, 1 tablespoon broth and cornstarch. Gently stir into slow cooker. Cook until thick, 5 minutes.

PER SERVING: 337 calories; 7 g fat (3 g sat.); 24 g protein; 46 g carbohydrate; 9 g fiber; 863 mg sodium; 107 mg cholesterol

PHOTOGRAPHY BY CHARLES SCHILLER

chicken and broccoli casserole

MAKES: 4 servings. **PREP:** 10 minutes.
SLOW-COOK: 3 hours on HIGH or 4 hours on LOW.

- 1 cup freshly shredded cheddar cheese
- 1 tablespoon cornstarch
- 1 pound boneless, skinless chicken breasts, cut into 1-inch pieces
- 1 package (10 ounces) frozen chopped broccoli
- 1 medium-size onion, chopped
- ½ cup low-sodium chicken broth
- ½ teaspoon salt
- ½ teaspoon black pepper
- 4 tablespoons crushed cheddar cheese crackers (such as Cheez-Its) (optional)
- 3 cups cooked white or brown rice (optional)

1. Toss together ½ cup of the cheddar cheese and the cornstarch; set aside.
2. Place chicken, broccoli, onion, broth, ¼ teaspoon each salt and pepper and the cheddar-cornstarch mixture into slow cooker. Cover and cook on HIGH for 3 hours or on LOW for 4 hours.
3. Remove lid and stir remaining ½ cup cheddar cheese and ¼ teaspoon each salt and pepper into slow cooker. Sprinkle crushed crackers over top and serve immediately with rice, if desired.

PER SERVING: 286 calories; 11 g fat (6 g sat.); 35 g protein; 9 g carbohydrate; 2 g fiber; 633 mg sodium; 96 mg cholesterol

white chicken chili

MAKES: 4 servings. **PREP:** 10 minutes. **COOK:** 6 minutes.
SLOW-COOK: 4 hours on HIGH or 6 hours on LOW.

- 1 tablespoon canola oil
- 1 large green pepper, chopped
- 1 poblano pepper, seeded and chopped
- 1 large jalapeño pepper, seeded and chopped
- 1 medium-size onion, chopped
- 1 tablespoon chopped garlic
- 1 tablespoon plus ½ teaspoon ground cumin
- 1½ teaspoons ground coriander
- 2 pounds bone-in split chicken breasts, skin removed
- 2 cans (14.5 ounces each) cannellini beans, drained and rinsed
- 1 cup low-sodium chicken broth
- 1 tablespoon lime juice
- ½ teaspoon salt
- ¼ cup reduced-fat sour cream (optional)
- ¼ cup cilantro leaves (optional)

1. Heat oil in a large nonstick skillet over medium-high heat. Place peppers, onion, garlic, 1 tablespoon cumin and 1 teaspoon coriander in skillet; cover. Cook, stirring, for 6 minutes.
2. Transfer vegetables to slow cooker; add chicken, beans and broth. Cover; cook on HIGH for 4 hours or on LOW for 6 hours.
3. Remove chicken with a slotted spoon. Remove any bones from liquid in cooker. Stir in remaining ½ teaspoon each cumin and coriander, lime juice and salt.
4. Shred chicken meat; stir into slow cooker. Serve with sour cream and cilantro, if desired.

PER SERVING: 440 calories; 8 g fat (1 g sat.); 52 g protein; 38 g carbohydrate; 11 g fiber; 824 mg sodium; 106 mg cholesterol

pasta and meat sauce

MAKES: 4 servings. **PREP:** 15 minutes.
SLOW-COOK: 5½ hours on HIGH or 6½ hours on LOW. **COOK:** 12 minutes.

- 1 large carrot, peeled and chopped
- 1 large rib celery, chopped
- 1 medium-size onion, chopped
- 3 cloves garlic, chopped
- 1 can (14.5 ounces) diced tomatoes
- 1 cup low-sodium beef broth
- 1½ tablespoons tomato paste
- 1 teaspoon sugar
- 1 teaspoon dried Italian seasoning
- ¾ teaspoon salt
- ⅛ teaspoon red pepper flakes
- 1¼ pounds beef chuck steak, trimmed and cut into 1-inch chunks
- 8 ounces fettuccine
  Parmesan cheese (optional)

1. Put carrot, celery, onion and garlic in a food processor and pulse until finely chopped; place in the slow cooker bowl. Add diced tomatoes, broth, tomato paste and sugar to slow cooker. Add ½ teaspoon Italian seasoning, ½ teaspoon salt and the red pepper flakes. Stir in beef and cook on HIGH for 5 hours or LOW for 6 hours.

2. Using a slotted spoon, remove beef chunks from slow cooker and set aside. When cool enough to handle, shred beef and stir back into slow cooker. Add remaining ½ teaspoon Italian seasoning and ¼ teaspoon salt. Cook another 30 minutes.

3. Meanwhile, cook pasta according to package directions, about 12 minutes; serve with meat sauce. Sprinkle with Parmesan cheese, if desired.

PER SERVING: 476 calories; 11 g fat (3 g sat.); 38 g protein; 55 g carbohydrate; 5 g fiber; 878 mg sodium; 84 mg cholesterol

moo shu pork

MAKES: 12 wraps. **PREP:** 10 minutes.
SLOW-COOK: 4 hours on HIGH or 6 hours on LOW.

- ½ cup hoisin sauce
- 3 large cloves garlic, minced
- 2 tablespoons dark Asian sesame oil
- 2 tablespoons reduced-sodium soy sauce
- 1 tablespoon cornstarch
- 1 bag (16 ounces) shredded coleslaw mix
- ½ bag (10 ounces) shredded carrots
- ¾ pound boneless pork loin chops
- 12 flour tortillas (6-inch)
  Scallion strips (optional)

1. Stir together hoisin, garlic, sesame oil, soy sauce and cornstarch; set aside.
2. Place coleslaw mix and carrots into slow cooker. Cut the pork into ⅛-inch-thick slices, then cut each slice in half lengthwise; sprinkle on top of cabbage mixture in slow cooker. Drizzle with ¼ cup of hoisin sauce mixture. Cover and cook on HIGH for 4 hours or LOW for 6 hours.
3. Remove cover; stir in remaining ½ cup hoisin sauce mixture.
4. Heat tortillas according to package directions. Place ½ cup pork mixture in center of each tortilla, top with scallion strips, if desired, and fold over.

PER WRAP: 231 calories; 6 g fat (2 g sat.); 17 g protein; 27 g carbohydrate; 3 g fiber; 843 mg sodium; 31 mg cholesterol

applesauce cake

MAKES: 8 servings. **PREP:** 15 minutes.
SLOW-COOK: 2½ hours on HIGH.

- 1½ cups all-purpose flour
- 1½ teaspoons pumpkin pie spice
- 1 teaspoon baking soda
- ½ teaspoon baking powder
- ¼ teaspoon salt
- 5 tablespoons unsalted butter, softened
- ½ cup light-brown sugar
- 1 egg
- ¼ cup buttermilk
- 1 cup unsweetened applesauce
  Bottled caramel sauce, whipped topping and pecans (optional)

1. Coat slow cooker bowl with nonstick cooking spray. Place 1 long sheet of nonstick foil in bottom of slow cooker bowl, with ends extending over handles.
2. Whisk together flour, pumpkin pie spice, baking soda, baking powder and salt; set aside.
3. Beat together butter and brown sugar on high speed for 1 minute. Beat in egg. Scrape down sides of bowl and, on low speed, beat in buttermilk (mixture will look curdled). Beat in applesauce. Add flour mixture to bowl and beat on low speed until combined.
4. Spread batter into slow cooker. Place a clean dish towel over slow cooker, then put cover on top. Cook on HIGH for 2¼ to 2½ hours or until toothpick inserted in center comes out clean. Use foil to lift cake out of slow cooker. Cut into slices. Garnish with caramel sauce, whipped topping and pecans, if desired.

PER SERVING: 226 calories; 8 g fat (5 g sat.); 4 g protein; 35 g carbohydrate; 1 g fiber; 279 mg sodium; 46 mg cholesterol

When baking in a slow cooker, it's wise to put a clean dish towel or several layers of paper towels over the cooker before covering it. The towels absorb the condensation created during cooking and prevent the cake top from getting soggy.

food **university**

CUTTING UP CHICKEN FOR A MEAL WITH LOTS OF FLAVOR THAT ONLY COSTS A LITTLE DOUGH, BUY A WHOLE BIRD AND BONE UP ON YOUR KNIFE SKILLS. IT'S WAY MORE COST-EFFECTIVE THAN PAYING FOR PRICEY PRE-CUT PIECES. SIMPLY READ THROUGH THE STEPS ONCE OR TWICE, THEN CUT, MARINATE, GRILL AND EAT. **BY JULIE MILTENBERGER**

adobo-spiced grilled chicken

MAKES: 10 pieces. **PREP:** 10 minutes.
MARINATE: 1 hour. **GRILL:** 30 minutes.

- 1 5½-pound chicken, cut up
- ¼ cup white balsamic or white wine vinegar
- 2 tablespoons Worcestershire sauce
- 1 teaspoon Adobo seasoning
- ⅓ cup olive oil

1. Place chicken pieces in a large resealable plastic bag. In a medium-size bowl, whisk together vinegar, Worcestershire and Adobo. Add oil, whisking until well blended. Add to chicken in bag and seal. Turn bag to coat chicken; marinate in fridge 1 hour.

2. Heat gas grill to medium-high heat. If using charcoal grill, stack coal on one side of grill and light fire.

3. Once grill is heated, clean grate with wire brush. Place chicken, skin-side down, on grill (if using charcoal, place directly over coals). Cover and cook 5 minutes.

4. Open grill; Turn chicken pieces over. On gas grill, reduce heat to low; for charcoal grill, move chicken to side of grill so pieces are not directly over coals. Continue to cook chicken an additional 20 to 25 minutes, covered, turning occasionally. Check internal temperature of chicken; thickest part of breast should register 160° (temperature should rise to 165° as it sits). Remove chicken to platter. Let rest 5 minutes.

PER PIECE (WITH SKIN): 333 calories; 23 g fat (5 g sat.); 28 g protein; 2 g carbohydrate; 0 g fiber; 217 mg sodium; 89 mg cholesterol

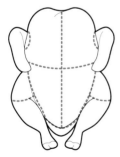

Most kitchen injuries are the result of a dull knife, so be sure to sharpen yours before you start. If desired, you can leave the breasts and legs whole, which yields four large portions plus wings.

Food styling: Megan Schlow. Prop styling: Megan Hedgpeth. Illustration: Brown Bird Design.

1 Rinse chicken and pat dry. Place on a cutting board with the wings away from you. Gently pull leg away from side of breast and slice through skin and meat.

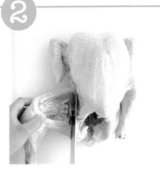

2 Bend leg joint away from body. Insert knife and cut down through joint in one quick motion, separating leg from body.

3 Turn leg skin-side down and slice along fat line between thigh and drumstick. Cut through leg joint. Repeat with opposite leg and the wings.

4 Starting at pointed end of breast, slice down through body cavity toward thickest part of breast, separating from backbone.

5 Turn breast skin-side down and split in half along breast bone (this will take firm pressure).

6 Turn over breast pieces and cut each in half, to create a total of 10 chicken pieces.

PHOTOGRAPHY BY YUNHEE KIM

october

Spiderweb Cookies
page 243

STIR UP SOME SPOOKY SWEETS—AND
MAKE SUPPERTIME ANYTHING BUT SCARY
WITH OUR TREAT BAG FULL OF QUICK-FIX,
HEALTHFUL FAMILY DINNERS.

Harvest Pot Pie
page 236

Chicken Parmesan
page 251

Strip Steak Diane
page 257

A THREE-CHEESE COMBO MAKES OUR MAC EXTRA RICH AND CREAMY.
BY KAREN TACK

mac and cheese

MAKES: 12 side-dish servings. **PREP:** 10 minutes. **COOK:** 6 minutes.
BAKE: at 350° for 20 minutes. **BROIL:** 3 minutes.

- 1 box (1 pound) penne rigate
- ¾ pound sharp cheddar cheese, shredded
- ½ pound Gruyère cheese, shredded
- ½ cup shredded Asiago or Parmesan cheese
- 3 tablespoons unsalted butter
- 3 tablespoons all-purpose flour
- 2 cups milk
- ½ teaspoon onion powder
- ½ teaspoon salt
- ⅛ teaspoon cayenne pepper

1. Heat oven to 350°. Coat a 2-quart broiler-safe oval baking dish with nonstick cooking spray. Bring a large pot of lightly salted water to boiling.
2. Once water boils, add penne. Cook 6 minutes, then drain. In a large bowl, toss together the cheddar, Gruyère and Asiago. Set aside.
3. Meanwhile, melt butter in medium-size saucepan over medium heat. Whisk in flour until smooth and slightly bubbly. In a thin stream, whisk in milk. Stir in onion powder, salt and cayenne. Bring to a boil over medium-high heat. Reduce heat and simmer 3 minutes. Remove from heat; whisk in 2½ cups of the cheese mixture.

4. In pasta pot, stir together the cooked penne and the cheese sauce. Pour half into prepared baking dish. Sprinkle with a generous cup of the cheese. Spoon remaining penne into dish and top with remaining cheese.
5. Bake at 350° for 20 minutes. Increase oven temperature to broil and broil 3 minutes, until top is lightly browned. Cool slightly before serving.

PER SERVING: 400 calories; 21 g fat (12 g sat.); 20 g protein; 33 g carbohydrate; 1 g fiber; 410 mg sodium; 65 mg cholesterol

PHOTOGRAPHY BY RITA MAAS

farm
fresh

INSPIRED BY A TRIP TO THE GREENMARKET, WE COOKED UP
FIVE VEGGIE-PACKED SUPPERS YOU'LL FALL FOR. **BY JULIE MILTENBERGER**

**Stuffed Tomatoes
(Recipe page 239)**
For a more
Mediterranean
flavor, use feta or
goat cheese
instead of blue.

The tangy glaze on Gingered Carrots and Cod would be great over any firm white fish or even salmon. (Recipe page 239)

PHOTOGRAPHY BY ANN STRATTON

harvest pot pie

MAKES: 6 servings. **PREP:** 15 minutes. **COOK:** 21 minutes. **BAKE:** at 400° for 25 minutes. **COOL:** 15 minutes.

- 2 **bunches Swiss chard (red is okay)**
- 2 **tablespoons olive oil**
- 1 **small onion, diced**
- 2 **medium-size carrots, sliced**
- 1 **package (20 ounces) ground turkey**
- ½ **teaspoon dried thyme**
- 1 **can (14.5 ounces) low-sodium chicken broth**
- 2 **tablespoons cornstarch**
- 2 **tablespoons Dijon mustard**
- ½ **teaspoon salt**
- ¼ **teaspoon ground black pepper**
- 1 **sheet frozen puff pastry (from a 17.3-ounce box), thawed**

1. Heat oven to 400°. Coat a 2-quart baking dish with nonstick cooking spray. Rinse chard well; trim stems, then separate at base of leaves. Cut into ½-inch pieces; set aside. Chop leaves.

2. Place half the leaves in a large nonstick skillet. Cover and cook over medium heat for 3 minutes, until wilted. Transfer to a bowl. Repeat with remaining chard leaves.

3. Add oil to same skillet; stir in onion, chard stems and carrots; cook 5 minutes. Stir in turkey and thyme, breaking apart with a spoon. Cook 7 minutes, until carrots are tender. Stir in wilted leaves; increase heat to medium-high.

4. In bowl, blend broth, cornstarch, mustard, salt and pepper. Add to skillet; bring to a simmer. Simmer 3 minutes, until thickened and clear. Transfer to prepared dish; top with puff pastry. Cut a few holes to vent.

5. Bake at 400° for 25 minutes, until browned. Cool 15 minutes before serving.

PER SERVING: 377 calories; 17 g fat (4 g sat.); 31 g protein; 26 g carbohydrate; 4 g fiber; 805 mg sodium; 39 mg cholesterol

curried chicken and cauliflower

MAKES: 6 servings. **PREP:** 15 minutes. **COOK:** 19 minutes.

1 can (14 ounces) light coconut milk

1 cup low-sodium chicken broth

2 tablespoons sugar

1 to 2 tablespoons yellow curry paste (such as Roland or Thai Kitchen)

2 tablespoons olive oil

1 pound boneless, skinless chicken breast halves, cut into 1-inch pieces

1 head cauliflower (about 2 pounds), trimmed and cut into florets

4 scallions, trimmed and sliced

1 tablespoon cornstarch

1 can (15 ounces) chickpeas, drained and rinsed

¾ teaspoon salt

Cooked basmati rice, optional

1. In a small bowl, whisk together coconut milk, ¾ cup of the chicken broth, sugar and curry paste (use 2 tablespoons of the paste for a spicier curry). Heat oil in a stockpot over medium-high heat. Add chicken and brown on all sides, about 4 minutes. Remove to a bowl with a slotted spoon.

2. Add cauliflower to pot and cook 1 minute. Reduce heat to medium. Stir in coconut milk mixture and bring to a simmer. Cover and simmer for 6 minutes.

3. Uncover pot and add chicken, with any accumulated juices, and scallions. Simmer, uncovered, 5 minutes. Meanwhile, whisk together remaining ¼ cup chicken broth and cornstarch.

4. Stir chickpeas, cornstarch mixture and salt into pot. Raise heat to medium-high and cook 3 minutes. Serve with basmati rice, if desired.

PER SERVING: 461 calories; 15 g fat (5 g sat.); 28 g protein; 54 g carbohydrate; 7 g fiber; 736 mg sodium; 44 mg cholesterol

cavatelli with brussels sprouts

MAKES: 6 servings. **PREP:** 15 minutes. **COOK:** 17 minutes.

1½ **pounds fresh Brussels sprouts, trimmed and halved (keep small ones whole)**
  1 **box (1 pound) cavatelli pasta**
  1 **package (8 ounces) bacon, chopped**
  1 **medium onion, chopped**
  2 **tablespoons olive oil**
  ¼ **cup fresh lemon juice**
  ½ **teaspoon salt**
  ⅛ **teaspoon ground black pepper**
      Grated Parmesan cheese (optional)

1. Heat a large pot of salted water to boiling. Add Brussels sprouts and cook 4 minutes. Remove with a slotted spoon to a bowl.

2. Add pasta to boiling water and cook 8 minutes, according to package directions. Reserve ¾ cup of the pasta water; drain pasta and return to pot.

3. While the pasta cooks, heat bacon in a large nonstick skillet over medium-high heat. Cook 8 minutes or until it begins to crisp. Push bacon to one side of pan and tilt pan. Carefully spoon out 2 tablespoons pan drippings and discard.

4. Reduce heat to medium and add onion and olive oil to skillet. Cook 2 minutes, stirring occasionally. Add Brussels sprouts to skillet and cook 3 minutes to brown slightly. Stir in pasta water and lemon juice and season with salt and pepper. Add to cooked pasta and gently toss to coat pasta with sauce. Serve warm with grated Parmesan cheese, if desired.

PER SERVING: 490 calories; 16 g fat (4 g sat.); 19 g protein; 68 g carbohydrate; 7 g fiber; 517 mg sodium; 18 mg cholesterol

To prepare these mini cabbages, just trim off the stem ends and discard any loose outer leaves.

gingered carrots and cod

MAKES: 4 servings. **PREP:** 15 minutes. **COOK:** 12 minutes.
MICROWAVE: 1½ minutes. **BAKE:** at 400° for 23 minutes.

- 4 **cod or scrod fillets (about 5 ounces each)**
- ¼ **cup honey**
- 1 **tablespoon chopped fresh ginger**
- 2 **tablespoons balsamic vinegar**
- 2 **tablespoons low-sodium soy sauce**
- ⅛ **plus ¼ teaspoon salt**
  Pinch ground black pepper
- 3 **tablespoons unsalted butter**
- 1 **large bunch carrots, peeled and cut on the diagonal into ½-inch slices**
- 1 **sweet yellow pepper, cored and cut into 1-inch pieces**
  Mashed potatoes, for serving (optional)

1. Heat oven to 400°. Coat a baking dish with nonstick cooking spray. Place cod in dish, spacing fillets at least ½ inch apart.
2. In a 2-cup measuring cup, combine honey, ginger, vinegar, soy sauce, ⅛ teaspoon of the salt and the pepper. Cover with plastic wrap and microwave on HIGH for 1½ minutes (mixture will bubble up). Remove from microwave and whisk in 1 tablespoon butter. Spoon 1 tablespoon sauce over each cod fillet. Sprinkle cod with remaining ¼ teaspoon salt. Cover dish with foil and bake at 400° for 20 to 23 minutes, until fish is opaque and flakes easily with a fork.
3. Meanwhile, melt remaining 2 tablespoons butter in a large nonstick skillet over medium-high heat. Add carrots; sauté 3 minutes. Add yellow pepper and sauté 2 minutes. Reduce heat to medium; add **¼ cup water** and cover. Cook 5 minutes, until tender.
4. Uncover skillet; stir in remaining sauce from measuring cup. Raise heat to medium-high and cook 2 minutes.
5. Divide carrot mixture evenly among 4 plates. Top each with a piece of cod. Serve with mashed potatoes, if desired.

PER SERVING: 293 calories; 10 g fat (6 g sat.); 22 g protein; 31 g carbohydrate; 3 g fiber; 645 mg sodium; 71 mg cholesterol

stuffed tomatoes

MAKES: 6 servings. **PREP:** 20 minutes.
COOK: 10 minutes. **BAKE:** at 325° for 30 minutes.

- 6 **large ripe tomatoes (10 to 12 ounces each)**
- 1 **pound ground sirloin**
- 2 **large cloves garlic, chopped**
- 1 **pouch (8.8 ounces) fully cooked brown rice (such as Uncle Ben's Ready Rice)**
- ¼ **cup pine nuts**
- ½ **teaspoon dried oregano**
- ½ **teaspoon salt, plus more for sprinkling**
- ¼ **teaspoon ground black pepper**
- ⅔ **cup blue cheese crumbles**
- 2 **tablespoons chopped fresh parsley**
  Crusty bread and salad, for serving

1. Heat oven to 325°. Rinse tomatoes and pat dry. Cut tops off tomatoes and scoop out pulp. Turn tomato shells upside down on paper towels to drain.
2. Heat a large nonstick skillet over medium heat. Add ground sirloin and garlic, breaking up meat with a wooden spoon. Cook 7 minutes, until meat is no longer pink.
3. Add rice, pine nuts, oregano, ½ teaspoon salt and the pepper to the skillet. Cover and cook on medium-low heat for 3 minutes.
4. Remove pan from heat and stir in blue cheese and 1½ tablespoons of the chopped parsley. Turn tomatoes right-side up and sprinkle insides with salt. Spoon filling into tomatoes, mounding slightly, ⅔ to ¾ cup each.
5. Place tomatoes in 13 × 9 × 2-inch baking dish. Cover dish with foil and bake at 325° for 25 minutes. Remove foil and bake an additional 5 minutes. Sprinkle with remaining ½ tablespoon parsley. Serve warm with salad and crusty bread.

PER SERVING: 291 calories; 12 g fat (5 g sat.); 22 g protein; 23 g carbohydrate; 4 g fiber; 513 mg sodium; 51 mg cholesterol

legends of the
fall

IT'S PRIME TIME FOR PUMPKINS—GO BEYOND PIE WITH SCONES, COOKIES AND MORE. **BY JULIE MILTENBERGER**

Pumpkin Buns
(Recipe page 245)

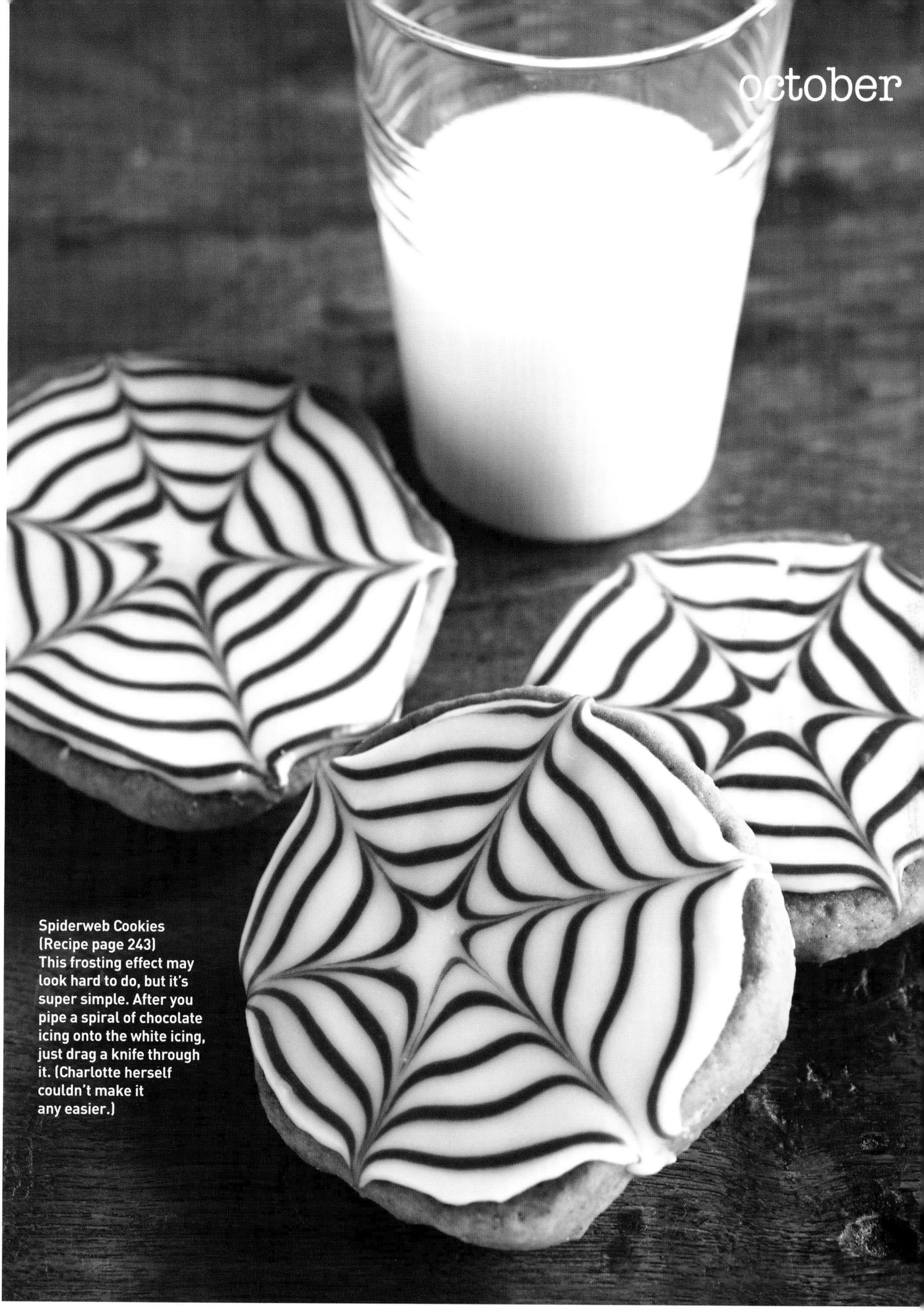

Spiderweb Cookies
(Recipe page 243)
This frosting effect may look hard to do, but it's super simple. After you pipe a spiral of chocolate icing onto the white icing, just drag a knife through it. (Charlotte herself couldn't make it any easier.)

Food styling: Sara Neumeier. Prop styling: Loren Simons.

PHOTOGRAPHY BY KATE MATHIS

ice cream sandwiches

MAKES: 12 servings. **PREP:** 10 minutes.
BAKE: at 350° for 35 minutes.
FREEZE: at least 3 hours or overnight.

- 1 cup canned solid-pack pumpkin
- 2 cups all-purpose flour
- ¼ cup cocoa powder
- 1½ teaspoons baking powder
- 1 teaspoon pumpkin pie spice
- ½ cup (1 stick) unsalted butter
- 1 cup sugar
- 1 egg
- ⅓ cup mini chocolate chips
- 2¼ cups reduced-fat vanilla-bean ice cream

1. Heat oven to 350°. Line a baking sheet with foil; coat foil with nonstick cooking spray. Spread pumpkin onto greased foil. Bake at 350° for 20 minutes. Remove from oven and cool slightly. Coat two large baking sheets with nonstick cooking spray. Set aside.

2. In a small bowl, whisk together the flour, cocoa, baking powder and pumpkin pie spice. Set aside. In a large bowl, combine baked pumpkin, butter and sugar. Beat with an electric mixer on medium speed until well blended. Beat in egg, then stir in flour mixture.

3. Drop batter by heaping tablespoonfuls onto prepared baking sheets. Bake at 350° for 15 minutes. Remove cookies from oven; press down with a flat-bottom glass or measuring cup. Transfer to wire racks and cool completely. Repeat with all dough.

4. Once cookies are cool, place mini chips in a small bowl. Top one cookie with 3 tablespoons of the ice cream (on flat side of cookie). Press the flat side of another cookie into ice cream. Roll edge of sandwich in chips. Repeat with all cookies and ice cream, rolling half of the sandwiches in mini chips. Wrap each sandwich in plastic. Freeze at least 3 hours or overnight.

PER SERVING: 267 calories; 12 g fat (7 g sat.); 5 g protein; 40 g carbohydrate; 2 g fiber; 33 mg sodium; 49 mg cholesterol

spiderweb cookies

MAKES: 14 cookies. **PREP:** 20 minutes.
BAKE: at 350° for 15 minutes each batch.

Cookies:
- 2⅔ cups all-purpose flour
- 1 teaspoon baking soda
- ¾ teaspoon salt
- ½ teaspoon ground allspice
- ¾ cup canned solid-pack pumpkin
- ¼ cup milk
- 1 cup granulated sugar
- ¼ cup (½ stick) unsalted butter, softened
- 2 eggs

Icing:
- 3 cups confectioners' sugar
- 3 tablespoons light corn syrup
- ½ teaspoon vanilla
- 3 tablespoons plus 4 teaspoons milk
- 2 tablespoons unsweetened cocoa powder

1. Cookies: Heat oven to 350°. Coat 2 baking sheets with nonstick cooking spray. In bowl, combine flour, baking soda, salt and allspice. In small bowl, stir together the pumpkin and milk. In large bowl, beat sugar and butter until blended, 1 minute. Beat in eggs. On low speed, alternately beat in flour mixture and pumpkin mixture, ending with flour mixture.

2. Drop ¼-cupfuls of dough onto prepared sheets, spacing 2 inches apart. Spread slightly with spatula.

3. Bake 1 sheet at a time in 350° oven 13 to 15 minutes, until toothpick inserted in centers tests clean. Remove cookies to rack to cool.

4. Icing: Blend confectioners' sugar, corn syrup, vanilla and 3 tablespoons plus 2 teaspoons milk until smooth. Remove ⅓ cup icing to small bowl and stir in cocoa and remaining 2 teaspoons milk. Transfer chocolate icing to plastic bag; snip off corner.

5. Turn cookies flat-side up. Spread white icing over one cookie. Beginning in center, pipe a spiral of chocolate icing onto cookie. Starting in center of spiral, drag a knife through spiral for spiderweb pattern. Repeat with all cookies. Let stand until set.

PER COOKIE: 273 calories; 5 g fat (3 g sat.); 4 g protein; 57 g carbohydrate; 1 g fiber; 230 mg sodium; 40 mg cholesterol

pumpkin-raisin scones

MAKES: 9 scones. **PREP:** 10 minutes. **BAKE:** at 400° for 16 minutes.

- 3 cups all-purpose flour
- ⅔ cup plus 1 tablespoon sugar
- 1 tablespoon baking powder
- 1 teaspoon baking soda
- ¾ teaspoon salt
- 1 teaspoon chopped crystallized ginger
- 4 tablespoons cold unsalted butter, cut into small cubes
- 1 cup canned solid-pack pumpkin
- ¾ cup buttermilk
- 1 egg
- ¾ cup regular or golden raisins

1. Heat oven to 400°. Line a baking sheet with parchment paper or a silicone baking-sheet liner.

2. Combine flour, the ⅔ cup sugar, the baking powder, baking soda, salt and ½ teaspoon of the crystallized ginger in a large bowl. Add butter; mix with pastry blender until mixture resembles coarse crumbs. In a small bowl, whisk together pumpkin, buttermilk and egg. Stir into dough, along with raisins.

3. Drop dough by ½-cupfuls onto prepared sheet, about 2 inches apart. In a small bowl, stir together remaining tablespoon sugar and remaining ½ teaspoon chopped crystallized ginger. Sprinkle sugar-ginger mixture evenly over scones.

4. Bake at 400° for 16 minutes or until golden brown. Remove to wire rack and let cool slightly. Serve warm or at room temperature.

PER SCONE: 300 calories; 6 g fat (4 g sat.); 6 g protein; 55 g carbohydrate; 2 g fiber; 500 mg sodium; 38 mg cholesterol

Crumb-Topped Loaf
(Recipe opposite)
The super moist cake
contrasts with a crunchy
walnut topping.

Stash half the batch—unbaked—in the freezer for another day.

crumb-topped loaf

MAKES: 12 servings. **PREP:** 20 minutes.
BAKE: at 350° for 55 minutes.
COOL: 10 minutes.

Loaf:
- 1½ cups all-purpose flour
- 2 teaspoons baking powder
- 1 teaspoon pumpkin pie spice
- ½ teaspoon salt
- 1 egg
- ½ cup granulated sugar
- 1 cup canned solid-pack pumpkin
- ¼ cup vegetable oil
- 1 teaspoon vanilla
- ½ cup walnuts, coarsely chopped

Topping:
- ¼ cup (½ stick) unsalted butter, softened
- ⅓ cup packed dark-brown sugar
- ½ cup all-purpose flour
- ⅓ cup walnuts, finely chopped
- 1 teaspoon confectioners' sugar (optional)

1. Loaf: Heat oven to 350°. Coat a 9 × 5 × 3-inch loaf pan with nonstick cooking spray.

2. Mix flour, baking powder, pie spice and salt in small bowl. Beat egg and sugar in large bowl. Beat in pumpkin, oil and vanilla until smooth. Make a well in center of flour mixture. Add egg mixture. Stir just until moistened and batter comes together. Fold in walnuts. Spoon batter into prepared pan.

3. Topping: Mix butter, brown sugar and flour in small bowl until crumbly. Stir in walnuts. Sprinkle over batter.

4. Bake loaf at 350° for 50 to 55 minutes, until wooden toothpick tests clean. Cool in pan on rack 10 minutes. Turn out onto rack to cool completely. Dust with confectioners' sugar; slice.

PER SERVING: 259 calories; 14 g fat (4 g sat.); 4 g protein; 31 g carbohydrate; 2 g fiber; 105 mg sodium; 28 mg cholesterol

pumpkin buns

MAKES: 24 buns. **PREP:** 20 minutes. **RISE:** 2 hours. **BAKE:** at 350° for 33 minutes.

- 1 envelope (¼ ounce) active dry yeast
- ¼ cup warm water (100° to 110°)
- 1 teaspoon plus 2 tablespoons granulated sugar
- 2 eggs
- ¼ cup (½ stick) unsalted butter, melted
- 1 can (15 ounces) solid-pack pumpkin
- 5½ cups all-purpose flour
- ¾ teaspoon salt

Filling:
- ½ cup (1 stick) unsalted butter, softened
- ¼ cup granulated sugar
- 1 cup packed light-brown sugar
- 1 tablespoon cinnamon

Glaze:
- 2 cups confectioners' sugar
- 3 tablespoons milk

1. Sprinkle yeast over warm water in large bowl. Add 1 teaspoon of the granulated sugar; let stand until foamy, about 5 minutes. Beat in remaining 2 tablespoons sugar, the eggs, butter and pumpkin.

2. Gradually add 5 cups of the flour and the salt, scraping side of bowl, until soft dough forms. Turn out onto floured surface and knead remaining ½ cup flour into dough, adding more if sticky. Knead for 10 minutes, until smooth. Dough will be soft.

3. Grease a bowl; add dough. Cover with plastic wrap and place in a warm spot until doubled, about 1¼ hours.

4. Coat two 13 × 9 × 2-inch baking pans with nonstick cooking spray. Make **Filling:** Mix butter, granulated and brown sugars, and cinnamon in a bowl.

5. Punch down dough. Roll out half onto a lightly floured surface to form a 16 × 10-inch rectangle. Spread with half of the filling. Starting on one long side, roll up jelly-roll fashion. Pinch seam to close. Repeat with second half of dough and filling.

6. Cut each log crosswise into 12 generous 1-inch pieces. Arrange 12 pieces, cut-side down, in each prepared pan. Cover with plastic wrap; let sit in a warm spot until buns double in size, about 30 to 45 minutes. (You can refrigerate one pan overnight or cover plastic with foil and freeze at this point. Thaw in fridge overnight, then let stand on counter while preheating oven.)

7. Heat oven to 350°. Uncover pans and bake buns until they are golden brown and bubbly, 28 to 33 minutes (thawed buns, 36 minutes). Transfer to a wire rack; let cool 10 minutes.

8. Glaze: Blend confectioners' sugar and milk. Drizzle over buns (about ⅓ cup per pan). Serve warm.

PER BUN: 249 calories; 7 g fat (4 g sat.); 4 g protein; 45 g carbohydrate; 2 g fiber; 85 mg sodium; 33 mg cholesterol

supper solutions

NO LAST-MINUTE SHOPPING ON THE WAY HOME. WITH A
WELL-STOCKED PANTRY, EVERYTHING YOU NEED FOR
DINNER IS RIGHT IN YOUR KITCHEN. **BY CINDY HELLER**

lentil salad with sausage

MAKES: 4 servings. **PREP:** 15 minutes.
COOK: 25 minutes.

1¼ cups lentils, rinsed
1 package (12 ounces) roasted red
  pepper and Asiago chicken
  sausage (such as Al Fresco)
1 can (8.5 ounces) quartered
  artichoke hearts, drained and
  rinsed
4 scallions, trimmed and thinly
  sliced
1 small sweet red pepper, finely
  chopped
1 large carrot, grated
¼ cup reduced-fat balsamic
  vinaigrette

1. Cook lentils according to package
directions, 20 to 25 minutes or until
tender; drain.
2. While lentils are cooking, cut
sausages into ½-inch-thick half-
moons and cook in a medium-size
nonstick skillet over medium-high
heat for 7 minutes or until lightly
browned; remove from skillet
and set aside.
3. Stir together lentils, sausages,
artichokes, scallions, red pepper and
carrot in a medium-size bowl. Drizzle
vinaigrette over top and stir until well
blended. Serve immediately.

PER SERVING: 419 calories; 9 g fat (3 g sat.);
36 g protein; 54 g carbohydrate; 11 g fiber;
1,115 mg sodium; 70 mg cholesterol

PHOTOGRAPHY BY MARK LUND

Dry polenta and cans of chicken broth and diced tomatoes—all ingredients in this soul-satisfying dish—are pantry staples.

Food styling: Simon Andrews. Prop styling: Megan Hedgpeth.

polenta and mushroom sauce

MAKES: 4 servings. **PREP:** 15 minutes. **BAKE:** at 350° for 40 minutes. **COOK:** 27 minutes.

- 1 **cup dry polenta**
- ½ **teaspoon salt**
- ½ **teaspoon black pepper**
- ½ **cup grated Parmesan cheese**
- 1 **cup dried porcini mushrooms**
- 1 **tablespoon olive oil**
- 1 **shallot, finely chopped**
- 10 **ounces white mushrooms, sliced**
- 3 **tablespoons flour**
- ½ **cup low-sodium chicken broth**
- 1 **can (14.5 ounces) diced tomatoes with basil, garlic and oregano (such as Del Monte), drained**
  Grated Parmesan cheese (optional)

1. Heat oven to 350°. Place polenta in an 8 × 8 × 2-inch baking dish and stir in **3½ cups water** and ¼ teaspoon each salt and pepper. Bake at 350° for 40 minutes or until most of the water has been absorbed. Stir in Parmesan cheese.
2. Place dried mushrooms in a small bowl; cover with **1 cup very hot water**. Soak for 15 minutes, then remove with a slotted spoon and chop; set aside. Reserve mushroom soaking water.
3. Heat oil in a large nonstick skillet over medium heat. Cook shallot 3 minutes. Add white mushrooms to pan; sprinkle

with remaining ¼ teaspoon each salt and pepper. Cook 7 minutes. Stir in flour and cook 2 minutes, stirring constantly. Whisk chicken broth, chopped porcini, mushroom liquid and diced tomatoes into skillet. Simmer over medium heat for 15 minutes. Spoon mushroom sauce over polenta. Top with grated Parmesan cheese, if desired.

PER SERVING: 350 calories; 10 g fat (3 g sat.); 15 g protein; 50 g carbohydrate; 5 g fiber; 1,054 mg sodium; 11 mg cholesterol

salmon cakes with corn salsa

MAKES: 6 servings. **PREP:** 10 minutes.
COOK: 8 minutes.

- 2 **cups frozen corn kernels, thawed**
- 1 **cup salsa**
- 6 **cans (3.75 ounces each) blueback salmon, drained**
- 1 **can (4.5 ounces) chopped green chiles, drained**
- 2 **tablespoons chopped cilantro**
- 2 **tablespoons light mayonnaise**
- 1 **egg, lightly beaten**
- ¼ **cup plain bread crumbs**

1. In a small bowl, combine corn and salsa; set aside.
2. Stir together salmon, chiles, cilantro, mayonnaise and egg just until blended. Form into 12 patties, a scant ¼ cup salmon mixture each. Place bread crumbs in a shallow dish and coat salmon cakes with crumbs. Lightly spritz tops and bottoms of cakes with nonstick cooking spray.
3. Heat a large nonstick skillet over medium-high heat. Cook salmon cakes 2 to 4 minutes on each side or until lightly browned. Serve immediately with salsa.

PER SERVING: 249 calories; 8 g fat (1 g sat.); 27 g protein; 16 g carbohydrate; 3 g fiber; 916 mg sodium; 124 mg cholesterol

linguine with clam sauce

MAKES: 8 servings. **PREP** 10 minutes. **COOK:** 14 minutes.

- 1 **pound linguine**
- 1 **tablespoon olive oil**
- 1 **medium onion, chopped**
- 3 **cloves garlic, chopped**
- 3 **cans (6.5 ounces each) chopped clams**
- 1 **tablespoon dried parsley**
- ½ **teaspoon dried oregano**
- ½ **teaspoon dried basil**
- ¼ **teaspoon red pepper flakes**
- ¼ **teaspoon salt**
- ⅛ **teaspoon black pepper**
- ¼ **cup plain bread crumbs**
  Chopped fresh flat-leaf parsley

1. Cook linguine 11 minutes. Drain and return to pot.
2. Meanwhile, heat ½ tablespoon oil in a 10-inch nonstick skillet over medium heat. Add onion and garlic; sauté 5 minutes.

3. Strain liquid from clams and add liquid to skillet, reserving clams. Add parsley, oregano, basil, pepper flakes, salt and pepper to pan. Simmer 5 minutes, then stir in clams; cook 2 minutes. Stir into pasta in pot; toss to mix. Cover to keep warm.
4. Heat remaining ½ tablespoon oil in a small skillet over medium-high heat and add bread crumbs. Cook, stirring, for 2 minutes or until lightly browned. Sprinkle over pasta and gently toss. Top with chopped parsley.

PER SERVING: 361 calories; 4 g fat (1 g sat.); 18 g protein; 65 g carbohydrate; 3 g fiber; 739 mg sodium; 17 mg cholesterol

warm sweet potato salad

MAKES: 6 servings. **PREP:** 15 minutes. **ROAST:** at 400° for 45 minutes.

- 3 **tablespoons cider vinegar**
- 3 **tablespoons maple syrup**
- 2 **teaspoons Dijon mustard**
- 3 **tablespoons olive oil**
- 2 **pounds sweet potatoes, peeled and cut into 1-inch pieces**
- 1 **large onion, thinly sliced**
- 1 **slice ham, ½ inch thick (about 8 ounces), cut into ½-inch pieces**
- ¾ **teaspoon dried thyme**
- ¼ **teaspoon salt**
- ¼ **teaspoon black pepper**
- 1 **package (10 ounces) frozen chopped spinach, thawed and squeezed dry**
- ½ **cup chopped walnuts, toasted**

1. Heat oven to 400°. Stir together vinegar, maple syrup and mustard. Slowly whisk in 2 tablespoons of the olive oil; set aside.

2. Place sweet potatoes, onion and ham in a large bowl. Drizzle with remaining 1 tablespoon olive oil; stir until coated. Spread on a rimmed baking sheet; sprinkle with thyme, salt and pepper. Roast at 400° for 45 minutes, stirring halfway through.

3. Remove from oven and place in a large bowl. Stir in spinach and walnuts. Drizzle with maple vinaigrette and serve immediately.

PER SERVING: 356 calories; 14 g fat (2 g sat.); 13 g protein; 45 g carbohydrate; 6 g fiber; 712 mg sodium; 18 mg cholesterol

bella cucina

YES, YOU LOVE YOUR LITTLE NEIGHBORHOOD ITALIAN PLACE. BUT IT'S JUST AS DELICIOUS—AND CHEAPER—TO MAKE YOUR FAVORITES SUCH AS CHICKEN PARM, PASTA FAGIOLI AND GARLIC BREAD AT HOME. **BY MICHAEL TYRRELL**

Chicken Parmesan
(Recipe opposite)

octob

october

loaÿeÿ garlic bread

MAKES: 24 pieces. **PREP:** 10 minutes.
MICROWAVE: 4 minutes. **COOK:** 2 minutes. **BAKE:** at 400° for 15 minutes.

- 6 slices bacon, each cut into 4 pieces
- 8 tablespoons (1 stick) butter
- 6 cloves garlic, peeled and finely chopped
- 1 loaf (12 ounces) crusty Italian bread, cut into 24 slices, about ½ inch thick
- ¾ pound mozzarella cheese, cut into 2 pieces, each cut into 12 slices

1. Heat oven to 400°. Coat 2 large baking sheets with nonstick cooking spray.
2. Place bacon on a microwave-safe plate lined with paper towels. Cover with another piece of paper towel. Microwave on HIGH for 4 minutes or until slightly crisp. Pat with clean paper towels to absorb fat and set aside. When cool enough to handle, cut into thin strips.
3. Melt butter in a small saucepan over medium-low heat. Add garlic and cook 1 to 2 minutes. Remove from heat.
4. Place bread on baking sheets. Spoon on butter and garlic. Top each with a slice of cheese; sprinkle with bacon. Bake at 400° for 12 to 15 minutes, until cheese melts and bacon is crisp. Cool slightly.

PER PIECE: 125 calories; 8 g fat (5 g sat.); 5 g protein; 8 g carbohydrate; 0 g fiber; 214 mg sodium; 22 mg cholesterol

chicken parmesan

MAKES: 6 servings. **PREP:** 20 minutes.
COOK: 12 minutes. **BAKE:** at 375° for 10 minutes.

- 1 cup seasoned bread crumbs
- 1 egg, lightly beaten
- 12 chicken tender fillets, about 1½ pounds
- 4 tablespoons vegetable oil
- 1 cup bottled marinara sauce
- 12 fresh basil leaves
- 1 cup shredded four-cheese blend
  Cooked ziti and marinara sauce (optional)

1. Heat oven to 375°.
2. Place bread crumbs in a shallow dish and egg in a shallow bowl. Dip chicken pieces in egg, shaking off excess. Coat with bread crumbs; place on a plate.
3. Heat 2 tablespoons of the oil in a large nonstick skillet over medium-high heat. Add half the chicken and cook for 3 minutes per side. Remove to a 13 × 9 × 2-inch baking dish. Repeat with remaining 2 tablespoons oil and remaining chicken.
4. Spoon marinara sauce over chicken in dish. Top each tender with a basil leaf, then sprinkle cheese over chicken.
5. Bake at 375° for 10 minutes, until bubbly and cheese melts. Serve with cooked ziti and marinara sauce, if desired.

PER SERVING: 453 calories; 26 g fat (11 g sat.); 39 g protein; 15 g carbohydrate; 2 g fiber; 911 mg sodium; 138 mg cholesterol

Food styling: Liza Jernow. Prop styling: Deborah Williams.

OCT.09 **251**

rotini with broccoli rabe and sausage

MAKES: 4 servings. **PREP:** 10 minutes.
COOK: 13 minutes.

- 2 tablespoons olive oil
- ½ pound sweet Italian sausage, crumbled
- 4 cloves garlic, thinly sliced
- 1 large bunch broccoli rabe, stems trimmed, rinsed and cut into 2-inch pieces
- ½ teaspoon salt
- ½ teaspoon dried oregano
- ¼ teaspoon black pepper
- 1 package (12 ounces) tri-color rotini pasta
  Grated Asiago cheese (optional)

1. Heat oil in a large nonstick skillet over medium-high heat. Add sausage and cook 5 minutes, stirring occasionally. Stir in garlic during last minute of cooking time. Add broccoli rabe, salt, oregano and pepper. Cook, uncovered, 8 minutes or until tender, stirring occasionally. If mixture gets too dry, add a few tablespoons of water.
2. Meanwhile, cook pasta following package directions, about 7 minutes. Drain, reserving ½ cup of the cooking liquid.
3. Add pasta water to sausage mixture to create a sauce, then stir together with pasta. Serve immediately with grated Asiago cheese, if desired.

PER SERVING: 494 calories; 13 g fat (3 g sat.); 25 g protein; 72 g carbohydrate; 3 g fiber; 656 mg sodium; 17 mg cholesterol

pork saltimbocca

MAKES: 4 servings. **PREP:** 10 minutes.
COOK: 6 minutes.

- 4 boneless pork chops, about 6 ounces each, cut ¾ inch thick
- ⅛ teaspoon salt
- ⅛ teaspoon black pepper
- 8 fresh sage leaves
- 3 ounces prosciutto
- 2 tablespoons olive oil
- ½ cup beef broth
- 2 teaspoons cornstarch
- ½ cup Marsala wine
- 1 cup shredded fontina cheese (4 ounces)
- 1 roll prepared polenta, grilled (optional)

1. Season pork with salt and pepper. Place 2 sage leaves and ¼ of the prosciutto on each chop. With the sharp side of a chef's knife pointed up, gently pound pork so that prosciutto adheres to it.
2. Heat oil in large nonstick skillet over medium-high heat. Place pork, prosciutto-side down, in skillet; cook 2 minutes. Turn and cook 2 more minutes. Remove to a plate.
3. Stir together beef broth and cornstarch. Off heat, add Marsala wine and beef broth mixture to the skillet. Scrape up browned bits from the bottom. Add pork back to skillet, prosciutto-side up, and top each chop with ¼ of cheese. Cover; simmer 2 minutes, until cheese melts and pork registers 155° on an instant-read thermometer. Top each piece with a tablespoon of sauce.
4. Serve with grilled polenta, if desired.

PER SERVING: 460 calories; 24 g fat (9 g sat.); 46 g protein; 6 g carbohydrate; 0 g fiber; 624 mg sodium; 145 mg cholesterol

shrimp piccata

MAKES: 4 servings. **PREP:** 15 minutes. **COOK:** 4 minutes, 30 seconds.

- 3 tablespoons all-purpose flour
- 1 teaspoon citrus-pepper blend or lemon pepper (such as McCormick)
- 1¼ pounds large shrimp, cleaned and deveined
- 2 tablespoons olive oil
- 2 cloves garlic, finely chopped
- ½ cup dry white wine
- ½ cup vegetable broth
- 3 tablespoons lemon juice
- 2 tablespoons capers
- 2 tablespoons unsalted butter
- 1 tablespoon chopped parsley
- 3 cups cooked white rice

1. Combine flour and pepper blend in a shallow dish. Toss shrimp in mixture until coated.

2. Heat oil in a large nonstick skillet over medium-high heat. Add shrimp and cook 2 minutes; turn and cook another minute. Remove shrimp to a plate. Cook in batches if necessary.
3. Add garlic to skillet and cook 30 seconds. Stir in wine, broth, lemon juice and capers. Bring to a simmer. Add shrimp and cook 1 minute, until heated through. Off heat, whisk in butter and stir in parsley. Serve with cooked white rice.

PER SERVING: 424 calories; 14 g fat (5 g sat.); 27 g protein; 41 g carbohydrate; 1 g fiber; 551 mg sodium; 225 mg cholesterol

Turkey Meatball Heroes
(Recipe opposite)

turkey meatball heroes

MAKES: 6 servings. **PREP:** 20 minutes.
BAKE: at 375° for 30 minutes.
BROIL: 3 minutes.

- 1⅓ pounds ground turkey
- ½ cup seasoned bread crumbs
- 2 eggs, lightly beaten
- ¼ cup grated Parmesan cheese
- ¾ teaspoon garlic salt
- ½ teaspoon dried Italian seasoning
- 6 crusty hoagie rolls, about 4 ounces each and 6 inches long, tops split and insides slightly scooped out
- ¾ cup prepared marinara sauce
- 6 slices provolone cheese, about 1 ounce each

1. Heat oven to 375°. Coat a 15 × 10-inch rimmed baking pan with nonstick cooking spray.
2. In a large bowl, mix together the turkey, bread crumbs, eggs, Parmesan cheese, garlic salt and Italian seasoning until well combined. Form into 24 meatballs, about one well-rounded tablespoon each. Place meatballs in the prepared baking pan. Bake, on middle rack in oven, at 375° for 30 minutes, turning halfway through baking time. Remove meatballs from oven; set oven to broil.
3. Place 4 meatballs inside each roll and spoon 2 tablespoons of sauce over the meatballs. Top each with a slice of cheese. Place sandwiches on a broiler pan and cook on the middle rack of the oven for 3 minutes or until lightly browned and cheese melts; be sure that rolls do not get too crispy. Serve immediately.

PER SERVING: 554 calories; 23 g fat (9 g sat.); 37 g protein; 48 g carbohydrate; 3 g fiber; 1,293 mg sodium; 173 mg cholesterol

Every home-style Italian restaurant has its own version of pasta fagioli— or "pasta and beans." Our version is flavored with lots of garlic and spicy Italian ham.

pasta fagioli

MAKES: 6 servings. **PREP:** 10 minutes. **COOK:** 11 minutes.

- 1 tablespoon olive oil
- 3 cloves garlic, finely chopped
- 2 cans (14½ ounces each) reduced-sodium chicken broth
- 2 cans (8 ounces each) no-salt-added tomato sauce
- 1 teaspoon Italian seasoning
- ½ pound ditalini pasta
- 4 carrots, peeled and sliced into coins
- 2 cans (15 ounces each) cannellini beans, drained and rinsed
- ¼ pound capicola (spicy Italian ham)
- ½ teaspoon salt
- ¼ teaspoon black pepper
  Grated Parmesan cheese (optional)

1. Heat oil in saucepan over medium-high heat. Add garlic and cook 1 minute. Stir in broth, **2 cups water,** the tomato sauce and Italian seasoning. Bring to a boil. Add pasta and carrots; simmer for 10 minutes, stirring occasionally.
2. Stir in beans, capicola, salt and black pepper. Heat through.
3. Serve warm with grated Parmesan cheese, if desired.

PER SERVING: 349 calories; 5 g fat (1 g sat.); 17 g protein; 59 g carbohydrate; 9 g fiber; 764 mg sodium; 12 mg cholesterol

the club scene

THINK BIG WHEN YOU SHOP AT BJ'S, SAM'S CLUB OR COSTCO—WE HAVE PERFECT RECIPES FOR THOSE GIANT PACKAGES OF BEEF, CHICKEN AND SHRIMP. **BY MICHAEL TYRRELL**

Now and Later: Broil two steaks—one for tonight's pizza (recipe opposite), the other for a salad tomorrow.

strip steak diane

MAKES: 4 servings. **PREP:** 15 minutes. **COOK:** 14 minutes.

- 2 tablespoons olive oil
- 2 large boneless strip steaks, about 12 ounces each
- ¼ teaspoon salt
- ⅛ teaspoon black pepper
- 2 cups sliced mushrooms (about 6 ounces)
- 1 large shallot, chopped
- 2 cloves garlic, finely chopped
- 2 ounces brandy
- 1 cup beef broth
- 1 tablespoon cornstarch
- 2 tablespoons chopped parsley

1. Heat 1 tablespoon of oil in a large skillet (not nonstick) over medium-high heat. Season the steaks with the salt and pepper. Add to skillet and sauté for 4 minutes per side or until internal temperature registers 135°on an instant-read thermometer. Remove to a plate and loosely cover.

2. Add remaining tablespoon oil to skillet. Stir in mushrooms, shallot and garlic; cook 3 minutes, stirring occasionally. Remove from heat; add brandy. Return to heat and scrape browned bits from bottom of skillet. Cook 1 minute. Mix together broth and cornstarch. Add broth mixture to mushrooms and cook 1 to 2 minutes, until thickened. Stir in parsley.

3. Thinly slice the steak and serve with the mushroom sauce.

PER SERVING: 446 calories; 28 g fat (10 g sat.); 32 g protein; 6 g carbohydrate; 1 g fiber; 448 mg sodium; 78 mg cholesterol

smoky philly cheesesteak pizza

MAKES: 8 pieces. **PREP:** 15 minutes. **COOK:** 5 minutes. **BAKE:** at 425° for 12 minutes. **BROIL:** 10 minutes.

- 1 tablespoon olive oil
- 1 large onion, peeled and cut into ¼-inch slices
- 1 large green pepper, seeds removed, cut into ¼-inch slices
- 1 tube (13.8 ounces) refrigerated pizza crust (such as Pillsbury)
- 2 large boneless strip steaks, about 12 ounces each
- ¼ teaspoon salt
- ⅛ teaspoon black pepper
- 3 tablespoons honey-Dijon mustard
- 4 ounces smoked Gouda cheese, shredded
- 4 ounces shredded cheddar cheese

1. Heat oven to 425°.

2. Heat a large nonstick skillet over medium-high heat. Add olive oil, onion and green pepper. Cook for 5 minutes, stirring occasionally. Set aside.

3. Spray a 16 × 12-inch baking sheet with nonstick cooking spray. Unroll pizza crust and stretch out to 1 inch from edge of baking sheet. Bake at 425° for 12 minutes. Remove from oven.

4. Heat broiler. Season steaks with salt and pepper. Broil for 7 to 8 minutes, turning after 4 minutes, until internal temperature of steaks registers 135° on an instant-read thermometer for medium-rare. Let rest for 5 minutes. Thinly slice 1 steak; reserve second steak for another use (such as steak salad).

5. Spread mustard over crust. Scatter 1½ cups of both cheeses, the onions, peppers and steak slices over the top. Sprinkle remaining cheese over pizza.

6. Broil for 1 to 2 minutes, until heated through and cheese is melted. Cut into 8 pieces and serve immediately.

PER PIECE: 371 calories; 19 g fat (9 g sat.); 20 g protein; 31 g carbohydrate; 1 g fiber; 702 mg sodium; 55 mg cholesterol

Freeze remaining chicken breasts individually so you can grill them for a quick sandwich or salad.

thai chicken curry with jasmine rice

MAKES: 4 servings. **PREP:** 10 minutes. **COOK:** 6 minutes.

- 1 can (14½ ounces) light coconut milk
- 1 tablespoon green curry paste (such as Thai Kitchen)
- 1 tablespoon fish sauce
- 1 tablespoon sugar
- 2 teaspoons cornstarch
- ¾ cup chicken broth
- 1½ pounds boneless, skinless chicken breasts, thinly sliced
- 1 package (16 ounces) frozen Asian stir-fry vegetables, thawed (such as Birds Eye Broccoli Stir-Fry)
- 3 cups cooked jasmine rice

1. Place 1 cup of the coconut milk in a large skillet and stir in the curry paste. Bring to a simmer and cook 1 minute. Add remaining coconut milk, the fish sauce and sugar. Stir cornstarch into the chicken broth and add to skillet.
2. Bring contents of skillet to a simmer. Add the chicken and cook 5 minutes or until cooked through. Add the thawed vegetables and heat through. Serve curry over the cooked jasmine rice.

PER SERVING: 443 calories; 13 g fat (6 g sat.); 43 g protein; 31 g carbohydrate; 3 g fiber; 798 mg sodium; 99 mg cholesterol

chicken murphy

MAKES: 4 servings. **PREP:** 15 minutes. **COOK:** 15 minutes.

- 2 tablespoons olive oil
- 4 cloves garlic, sliced
- 1 can (28 ounces) whole tomatoes
- ½ teaspoon salt
- ¼ teaspoon black pepper
- 1½ pounds boneless, skinless chicken breasts, cut into 2-inch chunks
- 1 large red sweet pepper, seeds removed, cut into ¼-inch slices
- ½ large sweet onion, peeled and cut into ¼-inch slices
- 4 hot cherry peppers, cut in half, seeds removed
- ½ pound orzo, cooked following package directions
  Grated Parmesan cheese, optional

1. Heat oil in a large skillet over medium-high heat. Add garlic and cook for 1 to 2 minutes, until lightly browned and fragrant. Stir in tomatoes with liquid, salt and pepper. Break up tomatoes with the back of a wooden spoon. Cook over medium-high heat for 3 minutes, stirring occasionally.
2. Add chicken, sweet peppers, onion and cherry peppers. Cook over medium-high heat, covered, for 5 minutes. Turn chicken over and stir peppers and onion. Cook for an additional 5 minutes or until chicken is no longer pink.
3. Serve with cooked orzo. Sprinkle with grated cheese, if desired.

PER SERVING: 528 calories; 10 g fat (2 g sat.); 50 g protein; 56 g carbohydrate; 5 g fiber; 927 mg sodium; 99 mg cholesterol

creole shrimp and rice

MAKES: 4 servings. **PREP:** 15 minutes.
COOK: 14 minutes.

- 3 tablespoons vegetable oil
- ¾ pound large shrimp, shelled and deveined
- 3 teaspoons Creole seasoning (such as McCormick)
- 2 large green peppers, seeded and chopped
- ½ large onion, chopped
- 3 ribs celery, thinly sliced
- 2 cloves garlic, finely chopped
- 1 can (14½ ounces) stewed tomatoes
- 4½ cups cooked white rice

1. Heat 2 tablespoons of the oil in a large nonstick skillet over medium-high heat. Add shrimp and season with 1 teaspoon of the Creole seasoning. Sauté for 2 minutes per side. Remove to a plate.
2. Add remaining tablespoon oil, the peppers, onion, celery and garlic. Cook for 5 minutes, stirring occasionally. Scrape up any browned bits in bottom of skillet. Add tomatoes and remaining 2 teaspoons Creole seasoning. Break up tomatoes with the back of a wooden spoon. Simmer, covered, for 5 minutes.
3. Stir in shrimp and heat through. Serve with cooked rice.

PER SERVING: 504 calories; 12 g fat (2 g sat.);
22 g protein; 77 g carbohydrate; 5 g fiber;
919 mg sodium; 126 mg cholesterol

shrimp scampi

MAKES: 4 servings. **PREP:** 10 minutes. **COOK:** 9 minutes.

- 3 tablespoons olive oil
- 3 tablespoons unsalted butter
- 6 cloves garlic, peeled and finely chopped
- ¾ pound large shrimp, shelled and deveined
- ⅓ cup dry white wine
- 1 tablespoon lemon juice
- ¼ teaspoon salt
- ¼ teaspoon black pepper
- 3 tablespoons chopped flat-leaf parsley
- ¾ pound angel hair pasta

1. Heat 2 tablespoons of the oil and 2 tablespoons of the butter in a large skillet over medium-high heat. Add garlic and cook 1 minute. Add shrimp and cook 1 minute on each side. Stir in wine, lemon juice, salt and pepper; cook 2 minutes. Stir in parsley and remove from heat.
2. While shrimp is cooking prepare pasta following package directions. Reserve ½ cup of the cooking liquid and drain.
3. Add pasta to shrimp in skillet and toss to coat. Stir in cooking liquid and remaining tablespoon each of the oil and butter. Stir until pasta is coated and butter melted. Serve immediately.

PER SERVING: 576 calories; 21 g fat (7 g sat.);
25 g protein; 67 g carbohydrate; 3 g fiber;
301 mg sodium; 149 mg cholesterol

This garlicky recipe calls for large shrimp. There are usually between 21 and 30 large shrimp in a pound.

food **university**

CANNING 101   ALL YOU NEED TO TURN LATE SUMMER VEGETABLES—WE PICKED TOMATOES AND ZUCCHINI—INTO FLAVOR-PACKED STAPLES ARE A CAN-DO ATTITUDE AND THE STEPS ON THE FOLLOWING PAGE.   **BY JULIE MILTENBERGER**

Canning may feel a bit *Little House on the Prairie*, but it's a great idea for filling your shelves on the cheap—and a fun way to spend an afternoon. Reuse the jars and bands from year to year, but replace lids annually for a tight seal. Your local hardware store or a well-stocked supermarket will have everything you need. The investment is small compared to the payoff.

garlic and basil tomatoes

MAKES: 4 pint jars (16 servings). **PREP:** 30 minutes.
PROCESS: in boiling water bath for 40 minutes.

- 2½ pounds ripe tomatoes
- 4 tablespoons bottled lemon juice
- 16 fresh basil leaves
- 2 teaspoons kosher salt
- ½ teaspoon garlic powder

1. Prepare boiling water canner (see steps A and B). Heat jars and lids in barely simmering water until ready for use. Have bands handy on countertop. Bring a second pot of water to boiling.
2. Wash tomatoes and dip in boiling water for 30 to 60 seconds, or until skins split. Keep water boiling. Plunge tomatoes into cool water, then peel. Core tomatoes and cut into quarters or wedges.
3. Remove jars from simmering water (step C). Pour 1 tablespoon lemon juice into each jar. Pack tomatoes into jars, tucking basil leaves between wedges, fitting tightly. Sprinkle ½ teaspoon kosher salt and ⅛ teaspoon garlic powder into each jar. Ladle some of the boiling water over tomatoes to fill jar, leaving a ½-inch headspace.
4. Remove air bubbles from jars, tapping lightly on countertop if needed. Wipe jar rims (step D), then center lids on jars. Screw on bands, adjusting until fingertip tight.
5. Process jars in boiling water bath, covered, for 40 minutes (step E). Remove jars to a kitchen cloth and cool. Check lid for seal after 24 hours; when pressed, lids should not pop up and down. Keep in cool place up to one year.

PER SERVING: 14 calories; 0 g fat (0 g sat.); 1 g protein; 3 g carbohydrate; 1 g fiber; 245 mg sodium; 0 mg cholesterol

zucchini pickles

MAKES: 2 pints (8 servings). **PREP:** 10 minutes. **STAND:** 2 hours.
COOK: 5 minutes. **PROCESS:** in boiling water bath for 15 minutes.

- 1 pound zucchini, thinly sliced
- 1 small onion, peeled and thinly sliced
- 2 tablespoons kosher salt
- 1½ cups white vinegar
- 1 cup sugar
- 1 teaspoon mustard seeds
- ½ teaspoon turmeric

1. Combine zucchini and onions in a large nonreactive bowl. Cover with cool water and stir in salt. Let stand at room temperature for 2 hours.
2. Prepare boiling water canner (see steps A and B). Heat jars and lids in barely simmering water until ready for use. Have bands handy on countertop.
3. Drain zucchini-onion mixture. In a medium-size saucepan, combine vinegar, sugar, mustard seeds and turmeric. Bring to a boil. Add zucchini and onions and simmer for 5 minutes. Pack pickle mixture into hot jars, leaving a ½-inch headspace. Discard excess liquid.
4. Remove air bubbles from jars, tapping lightly on countertop if needed. Wipe jar rims (step D), then center lids on jars. Screw on bands, adjusting until fingertip tight.
5. Process jars in boiling water bath, covered, for 15 minutes (step E). Remove jars to a kitchen cloth and cool. Check lid for seal after 24 hours; when pressed, lids should not pop up and down. Keep in cool place up to one year.

PER SERVING: 122 calories; 0 g fat (0 g sat.); 1 g protein; 28 g carbohydrate; 1 g fiber; 1,454 mg sodium; 0 mg cholesterol

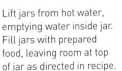

a Wash jars and lids with soapy water. Then place in a large pot of water. Bring to a simmer to sterilize.

b To process (seal) the jars, you will need a boiling water canner or a large covered pot fitted with a rack in the bottom.

c Lift jars from hot water, emptying water inside jar. Fill jars with prepared food, leaving room at top of jar as directed in recipe.

d Remove air bubbles from jars; wipe any food bits or liquid from jar rim— anything that might prevent lid from forming a complete seal.

e Place filled jars in boiling water canner or pot (there should be at least 2 inches of water over jars). Begin processing time.

november

Maple-Apple Sweet Potatoes
page 275

FEASTING BEGINS IN EARNEST THIS MONTH.
TRY SOMETHING NEW WITH YOUR THANKSGIVING
TURKEY, THEN TRANSITION TO THE WINTER HOLIDAYS
WITH A SELECTION OF FABULOUS SWEETS.

Holiday Carrot Cake
page 278

Beef and Sausage Stew
page 284

Chocolate Peppermint Cookies
page 293

THIS CAKE ISN'T TRICKY TO MAKE, BUT IT'S A REAL TREAT.
BY KAREN TACK

m&m's pumpkin cake

MAKES: 24 servings. **PREP:** 25 minutes. **BAKE:** at 350° for 65 minutes. **COOL:** about an hour. **DECORATE:** about an hour.

Cake:
- 4 cups all-purpose flour
- 1 tablespoon baking powder
- 1½ teaspoons baking soda
- 1 teaspoon cinnamon
- ½ teaspoon salt
- 1 can (15 ounces) pumpkin puree
- ½ cup milk
- 2 teaspoons vanilla extract
- 1 cup (2 sticks) unsalted butter, softened
- 2 cups sugar
- 5 eggs

Decoration:
- 1 can (16 ounces) vanilla frosting
  Orange gel food coloring (such as Wilton)
- 2 bags (7 ounces each) orange M&M's candies (about 2 cups)
- 34 yellow or brown M&M's
- 1 chocolate-covered candy bar (such as Snickers)

1. Cake: Heat oven to 350°. Coat two 1.5-liter Pyrex bowls with nonstick cooking spray; set aside.
2. Whisk together the flour, baking powder, soda, cinnamon and salt. Mix the pumpkin, milk and vanilla in a small bowl to blend.
3. Beat the butter in a large bowl with an electric mixer until smooth. Gradually add the sugar and beat until light and fluffy, about 3 minutes. Add the eggs, one at a time, beating well after each addition. Add the flour mixture, alternating with the pumpkin mixture, ending with the flour mixture. Beat just until smooth.
4. Divide the batter evenly between the prepared bowls. Bake at 350° in the center of the oven for 55 to 65 minutes, or until golden and a toothpick inserted in centers of cakes comes out clean. Transfer bowls to a wire rack and cool 15 minutes. Invert cakes onto racks and remove bowls; cool completely (about an hour).

5. Decoration: Trim the tops of the cakes with a serrated knife to make level. Tint the frosting orange with the food coloring. Place one cake layer, cut-side up, on a serving platter. Spread the cut side with ½ cup of the frosting. Place the other cake layer on top, cut-side down. Trim any excess to make round.
6. Spread a thin layer of frosting on half the cake, from top to bottom. Start with the nose: In the center of the frosted area, place 3 yellow or brown M&M's (see photo, left)—2 on the bottom and 1 on the top—to make a triangle nose. Place 2 orange candies above the nose. Then begin the eyes: Attach 3 yellow candies along the same line as the orange candies above nose, to the left. Then place 2 yellow candies above that row and end with a single yellow candy. Repeat on the other side of the nose. Below the nose, make an upside-down triangle using 6 orange candies. Make a yellow candy mouth, beginning with 7 candies arranged in a "V" around the orange triangle. Then use 12 additional yellow candies to finish the mouth. Fill in with more orange candies close together on the frosted area. When that area is covered, spread another area with the frosting and add more candies. Repeat until the entire cake is covered with orange candies.
7. Cut the candy bar in half crosswise on the diagonal to fashion a stem. Make a small hole in the top of the cake and press the candy bar half, cut-side down, into the top of the cake, for the stem. Refrigerate to firm frosting.

PER SERVING: 410 calories; 16 g fat (8 g sat.); 5 g protein; 61 g carbohydrate; 2 g fiber; 247 mg sodium; 67 mg cholesterol

THESE GINGER PEOPLE ARE NICELY SPICED AND CUTE AS CAN BE.
BY JULIE MILTENBERGER

gingerbread men

MAKES: 2½ dozen assorted-size cookies.
PREP: 20 minutes. **BAKE:** at 350° for 13 minutes.
DECORATE: 1 hour.

- 2¾ cups all-purpose flour
- ¾ teaspoon baking soda
- 1 tablespoon ground ginger
- 1 teaspoon ground cinnamon
- ½ teaspoon ground cloves
- ¼ teaspoon salt
- ½ cup (1 stick) unsalted butter, softened
- ½ cup packed dark-brown sugar
- 1 large egg
- ½ cup original molasses (such as Grandma's brand)
   Royal Icing (see recipe, right), Red Hot cinnamon candies for decorating

1. In a medium-size bowl, whisk together the flour, baking soda, ginger, cinnamon, cloves and salt. Set aside.
2. In a large bowl, beat butter and sugar until smooth. Beat in egg, then molasses. Stir flour mixture into butter mixture. Divide dough into 2 halves. Wrap; chill 2 hours.
3. Heat oven to 350°. On a well-floured surface, roll half of dough to ⅛-inch thickness. Cut shapes with assorted-size gingerbread cookie cutters; transfer to ungreased baking sheets. Reroll scraps; cut. Repeat with rest of dough.
4. Bake at 350° for 13 minutes. Transfer cookies to racks to cool. Decorate with Royal Icing and assorted candies.

royal icing

MAKES: about 1½ cups. **PREP:** 10 minutes.

- 2 cups confectioners' sugar
- 1½ tablespoons powdered egg whites

In a medium-size bowl, combine confectioners' sugar, powdered egg whites and **3 tablespoons water.** Beat on medium speed for 1 minute to blend, then increase speed to high and beat 5 minutes until thick and shiny. Transfer to a pastry bag fitted with a round tip or a resealable plastic bag; snip small corner off bag. Pipe icing over cookies and add Red Hot cinnamon candies to decorate.

PER ONE 3½-INCH COOKIE: 134 calories; 3 g fat (2 g sat.); 2 g protein; 25 g carbohydrate; 0 g fiber; 62 mg sodium; 15 mg cholesterol

Food styling: Karen Tack. Prop styling: Leslie Siegel.

PHOTOGRAPHY BY RITA MAAS

american pies

PERFECT TAKES ON THE CLASSICS—FLAKY CRUST
AND DELICIOUS PUMPKIN, APPLE OR PECAN FILLING.

**Pecan Pie
(Recipe page 271)**
The rich, nutty
center of this pie is
as much confection
as it is pie filling.

The creamy filling of this pumpkin pie is infused with the flavor of butterscotch and sweet spices. The cut-out church-window crust is made with a lattice cutter, which comes in a variety of designs. You can also cut the top crust with a cookie cutter.

Lattice-Topped Pumpkin Pie
(Recipe page 270)

Photos (from left): Andy Lyons; Lara Robby

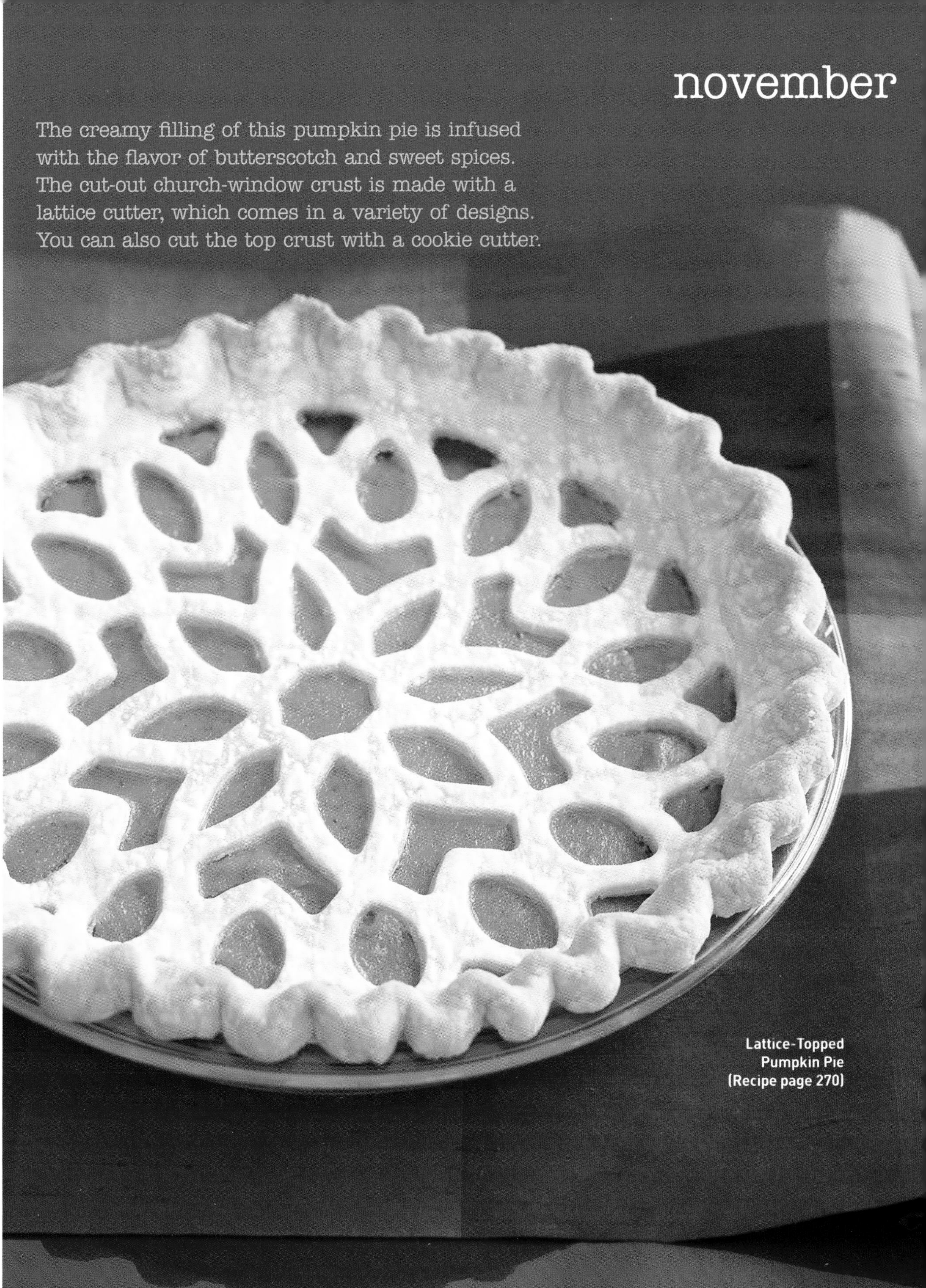

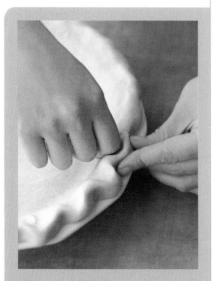

basic pastry

MAKES: enough for 2-crust pie.
PREP: 15 minutes.
REFRIGERATE: 30 minutes.

- 2½ cups all-purpose flour
- 1 teaspoon salt
- ½ cup (1 stick) unsalted butter, cut into pieces and chilled
- ½ cup solid vegetable shortening, cut into pieces and chilled
- 6 to 7 tablespoons cold water

1. Mix flour and salt in bowl.
2. With pastry blender or fingertips, rub butter and shortening into flour mixture until texture of coarse meal.
3. Gradually add water, tossing with fork, until mixture begins to mass together.
4. Divide dough in half; shape and flatten into disks. Wrap in plastic wrap. Refrigerate until well chilled, about 30 minutes.

Food Processor Method: Combine flour and salt in food processor. Pulse with on-and-off motion just to mix. Add butter and shortening. Whirl until texture of coarse meal, about 30 seconds. With machine running, add water in a slow and steady stream just until mixture begins to mass together.

PER SERVING: 118 calories; 8 g fat (3 g sat.); 1 g protein; 10 g carbohydrate; 0 g fiber; 98 mg sodium; 10 mg cholesterol

lattice-topped pumpkin pie

MAKES: 12 servings. **PREP:** 10 minutes. **COOK:** 5 minutes.
BAKE: at 425° for 25 minutes; at 350° for 35 minutes.

- 1 Basic Pastry (see recipe, left)
- ¾ cup butterscotch chips
- ½ cup heavy cream
- 1 can (15 ounces) solid-pack pumpkin puree
- 1 egg plus 1 egg yolk
- ¼ cup sugar
- 1 teaspoon pumpkin pie spice
- ¼ teaspoon salt
- ¼ teaspoon ground ginger
  Pinch ground nutmeg
  Whipped cream (optional)

1. Heat oven to 425°. Roll out 1 pastry to an 11-inch circle and fit into a 9-inch round pie plate. Decoratively crimp edge. Refrigerate until ready to fill.
2. In a small saucepan, combine butterscotch chips and heavy cream. Heat over medium heat about 5 minutes, whisking occasionally, until smooth. Let cool slightly.
3. Meanwhile, whisk pumpkin puree, egg and egg yolk, sugar, pumpkin pie spice, salt, ginger and nutmeg. Whisk in butterscotch mixture until incorporated. Spoon into crust and spread smooth.

4. Roll out second crust to a 10-inch circle. Spread on top of a lattice pie cutter (see Note), then use rolling pin to cut and create lattice pattern. Carefully remove crust from lattice cutter (try not to stretch) and place on top of pie. Fold over edge and crimp.
5. Bake at 425° for 25 minutes, then reduce oven temperature to 350° and bake an additional 35 minutes, until crust is browned and pie puffs slightly. Cover edge of pie with foil if browning too quickly. Cool at room temperature on a wire rack. Serve with whipped cream alongside, if desired.

Note: Lattice pie cutters are available at baking and home supply stores. Or you can cut decorative holes in the second crust with a cookie cutter and bake as directed.

PER SERVING 250 calories; 15 g fat (8 g sat.); 2 g protein; 27 g carbohydrate; 1 g fiber; 221 mg sodium; 54 mg cholesterol

pecan pie

MAKES: 12 servings.
PREP: 10 minutes.
BAKE: at 350° for 55 minutes.

- 4 eggs
- ½ cup packed dark-brown sugar
- ½ cup granulated sugar
- 1 cup light corn syrup
- 1½ teaspoons vanilla extract
- 1½ cups pecan halves
- ½ Basic Pastry
  (see recipe, page 270)
  Whipped cream or topping
  (optional)

1. Heat oven to 350°.
2. Beat eggs slightly in bowl. Add both kinds of sugar, the corn syrup and vanilla. Stir in pecans. Roll out pastry to a 12-inch circle. Fit into a 9-inch deep-dish pie plate. Decoratively crimp pastry edge; set pie plate on heavy-duty baking sheet. Pour filling into pie shell.
3. Bake at 350° for 55 minutes, until knife inserted midway between center and rim tests clean. Cool on rack to room temperature. Serve with whipped cream or topping, if desired.

PER SERVING: 380 calories; 19 g fat (5 g sat.); 5 g protein; 50 g carbohydrate; 2 g fiber; 142 mg sodium; 81 mg cholesterol

apple crumb pie

MAKES: 12 servings. **PREP:** 20 minutes.
BAKE: at 375° for 30 minutes; at 350° for 30 minutes. **COOL:** 1½ hours.

- ½ Basic Pastry (see recipe, page 270)

Crumb:
- 1½ cups all-purpose flour
- ¾ cup packed light-brown sugar
- ¾ teaspoon ground cinnamon
- ¼ teaspoon salt
  Pinch ground cloves
- ¾ cup (1½ sticks) unsalted butter, cut into pieces and chilled
- ⅓ cup chopped walnuts (optional)

Filling:
- 6 Golden Delicious apples (2¾ pounds), peeled, cored and cut into ½-inch dice
- ¾ cup packed light-brown sugar
- ¼ cup all-purpose flour
- ½ teaspoon ground cinnamon
  Pinch ground cloves
- 1 tablespoon confectioners' sugar

1. Arrange a rack in the lowest slot of your oven. Heat oven to 375°. Roll out pastry to an 11-inch circle and fit into a 9-inch pie plate. Decoratively crimp edge. Refrigerate until you are ready to add filling.

2. Crumb: Combine flour, brown sugar, cinnamon, salt and cloves in bowl. Rub in butter with fingertips until crumbly. Stir in nuts, if using.
3. Filling: In a large bowl, toss together apples, brown sugar, flour, cinnamon and cloves.
4. Spoon filling into pie shell, mounding slightly in the center. Top filling with crumb topping. Place on small foil-lined baking sheet.
5. Bake at 375° for 30 minutes. Reduce temperature to 350°; bake 30 minutes more, until fruit is tender. Loosely tent pie with aluminum foil during last 20 minutes. Let cool for at least 1½ hours. (Can be made a day ahead. Cover pie and store at room temperature.) Dust with confectioners' sugar before serving.

PER SERVING: 421 calories; 19 g fat (9 g sat.); 4 g protein; 63 g carbohydrate; 3 g fiber; 130 mg sodium; 34 mg cholesterol

turkey time

ANY WAY YOU SERVE IT—
ROASTED,
GRILLED
OR FRIED—
THEY'LL GOBBLE IT UP.

PHOTOGRAPHY BY DAVID PRINCE

Preparing the Bird

To thaw, place frozen 12- to 16-pound (nonbasted) turkey in its packaging on a tray in the refrigerator; it will take 24 hours for each 4 to 5 pounds. When thawed, remove giblets and neck; rinse well with cold water. Brine turkey: In a large stockpot, combine **⅔ cup kosher salt, ⅔ cup firmly packed dark-brown sugar, 1 cup hot water, 3 cups cold water, 1 onion, halved and thinly sliced, 2 cloves garlic (slightly crushed), 1 jalapeño (sliced)** and **12 whole black peppercorns (crushed).** Place turkey in pot. Add enough water to cover by 1 inch. Cover and refrigerate overnight but not longer than 8 hours. Dry turkey inside and out, including cavities, and proceed with one of the following methods.

roasted turkey

MAKES: 12 servings. **PREP:** 15 minutes.
ROAST: at 450° for 30 minutes; at 350° for 1½ hours.

- 1 **brined 12- to 16-pound turkey, patted dry**
- 1 **onion, chopped**
- 2 **carrots, peeled and halved lengthwise**
- 2 **ribs celery, halved crosswise**
  Cooking oil

1. Heat oven to 450°.
2. Place onion, carrots and celery inside turkey cavity. Twist wing tips behind back. Tie up legs or tuck them into flap of skin. Place turkey, breast-side up, on rack in large roasting pan. Brush with oil. Roast at 450° for 30 minutes.
3. Reduce oven temperature to 350°. Roast turkey at 350°, basting every 15 minutes with pan liquid, for 1½ hours or until instant-read thermometer inserted into thickest part of thigh registers 180°. When turkey is ¾ done, loosely cover breast and top of drumsticks with lightweight foil to prevent overcooking. Remove from oven; tent with foil. Let stand 20 minutes before carving.

PER SERVING: 609 calories; 31 g fat (8 g sat.); 73 g protein; 4 g carbohydrate; 1 g fiber; 1,021 mg sodium; 244 mg cholesterol

grilled turkey

MAKES: 12 servings. **PREP:** 15 minutes.
GRILL: 2¼-3 hours.

- 1 **brined 12- to 16-pound turkey, patted dry**

1. For charcoal grill, arrange medium-hot coals around a drip pan or foil pan. Test for medium heat above the pan. Twist turkey wing tips behind back. Tie up legs or tuck into flap of skin. Place turkey on grill rack over pan. Cover; grill for 2 to 3 hours or until an instant-read thermometer in thigh registers 180° and meat is no longer pink. Add coals every 45 to 60 minutes and cut band of skin or string the last 1 hour of grilling. (For a gas grill, preheat grill, reduce heat to medium. Adjust for indirect cooking. Grill as above.)
2. Remove from grill. Cover with foil; let stand for 15 minutes before carving.

PER SERVING: 580 calories; 29 g fat (8 g sat.); 73 g protein; 2 g carbohydrate; 0 g fiber; 1,008 mg sodium; 244 mg cholesterol

fried turkey

MAKES: 12 servings **PREP:** 15 minutes.
FRY: 3 minutes per pound

- 1 **brined 12- to 16-pound turkey, patted dry**
- 3 **quarts peanut oil or other cooking oil**
- 1 **turkey fryer**

1. Consult the manufacturer's instructions for details. Place turkey fryer on an open and level dirt, cement or grassy area.* Heat oil to 400°. (Oil can take about 40 minutes to heat.) When the oil reaches 400°, very slowly lower turkey in basket into oil. Oil will rise and bubble initially. Check temperature; increase or lower as needed to maintain 375°. Fry turkey 3 minutes per pound. Carefully remove from oil to check for doneness. Insert an instant-read thermometer into thickest part of thigh, not touching bone. Temperature should read 180°. Remove from oil; drain on rack for a few minutes. Loosely cover with foil and let stand for 20 minutes before carving.

PER SERVING: 739 calories; 47 g fat (11 g sat.); 73 g protein; 2 g carbohydrate; 0 g fiber; 1,008 mg sodium; 244 mg cholesterol

* Certain electric turkey fryers can be used indoors. Propane fryers (above) should never be used indoors or in a garage. Do not fry on a wood deck, which could catch fire.

green bean salad

MAKES: 8 servings. **PREP:** 15 minutes.
COOK: 11 minutes.

Vinaigrette:
- 2 tablespoons red wine vinegar
- 2 teaspoons Dijon mustard
- ¼ teaspoon salt
- ¼ teaspoon black pepper
- 5 tablespoons extra-virgin olive oil
- 4 tablespoons snipped fresh chives

Green Beans:
- 2 pounds green beans, trimmed
- 1 tablespoon extra-virgin olive oil
- 2 large shallots, thinly sliced
- ⅓ cup dried cranberries
- 2 cloves garlic, finely chopped
- 3 ounces Parmesan, shaved with a vegetable peeler

1. Vinaigrette: In a small bowl, whisk vinegar, mustard, salt and pepper. Drizzle in the olive oil, whisking continuously until dressing is emulsified. Add chives; set aside.

2. Green Beans: Bring large pot of lightly salted water to boil. Add beans; simmer 5 minutes or until crisp-tender. Drain; place in serving bowl. Toss with vinaigrette dressing.

3. Heat the oil in a medium-size skillet over medium heat. Add shallots, cranberries and garlic. Cook about 6 minutes or until softened. Pour over beans and toss. Top with Parmesan cheese and serve.

PER SERVING: 198 calories; 14 g fat (3 g sat.);
6 g protein; 14 g carbohydrate; 4 g fiber;
333 mg sodium; 9 mg cholesterol

scallion and cheddar popovers

MAKES: 8 servings. **PREP:** 10 minutes. **BAKE:** at 450° for 15 minutes; at 350° for 15 minutes.

- 1 cup all-purpose flour
- ½ teaspoon salt
- 2 eggs
- 1 cup milk
- 1 cup shredded sharp Cheddar cheese
- 3 scallions, trimmed and chopped

1. Coat 8 cups of a popover or standard muffin pan with nonstick cooking spray. Fill empty cups with ½ inch of water (so as not to burn pan). Heat oven to 450°.

2. In bowl, whisk together flour and salt. In second bowl, whisk together eggs and milk. Add to flour mixture; stir just until blended. Fold in cheese and scallions.

3. Fill prepared cups about ¾ full (about ⅓ cup batter in each). Bake at 450° for 15 minutes. Reduce oven temperature to 350° and bake for 10 to 15 minutes, until browned and puffed. Keep oven closed until end of baking time or popovers will deflate.

2. Remove popovers from oven and immediately remove from pan. Pierce sides once with a knife to release steam. Serve warm. If needed, reheat at 350° for 5 minutes to crisp outside edges.

PER SERVING: 150 calories; 7 g fat (0 g sat.);
8 g protein; 14 g carbohydrate; 1 g fiber;
263 mg sodium; 71 mg cholesterol

This menu features all of the traditional Thanksgiving foods but with fresh touches, like dried cranberries adding color and flavor to a crunchy and cool green bean salad.

corn bread dressing

MAKES: 8 servings. **PREP:** 25 minutes.
BAKE: at 400° for 1 hour. **COOK:** 22 minutes.

    2 boxes (8.5 ounces each) corn muffin
       mix (such as Jiffy)
    2 eggs
    ⅔ cup milk
    8 ounces bacon, chopped
  1½ cups frozen corn kernels, thawed
    1 small onion, chopped
    3 cloves garlic, minced
    2 medium-size carrots, diced (about ½ cup)
    1 rib celery, diced
  1½ teaspoons chopped fresh sage
    ½ teaspoon salt
    ½ teaspoon black pepper
       Pinch cayenne
    3 cups low-sodium chicken broth

1. Heat oven to 400°. Coat two 8 × 8 × 2-inch
baking dishes and one 13 × 9 × 2-inch dish
with nonstick cooking spray; set aside.
2. Stir together corn muffin mix with eggs
and milk. Divide batter between square
baking dishes and bake at 400° for about
15 minutes or until lightly browned; cool

completely on wire racks. Cut corn bread
into ½-inch cubes and spread onto a
rimmed baking sheet.
3. Bake at 400° for 15 minutes or until
slightly crisp. Remove from oven and let
cool. Leave oven on 400°.
4. Meanwhile, cook bacon in a large
nonstick saucepan over medium-high heat
for 10 minutes, then transfer to a paper-
towel-lined plate.
5. Pour out all but 1 tablespoon of the bacon
fat and place saucepan over medium-high
heat. Add corn and onion and cook 5 minutes.
Add garlic, carrots, celery, sage, salt, pepper
and cayenne to skillet; cook, stirring, for
7 minutes or until vegetables are softened.
6. Add the broth and bacon to saucepan
and stir to combine. Add corn bread and
stir gently until liquid is absorbed.
7. Pour contents of pot into prepared
13 × 9 × 2-inch baking dish and bake at
400° for about 30 minutes or until top is
golden brown.

PER SERVING: 378 calories; 13 g fat (0 g sat.);
11 g protein; 53 g carbohydrate; 2 g fiber;
1,188 mg sodium; 73 mg cholesterol

maple-apple sweet potatoes

MAKES: 8 servings. **PREP:** 15 minutes.
COOK: 12 minutes.

    3 pounds sweet potatoes, peeled and
       cut into 1-inch chunks
    6 tablespoons unsalted butter
    ¾ cup maple syrup
    ½ teaspoon pumpkin pie spice
    ½ teaspoon salt
    ½ cup toasted pecans, coarsely chopped

1. Bring a large pot of lightly salted
water to boiling. Add sweet potatoes and
boil 12 minutes, until tender. Drain and
return to pot.
2. Meanwhile, in a small skillet, melt
butter over medium heat. Stir in maple
syrup, pumpkin pie spice and salt. Cook
for 1 minute; stir until sauce is smooth.
3. Add butter mixture to pot and mash to
desired consistency. Transfer sweet
potatoes to a serving dish. Sprinkle top
evenly with chopped pecans.
Do-Ahead Tip: If not serving right away,
do not top with pecans; spoon potatoes
into an ovenproof casserole. Let cool
completely; cover and refrigerate for
up to 2 days. To serve, bring to room
temperature. Reheat at 325° for
30 minutes. Sprinkle toasted nuts over
top immediately before serving.

PER SERVING: 295 calories; 10 g fat (6 g sat.);
3 g protein; 51 g carbohydrate; 4 g fiber;
195 mg sodium; 23 mg cholesterol

the
sweet spot

HOLIDAY DESSERTS THAT LOOK INCREDIBLE AND TASTE EVEN BETTER.

Double Chocolate Cake
(Recipe page 281)

Caramel and Chocolate Tartlets [Recipe page 281] There is chocolate in the crust and drizzled over the caramel-cream top of these tiny tarts.

holiday carrot cake

MAKES: 16 servings. **PREP:** 25 minutes.
BAKE: at 350° for 44 minutes.
COOL: 10 minutes.

Cake:

- 2½ cups all-purpose flour
- 1 teaspoon baking soda
- 1 teaspoon baking powder
- 1½ teaspoons pumpkin pie spice
- ½ teaspoon salt
- 1 cup granulated sugar
- ¾ cup packed light-brown sugar
- 1½ cups vegetable oil
- 4 eggs
- 2 teaspoons vanilla extract
- 3 medium-size carrots, peeled and shredded (about 2 cups)
- ¾ cup walnuts, chopped
- ½ cup sweetened dried cranberries

Frosting:

- 2 packages (8 ounces each) cream cheese, at room temperature
- ½ cup (1 stick) unsalted butter, softened
- 1 teaspoon vanilla extract
- 3 cups confectioners' sugar
  Cranberries and walnuts, for garnish

1. Heat oven to 350°. Coat two 9 × 2-inch round cake pans with cooking spray. Line bottoms with waxed paper. Coat paper with spray.

2. Cake: In medium-size bowl, whisk flour, baking soda, baking powder, pumpkin pie spice and salt. In large bowl, beat sugars, oil, eggs and vanilla on medium speed until blended. On low, beat in flour mixture until smooth. Stir in carrots, nuts and cranberries. Divide batter between pans, spreading evenly.

3. Bake at 350° for 42 to 44 minutes or until toothpick inserted in center comes out clean. Cool on wire rack 10 minutes. Turn out and cool completely.

4. Frosting: In large bowl, beat cream cheese, butter and vanilla until creamy. Gradually beat in confectioners' sugar until smooth.

5. With serrated knife, cut each cake horizontally in half. Place one layer on cake plate and spread with 1 cup frosting. Repeat two more times with layers and frosting. Place remaining layer, cut-side down, on top and spread with remaining frosting. Garnish with berries and nuts.

PER SERVING: 654 calories; 42 g fat (12 g sat.); 6 g protein; 67 g carbohydrate; 2 g fiber; 295 mg sodium; 99 mg cholesterol

irish coffee chiffon pie

MAKES: 8 servings. **PREP:** 25 minutes. **BAKE:** at 325° for 15 minutes. **COOK:** 5 minutes. **REFRIGERATE:** at least 2 hours.

Crust:

- 8 cinnamon graham cracker boards, finely crushed (about 1⅔ cups)
- 6 tablespoons unsalted butter, melted
- 2 tablespoons sugar

Filling:

- ⅔ cup sugar
- 4 egg yolks
- 1 envelope unflavored gelatin
- ⅛ teaspoon salt
- ⅓ cup Baileys with a Hint of Coffee
- 2 tablespoons powdered egg whites mixed with 6 tablespoons warm water
- 1 cup heavy cream
  Cocoa powder and chocolate-covered coffee beans, to garnish (optional)

1. Heat oven to 325°.

2. Crust: In a medium-size bowl, stir together graham cracker crumbs, butter and sugar until moistened. Press into the bottom and up side of 9-inch tart pan with removable bottom. Bake at 325° for 15 minutes, until lightly browned. Remove from oven and cool completely.

3. Filling: In small saucepan, stir together ⅓ cup of the sugar, **½ cup water,** egg yolks, gelatin and salt. Heat over medium-low heat, stirring, until slightly thickened and temperature registers 160° on an instant-read thermometer, about 5 minutes. Strain into a large glass or plastic bowl and stir in Baileys.

4. Beat egg white mixture until soft peaks form. Gradually beat in remaining ⅓ cup sugar until the peaks are stiff. In medium-size bowl, beat the heavy cream to form soft peaks; refrigerate.

5. Place bowl of egg yolk mixture in large bowl of ice water. Stir occasionally until mixture mounds slightly, 8 to 10 minutes.

6. Fold beaten whites into yolk mixture. Fold in whipped cream until no streaks of white remain. Spoon into crust; cover. Refrigerate for at least 2 hours. Garnish with cocoa power and chocolate-covered coffee beans, if desired.

PER SERVING: 376 calories; 25 g fat (14 g sat.); 4 g protein; 34 g carbohydrate; 0 g fiber; 154 mg sodium; 172 mg cholesterol

twisted berry-nut bread

MAKES: 16 servings. **PREP:** 40 minutes.
RISE: 2 hours. **BAKE:** at 350° for 30 minutes.

Dough:

- ¾ cup milk
- ⅓ cup sugar
- 3 tablespoons unsalted butter
- ½ teaspoon salt
- 1 packet (¼ ounce) active dry yeast
- ¼ cup warm water (105° to 115°)
- 3 eggs
- 4¼ cups all-purpose flour, plus more for dusting

Filling:

- ¾ cup seedless raspberry jam
- ¾ cup chopped walnuts, toasted
- 1 tablespoon sugar

1. Dough: Heat milk, sugar, butter and salt in a small saucepan over medium heat until butter melts. Let cool 30 minutes.

2. Sprinkle yeast over warm water in large bowl; stir to dissolve. Add milk mixture, 2 of the eggs and 1¼ cups flour. Beat 3 minutes on medium-low until smooth, scraping down side of bowl. Stir in about 3 cups flour to form dough.

3. Turn dough out onto floured surface. Knead dough until smooth and elastic, 3 to 5 minutes, adding flour as needed to prevent sticking. Place dough in large oiled bowl, turning dough to coat. Cover with plastic wrap and let rise in warm place, away from drafts, until doubled, 1 hour.

4. Punch dough down; place on floured surface. Cover; let rest 15 minutes.

5. Lightly coat 15 × 10 × 1-inch baking sheet with nonstick cooking spray.

6. Filling: Roll dough into 14-inch square. Brush with jam, leaving 1-inch border. Sprinkle with walnuts.

7. Beginning with one edge, roll dough, jelly-roll-style. Pinch seam closed, then carefully transfer to prepared baking sheet, seam-side down; reshape into 14-inch roll. Cut roll in half lengthwise. With cut-sides facing up and beginning in middle and working to one edge, loosely cross strips back and forth, keeping cut-sides up as much as possible; pinch ends together and under to seal. Repeat with remaining half of strips. Cover with plastic wrap and let rise in warm place until doubled, 30 to 45 minutes.

8. Heat oven to 350°. Lightly beat remaining egg. Brush over top of bread, then sprinkle with sugar.

9. Bake at 350° for about 30 minutes or until lightly golden and loaf sounds hollow when tapped. Remove to wire rack to cool completely.

PER SERVING: 229 calories; 6 g fat (2 g sat.);
6 g protein; 38 g carbohydrate; 1 g fiber;
92 mg sodium; 46 mg cholesterol

double chocolate cake

MAKES: 16 servings. **PREP:** 30 minutes.
BAKE: at 350° for 50 minutes.
COOK: 3 minutes. **MICROWAVE:** 1 minute.

Cake:
- 2 cups all-purpose flour
- ½ cup unsweetened cocoa powder
- 1 box (3.4 ounces) chocolate cook-and-serve pudding and pie mix
- 1 tablespoon baking powder
- ½ teaspoon salt
- ¾ cup (1½ sticks) butter substitute (such as I Can't Believe It's Not Butter for Baking) or unsalted butter, softened
- 1½ cups sugar
- 3 eggs
- 1 cup milk
- 2 teaspoons vanilla extract

Chocolate Glaze:
- 6 tablespoons heavy cream
- 1 small bag (6 ounces) semisweet chocolate chips

Drizzle:
- 3 squares (1 ounce each) white baking chocolate, broken apart
- 1 teaspoon vegetable oil

1. Cake: Heat oven to 350°. Coat a 10-inch fluted tube pan with nonstick cooking spray.
2. Combine flour, cocoa, pudding mix, baking powder and salt in bowl.
3. Beat butter and sugar until light, 2 minutes. Beat in eggs, one at a time, beating well after each. Alternately beat in flour mixture and the milk, beginning and ending with flour mixture. Stir in vanilla and pour into prepared pan.
4. Bake at 350° for 46 to 50 minutes or until cake springs back when pressed. Cool cake in pan 15 minutes. Remove cake from pan to rack; let cool completely.
5. Chocolate Glaze: Place cream in small saucepan. Bring just to a boil over medium heat, about 3 minutes. Add chocolate; stir until melted and smooth. Return to low heat, if needed. Spoon over cake; let stand.
6. Drizzle: Combine white chocolate and oil in small microwave-safe bowl. Microwave about 1 minute, stirring halfway through, until melted. Stir until smooth. Let cool slightly, 5 to 10 minutes. Drizzle over Chocolate Glaze; let set.

PER SERVING: 352 calories;16 g fat (7 g sat.); 5 g protein; 49 g carbohydrate; 2 g fiber; 269 mg sodium; 50 mg cholesterol

caramel and chocolate tartlets

MAKES: about 40 tartlets. **PREP:** 15 minutes.
BAKE: at 350° for 10 minutes.
COOK: 18 minutes. **MICROWAVE:** 30 seconds.
REFRIGERATE: 1 hour.

- 1 package (17.5 ounces) sugar cookie mix (such as Betty Crocker)
- ¾ cup pecans, toasted and finely chopped
- 2 tablespoons flour
- ½ cup (1 stick) unsalted butter, melted
- ½ cup plus 1 tablespoon sugar
- 2 cups heavy cream
- 2 tablespoons salted butter
- Pinch salt
- 2 bars (1.55 ounces each) milk chocolate, chopped

1. Heat oven to 350°. Coat two mini muffin pans with nonstick spray; set aside.
2. Stir together cookie mix, pecans and flour. Stir in unsalted butter until combined. Press 1 tablespoon cookie mixture into bottom and up sides of each muffin cup. Bake at 350° for 10 minutes or until golden. Cool 15 minutes in pan on rack; turn cookie cups out. Repeat with remaining mix.
3. Meanwhile, combine ½ cup sugar and **2 tablespoons water** in a saucepan. Cook over medium-high heat for about 5 to 8 minutes, or until mixture becomes a dark caramel color, swirling as it begins to brown. Remove from heat and carefully add ¾ cup cream, salted butter and salt. Caramel will seize up, so return saucepan to medium heat and cook for 10 minutes or until caramel has dissolved. Place in refrigerator for about 15 minutes to cool.
4. With mixer on high, beat 1 cup heavy cream and 1 tablespoon sugar until stiff peaks form. Fold cooled caramel into whipped cream. Place in resealable plastic bag and set aside.
5. Microwave chocolate and remaining ¼ cup cream for about 30 seconds, until melted; stir until smooth. Pour ½ teaspoon into each cookie cup; set aside rest. Snip off 1 corner of resealable bag and fill cups with caramel mixture. Reserve remaining caramel mixture for another use. Drizzle remaining chocolate over tartlets; refrigerate for 1 hour or until firm.

PER TARTLET:158 calories; 11 g fat (5 g sat.); 1 g protein; 15 g carbohydrate; 0 g fiber; 44 mg sodium; 25 mg cholesterol

souper stars

HEARTY, DELICIOUS DISHES THAT WILL BOWL YOU OVER. BY JULIE MILTENBERGER

Red Lentil Soup (Recipe page 287) Have lots of crusty bread handy to dip in the thick, fragrant broth.

Food styling: Megan Schlow. Prop styling: Lynda White.

French Onion Soup
(Recipe page 287)
A crock of onion soup with a
cheesy, crusty crouton hits
the spot on a cold fall night.

PHOTOGRAPHY BY ALEXANDRA GRABLEWSKI

This colorful and comforting stew contains sweet potatoes—the most nutrient-packed vegetables.

roasted cauliflower soup

MAKES: 8 servings. **PREP:** 15 minutes.
ROAST: at 400° for 30 minutes.
COOK: 20 minutes.

- 1 large head cauliflower (3 pounds), cut into florets (10 cups)
- 1 large onion, sliced
- 2 cloves garlic, each halved
- 2 tablespoons olive oil
- 2 cans (14.5 ounces each) chicken broth
- 1 bay leaf
- 1 teaspoon chopped fresh thyme
- 1 cup half-and-half
- 1 teaspoon salt
- ⅛ teaspoon black pepper

1. Heat oven to 400°. In large roasting pan, toss cauliflower, onion slices and garlic with olive oil.
2. Roast at 400° for 30 minutes, stirring halfway through.
3. In large saucepan, combine roasted cauliflower mixture, chicken broth, **1 cup water,** bay leaf and thyme. Cover; bring to boiling. Reduce heat; simmer, covered, 20 minutes.
4. Discard bay leaf. In blender or food processor, puree soup in batches. Return soup to saucepan. Stir in half-and-half, salt and pepper; cook over medium heat until heated through.

PER SERVING: 98 calories; 9 g fat (3 g sat.); 2 g protein; 4 g carbohydrate; 1 g fiber; 741 mg sodium; 13 mg cholesterol

beef and sausage stew

MAKES: 8 servings. **PREP:** 10 minutes.
COOK: 1 hour 20 minutes.

- 2 teaspoons vegetable oil
- 1 pound lean beef chuck for stew, cut into ½-inch chunks
- 1 pound turkey sausage, cut into 1-inch chunks
- 1 cup chopped onion
- 1 cup chopped sweet green pepper
- 1 clove garlic, finely chopped
- 1 tablespoon chili powder
- 1 can (16 ounces) stewed tomatoes
- 1½ pounds sweet potatoes, peeled and cut into 1½-inch chunks
- 1 tablespoon all-purpose flour
- ½ cup shredded Cheddar cheese
- ¼ cup chopped pickled jalapeño peppers

1. Heat oil in large Dutch oven. Add half of beef and sausage; sauté until browned, about 6 minutes. Remove to plate. Repeat with second half of meat.
2. Add onion, green pepper, garlic and **1 tablespoon water** to drippings in pot; cook, stirring occasionally, about 7 minutes. Stir in chili powder; cook 1 minute. Stir in tomatoes and **2 cups water.** Bring to boiling. Return beef and sausage to pot. Cover; simmer for 40 minutes. Stir in potatoes; cook until potatoes are tender, 10 to 15 minutes.
3. Whisk flour and 2 tablespoons water until smooth. Stir into pot; cook, until thickened, 5 minutes.
4. To serve, top each serving with cheese and jalapeño, dividing equally.

PER SERVING: 360 calories; 17 g fat (6 g sat.); 23 g protein; 48 g carbohydrate; 1 g fiber; 687 mg sodium; 89 mg cholesterol

This satisfying tomato-based stew goes from pan to table in under 15 minutes.

turkey marengo stew

MAKES: 4 servings. **PREP:** 10 minutes. **COOK:** 13 minutes.

1 small onion, thinly sliced
½ pound presliced white mushrooms
2 tablespoons vegetable oil
1 pound turkey cutlets, cut into ¾-inch chunks
1 can (14.5 ounces) diced tomatoes
1 can (14.5 ounces) no-salt-added diced tomatoes
¾ teaspoon salt
¼ teaspoon black pepper

¼ teaspoon garlic powder
¼ teaspoon dried thyme
½ cup small pitted green olives, halved
8 ounces uncooked medium egg noodles (about 4 cups)

1. Sauté onion and mushrooms in oil in large skillet over medium-high heat, 5 minutes. Add turkey; cook 3 minutes.
2. Stir in tomatoes, salt, pepper, garlic powder and thyme. Stir in olives; cover and cook, stirring occasionally, 5 minutes or until turkey is cooked through.
3. Meanwhile, cook noodles following package directions. Serve mixture over noodles.

PER SERVING: 168 calories; 13 g fat (1 g sat.); 37 g protein; 50 g carbohydrate; 5 g fiber; 992 mg sodium; 85 mg cholesterol

Creamy Veggie Soup
(Recipe opposite). Combining
leeks, lettuce and peas creates
this gorgeous green color.

creamy veggie soup

MAKES: 8 servings. **PREP:** 10 minutes.
COOK: 35 minutes. **STAND:** 5 minutes.

- 3 vegetable bouillon cubes
- 1 tablespoon vegetable oil
- 2 leeks, washed, green tops removed and white part chopped (about 2 cups)
- 1 box (10 ounces) frozen peas
- 1 bag (10 ounces) romaine salad blend
- ½ cup heavy cream
- ½ teaspoon salt
- ¼ teaspoon pepper
- ¼ teaspoon ground nutmeg
- ½ cup dried mashed-potato flakes
- ½ cup sour cream
  Chives, chopped

1. Place bouillon cubes in large heatproof bowl. Add **1 cup boiling water.** Stir to completely dissolve the bouillon cubes.
2. Heat vegetable oil in Dutch oven over low heat. Add leeks; cover and cook, stirring occasionally, until tender, about 20 minutes.
3. Increase heat to medium. Add vegetable bouillon liquid, **5 cups water** and the peas to Dutch oven; cook 10 minutes or until heated through. Add romaine. Bring to boiling. Remove from heat. Let soup stand for 5 minutes.
4. Working in batches, puree soup in food processor or blender. Return soup to Dutch oven. Stir in heavy cream, salt, pepper, nutmeg and potato flakes. Gently cook until heated through and slightly thickened, about 5 minutes.
5. To serve, ladle into soup bowls. Garnish with sour cream and chives.

PER SERVING: 162 calories; 12 g fat (6 g sat.); 4 g protein; 12 g carbohydrate; 3 g fiber; 829 mg sodium; 27 mg cholesterol

french onion soup

MAKES: 6 servings. **PREP:** 10 minutes.
COOK: 28 minutes. **BROIL:** 7 minutes.

- 3 tablespoons unsalted butter
- 4 large onions (about 2½ pounds), halved and thinly sliced
- 1 teaspoon sugar
- 2 tablespoons all-purpose flour
- 2 cans (14.5 ounces each) beef broth (see Note)
- ¼ cup sherry or red wine
- 6 ½-inch-thick slices French bread, sliced diagonally
- ¼ pound Gruyère or Swiss cheese

1. Melt butter in a large deep pot over medium heat. Add onions and stir to coat. Cover; cook 15 minutes, stirring occasionally, until onions are very soft and begin to turn golden brown.
2. Uncover; increase heat to medium-high. Stir in sugar. Cook, uncovered, 6 to 7 minutes, stirring often. Sprinkle with flour; cook 1 minute. Stir in broth, sherry or wine and **1 cup water.** Simmer, uncovered, for 5 minutes.
3. Heat broiler. Spread bread slices on a baking sheet; toast under broiler for 1 to 2 minutes per side; set aside. Place six ovenproof bowls or crocks on a baking sheet. Divide soup evenly among bowls (about a cup in each).
4. Use a vegetable peeler to thinly slice pieces of cheese. Place slice of toast on each serving of soup; top with cheese. Heat under broiler for 3 minutes or until cheese is melted and bubbly. Carefully remove from oven and serve warm.
Note: If desired, you can substitute reduced-sodium broth.

PER SERVING: 260 calories; 10 g fat (6 g sat.); 12 g protein; 28 g carbohydrate; 4 g fiber; 797 mg sodium; 31 mg cholesterol

red lentil soup

MAKES: 4 servings. **PREP:** 10 minutes.
COOK: 20 minutes.

- 2 tablespoons oil
- 1 large onion, chopped
- ½ bag (16 ounces) baby carrots, coarsely chopped (about 1½ cups)
- ½ teaspoon ground cumin
- 3 large vegetable bouillon cubes
- 1 package (1 pound) red lentils, picked over and rinsed
- 1 bunch (about ¾ pound) fresh kale, rinsed, tough stems removed, leaves coarsely chopped (about 8 cups)
- ½ teaspoon salt
- ¼ teaspoon hot pepper sauce

1. In large deep pot, heat oil over medium-high heat. Add onion, carrots and cumin; cook 5 minutes or until softened.
2. Add bouillon cubes and **8 cups water.** Bring to a simmer. Add lentils. Cover, reduce heat to medium-low and cook 10 minutes.
3. Uncover pot. Raise heat to high; stir in kale and salt. Cook 5 minutes, uncovered, stirring occasionally, or until kale is tender. Remove from heat; stir in hot sauce.

PER SERVING: 269 calories; 5 g fat (1 g sat.); 17 g protein; 44 g carbohydrate; 11 g fiber; 936 mg sodium; 0 mg cholesterol

cheese sampler

THE ONE INGREDIENT THAT MAKES AN EVERYDAY MEAL SOMETHING SPECIAL. BY MICHAEL TYRRELL

White Pizza with Clams
(Recipe opposite)
Hold the marinara and
add some seafood for
an awesome New
England-inspired pie.

chicken roll-ups

MAKES: 6 servings. **PREP:** 20 minutes. **BAKE:** at 350° for 40 minutes.

- ¼ cup all-purpose flour
- ¾ cup plain bread crumbs
- 2 eggs
- 4 ounces smoked mozzarella, cut into 6 pieces about 2 inches long
- 6 boneless, skinless, thin-sliced chicken breasts (about 4 ounces each), pounded to ¼-inch thickness
- ¾ cup (1½ sticks) unsalted butter
- 1 teaspoon dried parsley
- ¾ teaspoon dried thyme
- ¼ plus ⅛ teaspoon salt
- ½ cup dry white wine
- ¾ pound dried angel hair pasta
- ¼ cup grated Parmesan cheese

1. Heat oven to 350°. Coat a 13 × 9 × 2-inch baking dish with nonstick cooking spray.
2. Place flour and bread crumbs in separate shallow plates. Beat eggs in a medium-size bowl.
3. Place a piece of mozzarella on one short end of each chicken breast and roll up tightly. Tuck loose ends in.

4. Coat each chicken roll with flour, dip in the egg and roll in the bread crumbs. Place, seam-side down, in prepared dish.
5. Melt butter in a small saucepan and stir in parsley, thyme and ¼ teaspoon of the salt. Pour mixture over the chicken rolls. Bake at 350° for 15 minutes. Pour wine over the chicken and bake for an additional 25 minutes.
6. Meanwhile, prepare angel hair pasta following package directions. Drain and place in large serving bowl.
7. Remove chicken from baking dish and place on serving platter. Season with remaining ⅛ teaspoon salt. Pour butter-and-wine mixture from baking dish over pasta and toss with Parmesan cheese. Serve immediately.

PER SERVING: 697 calories; 33 g fat (19 g sat.); 43 g protein; 54 g carbohydrate; 3 g fiber; 559 mg sodium; 195 mg cholesterol

A delicious new go-to for when you want something fancy that can be made ahead.

white pizza with clams

MAKES: 6 slices. **PREP:** 10 minutes.
COOK: 2 minutes 30 seconds.
BAKE: at 400° for 12 minutes.

- 2 tablespoons olive oil
- 3 cloves garlic, finely chopped
- 2 cans (6.5 ounces each) chopped clams, drained
- 1 prepared 10-ounce pizza crust (such as Boboli)
- 1 cup reduced-fat shredded mozzarella cheese
- ½ cup shredded Asiago cheese
- ½ cup ricotta cheese
- 1 tablespoon chopped flat-leaf parsley

1. Heat oven to 400°. Heat oil in a medium-size skillet over medium-high heat. Add garlic; cook for 30 seconds. Stir in clams and cook for 2 minutes.
2. Place pizza crust on a baking sheet. Spoon clams over top. Scatter mozzarella and Asiago cheeses evenly over the clams. Dollop heaping teaspoonfuls of ricotta cheese over the top.
3. Bake pizza at 400° for 12 minutes, or until cheese is bubbly. Cool slightly; sprinkle with parsley and cut into 6 slices. Serve immediately.

PER SLICE: 395 calories; 17 g fat (6 g sat.); 30 g protein; 28 g carbohydrate; 1 g fiber; 567 mg sodium; 72 mg cholesterol

Before they're baked, the rolls are drizzled with an herbed butter-and-wine sauce. After they're baked, a crisp crust gives way to a center of melty smoked mozzarella.

Instead of the usual fettuccine and Parmesan, we went for short pasta and Gorgonzola—and extra veggies too.

straw and hay penne

MAKES: 8 servings. **PREP:** 10 minutes. **COOK:** 13 minutes.

½ pound dried penne pasta
½ pound dried spinach penne pasta
1 package (10 ounces) frozen peas, thawed
1 sweet red pepper, cored, seeded and thinly sliced
1½ cups heavy cream
6 ounces Gorgonzola cheese, crumbled
½ cup grated Romano cheese, plus additional for serving (optional)
¼ teaspoon salt

¼ teaspoon ground nutmeg
⅛ teaspoon cayenne pepper

1. Cook pasta following package directions in boiling salted water until firm but tender, about 13 minutes. Add peas and red pepper during last 2 minutes of cooking time.

2. Meanwhile, prepare sauce. In a saucepan, heat cream over medium-high heat. When the cream starts to simmer, stir in Gorgonzola, ½ cup Romano cheese, the

salt, nutmeg and cayenne. Heat through, stirring until all cheese is melted and sauce is smooth.

3. Drain pasta and vegetables. Return pasta to pot and toss with the sauce. Serve pasta immediately, with additional Romano cheese, if desired.

PER SERVING: 506 calories; 27 g fat (16 g sat.); 21 g protein; 47 g carbohydrate; 7 g fiber; 572 mg sodium; 88 mg cholesterol

No worries if you don't have a fondue pot handy—this is a stovetop version.

This is heaven on a chilly weekend morning when the family is hanging out in their PJ's.

swiss and gouda fondue

MAKES: 3½ cups. **PREP:** 10 minutes.
COOK: 2 minutes.

- 1½ cups dry white wine
- 1 tablespoon fresh lemon juice
- ¾ pound Jarlsberg cheese, shredded
- ½ pound Gouda cheese, shredded
- 2 tablespoons cornstarch
- ¼ teaspoon garlic powder
  Pinch ground nutmeg
  Pinch cayenne pepper
  Cored and sliced apples
  Crackers or bread toasts

1. Place wine and lemon juice in a medium-size nonaluminum saucepan over medium heat. Bring to a simmer.
2. In a large bowl, toss together the shredded cheeses and cornstarch. Add cheese to wine mixture, one handful at a time, stirring with a wooden spoon until melted. Stir in garlic powder, nutmeg and cayenne. Simmer over medium heat for 2 minutes, stirring frequently, until smooth and thickened. Serve warm with sliced apples and crackers.

PER TABLESPOON FONDUE: 36 calories; 2 g fat (1 g sat.); 2 g protein; 1 g carbohydrate; 0 g fiber; 54 mg sodium; 7 mg cholesterol

cheesy pepperoni strata

MAKES: 8 servings. **PREP:** 15 minutes.
REFRIGERATE: 3 to 4 hours. **BAKE:** at 375° for 40 minutes.

- 6 eggs
- 1¾ cups milk
- ¼ teaspoon garlic salt
- 1 loaf crusty Italian bread (12 ounces), cut into ½-inch-thick slices
- 6 ounces sliced pepperoni, chopped
- 1 package (10 ounces) frozen chopped spinach, thawed
- 2 cups shredded Cheddar cheese

1. In a large bowl, whisk eggs, milk and garlic salt. Coat a 13 × 9 × 2-inch baking dish with nonstick cooking spray. Set aside.
2. Arrange half the bread slices in bottom of prepared baking dish. Scatter half the pepperoni, spinach and cheese over the bread. Repeat layers. Pour the egg mixture evenly over the top. Cover and refrigerate for 3 to 4 hours.
3. Heat oven to 375°. Cover baking dish with foil; bake at 375° for 15 minutes. Uncover; bake 25 minutes, until bubbly and lightly browned. Cool slightly before serving.

PER SERVING: 430 calories; 26 g fat (13 g sat.); 22 g protein; 26 g carbohydrate; 2 g fiber; 927 mg sodium; 220 mg cholesterol

sugar **rush**

THIS YEAR WE DUG INTO THE CANDY JAR TO CREATE SWEET, ONE-OF-A-KIND COOKIES.

**Peanut Butter Crunch
Cheesecake Squares
(recipe opposite)**

chocolate peppermint cookies

MAKES: 2½ dozen cookies. **PREP** 10 minutes. **MICROWAVE:** 2 minutes.
BAKE at 325° for 18 minutes.

- 4 ounces semisweet chocolate, broken up
- ½ cup (1 stick) unsalted butter, softened
- 1 cup sugar
- 2 eggs
- 1¾ cups all-purpose flour
- ¼ teaspoon salt
- 2 tablespoons unsweetened cocoa powder
- 1 teaspoon mint extract
- 4 ounces white chocolate, broken up
- ½ teaspoon vegetable oil
- 12 starlight candies, crushed, or ⅓ cup crushed candy canes

1. Heat oven to 325°. Butter two large baking sheets.
2. Place chocolate in microwave-safe bowl. Microwave for 1 minute, then stir until smooth. Let cool 5 minutes.
3. Beat butter and sugar in a large bowl until blended. Beat in cooled chocolate.
Add eggs and beat until smooth. Stir in flour, salt and cocoa powder until a soft dough forms. Beat in mint extract.
4. Drop dough by tablespoonfuls onto prepared baking sheets. Bake at 325° for 18 minutes or until dry on top. Transfer to wire rack to cool.
5. While cookies cool, combine white chocolate and oil in glass bowl. Microwave 30 seconds, stir; then microwave another 30 seconds. Stir until smooth. Spoon about 1 teaspoon white chocolate onto each cookie, then top each with ½ teaspoon of the crushed candies. Let stand to harden for 30 minutes. Store in an airtight container up to 2 weeks.

PER COOKIE: 135 calories; 6 g fat (4 g sat.); 2 g protein; 19 g carbohydrate; 1 g fiber; 29 mg sodium; 23 mg cholesterol

peanut butter crunch cheesecake squares

MAKES: 36 cookies. **PREP:** 20 minutes.
BAKE: at 350° for 39 minutes.

- ½ cup all-purpose flour
- ¼ cup pecans, finely chopped
- 3 tablespoons light-brown sugar
- 3 tablespoons butter, melted
- 1 package (8 ounces) cream cheese, softened
- ¼ cup granulated sugar
- 1 egg
- 1 tablespoon lemon juice
- ¾ teaspoon vanilla extract
- 12 fun-size Butterfingers, coarsely chopped (about ¾ cup)
- 5 fun-size Butterfingers, finely chopped

1. Heat oven to 350°. Line an 8 × 8-inch baking pan with nonstick foil, allowing foil to hang over two sides.
2. In a medium-size bowl, whisk together the flour, pecans and light-brown sugar. Stir in the butter and mix until all dry ingredients are moistened and a crumbly dough forms. Press into the bottom of the prepared baking pan. Bake at 350° for 14 minutes, until lightly browned. Remove from oven.
3. In another medium-size bowl, beat the cream cheese and sugar until smooth. Beat in egg, lemon juice and vanilla until combined. Stir in ¾ cup coarsely chopped candy. Pour into the baked crust. Bake at 350° for 25 minutes. Remove from oven and sprinkle the finely chopped candy over the top.
4. Cool completely. Gently lift from pan and pull back foil. Cut into 36 squares. Refrigerate until serving.

PER COOKIE: 70 calories; 5 g fat (2 g sat.); 1 g protein; 7 g carbohydrate; 0 g fiber; 29 mg sodium; 15 mg cholesterol

If you love peppermint bark, you will love these candy-topped, double-chocolate cookies.

These chocolate-coated coconut and almond cookies may remind you of a favorite candy bar.

almond chocoroons

MAKES: 2½ dozen cookies.
PREP: 5 minutes. **COOK** 4 minutes.
BAKE: at 350° for 15 minutes.
MICROWAVE: 1 minute 15 seconds.

- 3 cups shredded coconut
- 1½ tablespoons cornstarch
- ¾ cup sugar
- 3 egg whites
- ½ teaspoon vanilla extract
- 10 ounces bittersweet chocolate, chopped
- 2 tablespoons vegetable shortening
- 1 cup raw almonds

1. Heat oven to 350°.
2. Mix coconut, cornstarch, sugar, egg whites and vanilla extract in heatproof bowl (or a double boiler).
3. Set bowl over a pot of boiling water. Heat for 4 minutes, stirring often. Remove from heat and set aside.
4. Spoon out coconut mixture by the tablespoonful and place on an ungreased baking sheet.
5. Bake at 350° for about 15 minutes or until lightly golden but still soft. Remove immediately to a wire rack to cool.
6. Place chocolate and vegetable shortening in a small microwave-safe bowl and heat for 1 minute and 15 seconds. Stir until smooth, microwaving in 15-second increments if needed.
7. Place one cookie on a fork and gently press 1 to 2 almonds on top so they adhere to the cookie. Holding the fork over the bowl of chocolate, carefully spoon chocolate over top, allowing excess to drip back into bowl. Place cookie on a rack over a waxed-paper-lined baking sheet. Repeat with remaining cookies. Place rack in refrigerator for chocolate to set, at least 20 minutes.

PER COOKIE: 131 calories; 9 g fat (4 g sat.); 2 g protein; 14 g carbohydrate; 2 g fiber; 25 mg sodium; 0 mg cholesterol

rocky road shortbread

MAKES: 16 cookies. **PREP:** 15 minutes. **BAKE:** at 350° for 18 minutes. **MICROWAVE:** 1 minute.

- 1¼ cups all-purpose flour
- ⅓ cup walnuts, finely chopped
- ¼ teaspoon salt
- ½ cup (1 stick) butter, softened
- ⅓ cup sugar
- 1 teaspoon vanilla extract
- ¾ cup mini marshmallows
- ½ cup coarsely chopped walnuts
- ½ cup semisweet chocolate chips

1. Heat oven to 350°. Coat a large baking sheet with nonstick cooking spray; set aside.
2. Blend flour, walnuts and salt in a bowl.
3. In second bowl, beat together butter, sugar and vanilla for 2 minutes or until creamy and smooth. Stir in flour mixture.
4. Roll 1 tablespoon dough into a ball; place on prepared baking sheet. Repeat with remaining dough. Gently flatten each ball to a ½-inch thickness and smooth its edges. Bake at 350° for 16 minutes or until lightly browned at edges.
5. Meanwhile, stir together marshmallows and coarsely chopped walnuts in a small bowl. Melt semisweet chocolate chips in another small bowl in microwave oven for 1 minute, stirring halfway through.
6. Remove cookies from oven and spread each with 1 teaspoon of the chocolate, then sprinkle with the marshmallow mixture. Return to the oven for 1 to 2 minutes, until the marshmallows soften. Let cool on baking sheet on wire rack for 2 minutes before transferring to wire rack to cool completely.

PER COOKIE: 169 calories; 11 g fat (5 g sat.); 3 g protein; 16 g carbohydrate; 1 g fiber; 40 mg sodium; 15 mg cholesterol

oatmeal chocolate raisin cookies

MAKES: 36 cookies. **PREP:** 15 minutes.
BAKE: at 375° for 13 minutes.

- 1¼ cups all-purpose flour
- 1 teaspoon baking soda
- ¾ teaspoon ground cinnamon
- ½ teaspoon salt
- ¾ cup (1½ sticks) unsalted butter, softened
- ⅔ cup granulated sugar
- ⅔ cup packed light-brown sugar
- 2 eggs
- 1 teaspoon vanilla extract
- 2¼ cups old-fashioned rolled oats
- 1 cup dark-chocolate-covered raisins (such as Raisinets), coarsely chopped

1. Heat oven to 375°.
2. Whisk together flour, baking soda, cinnamon and salt. Set aside.
3. Beat butter and sugars until smooth. Beat in eggs and vanilla. On low speed, beat in flour mixture until blended. Stir in oats and chocolate-covered raisins.
4. Drop by well-rounded tablespoonfuls onto ungreased nonstick baking sheets, 2 inches apart. Bake at 375° for about 11 to 13 minutes or until lightly browned around the edges. Cool on the baking sheets for 2 minutes. Remove cookies to a wire rack; cool completely.

PER COOKIE: 124 calories; 5 g fat (3 g sat.); 2 g protein; 18 g carbohydrate; 1 g fiber; 75 mg sodium; 22 mg cholesterol

stained glass cookies

MAKES: about 36 cookies. **PREP:** 15 minutes. **REFRIGERATE:** 2 hours.
BAKE: at 375° for 10 minutes.

- 1 cup (2 sticks) unsalted butter, softened
- ½ cup sugar
- 1 large egg yolk
- 1 teaspoon vanilla extract
- 2¼ cups all-purpose flour
- 2 ounces each red and green hard candies (such as Jolly Ranchers)

1. In a large bowl, blend butter and sugar with an electric mixer on medium-high speed until fluffy. Add egg yolk and vanilla; beat until incorporated. On low speed, add flour; mix until dough comes together in a ball.
2. Divide dough into 3 pieces; shape into disks. Wrap each in plastic; refrigerate for at least 2 hours and up to 2 days.
3. Heat oven to 375°. Line two large baking sheets with parchment paper.
4. Crush candies (keep colors separate) in a food processor until finely ground. Transfer to two small bowls.

5. Knead one piece of dough on a lightly floured work surface to soften. With a lightly floured rolling pin, roll out dough to ⅛ to ¼ inch thick. Cut out shapes with a 3-inch cookie cutter. Place on prepared baking sheets and cut out center of each cookie with a 1¼-inch cutter. Refrigerate the scraps.
6. Using a very small spoon, carefully fill each cutout with candy so it is resting on the parchment paper and is level with the dough (about 1 teaspoon in each). Bake at 375° for 8 to 10 minutes or until firm and golden. Cool completely on baking sheets. Repeat with the remaining dough, then chilled scraps, using fresh parchment each time. Store at room temperature in an airtight container for several days.

PER COOKIE: 94 calories; 5 g fat (3 g sat.); 1 g protein; 11 g carbohydrate; 0 g fiber; 2 mg sodium; 19 mg cholesterol

Crushed hard candies melt during baking to created the stained-glass effect.

food **university**

THESE DAYS MANY PEOPLE GRILL OR DEEP-FRY THEIR BIRD AND DON'T HAVE PAN DRIPPINGS TO JUMP-START THE GRAVY. BUT NO WORRIES—WITH THIS RECIPE, YOU'LL STILL GET THAT GENUINE HOMEY FLAVOR. **BY JULIE MILTENBERGER**

When I was growing up, we made gravy the old-fashioned way—in the roasting pan after the turkey was on the serving platter. We'd combine flour and cool water in an old jam jar, and it was my job to shake it like crazy. Then we'd whisk the mixture with some chicken broth and the browned bits in the pan.

the perfect gravy

MAKES: about 3¼ cups. **PREP:** 5 minutes. **COOK:** 4 minutes.

- 3 tablespoons unsalted butter
- 2 cans (14½ ounces each) low-sodium chicken broth
- ½ teaspoon gravy starter (such as Kitchen Bouquet)
- ⅓ cup quick-mixing flour (such as Wondra; see Note)
- ½ teaspoon salt
- ¼ teaspoon dried poultry seasoning
- ⅛ teaspoon black pepper

1. Melt butter in a medium-size saucepan over medium heat (see step A), about 1 minute. Add 1 can of the broth; bring to simmer.
2. In a large measuring cup or bowl with a pouring spout, whisk remaining can of broth, gravy starter and flour.
3. Pour flour mixture into simmering broth while stirring (step B). Add salt, poultry seasoning and pepper.
4. Increase heat to medium-high and bring mixture to a full boil. Once boiling, cook 3 minutes, until thickened (step C). Transfer to gravy boat and serve warm.
Note: Look for quick-mixing Wondra flour in the baking aisle. For thicker gravy, use ½ cup.

PER ¼ CUP: 40 calories; 3 g fat (2 g sat.); 1 g protein; 3 g carbohydrate; 0 g fiber; 265 mg sodium; 9 mg cholesterol

For even richer-tasting gravy, make a simple turkey stock. Ask the butcher for 2 pounds turkey wings. Roast at 450° for 1 hour; transfer to a stockpot. Cover with water; add chopped celery, onion, carrots and ½ teaspoon salt. Bring to a simmer. Cook 30 minutes, then strain out solids. Refrigerate broth; skim off fat. Substitute for canned broth in recipe at left.

Heat butter in a medium-size saucepan over medium heat until melted but not browned.

Gradually add flour mixture to simmering broth, stirring with a wooden spoon to incorporate.

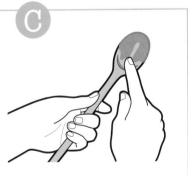

To test thickness, draw your finger through gravy on back of spoon. When distinct line forms, the gravy is ready.

PHOTOGRAPHY BY LUCY SCHAEFFER

december

Snowman Cake
page 301

CELEBRATE WITH PERFECTLY PAIRED
PARTY FOOD AND DRINKS, PLUS AN
ELEGANT SIT-DOWN DINNER AND FOOD
GIFTS TO MAKE AND GIVE.

**Beef Tenderloin
with Blue Cheese Butter**
page 307

**Asparagus Rolls and
Ginger-Lemon Fizz**
page 302

**Classic Yellow Cake and Milk
Chocolate Frosting**
page 317

THIS FRIENDLY FELLOW IS ALMOST TOO CUTE TO EAT.
HE'LL MELT HEARTS AT ANY HOLIDAY PARTY.

snowman cake

MAKES: 24 servings. **PREP:** 15 minutes. **BAKE:** at 350° for 43 minutes.

Equipment:
- 2 8-ounce ovenproof glass bowls
- 2 12-ounce ovenproof glass bowls
- 2 4-cup ovenproof bowls or metal ball pans (such as Wilton)
- 9 foil cupcake liners
- Chopstick or wooden skewer

Ingredients:
- 2 boxes (18.25 ounces each) yellow cake mix
- 8 large eggs
- 2 cups buttermilk
- ⅔ cup vegetable oil
- 1 bag (14 ounces) flaked coconut
- 1 roll strawberry fruit leather (such as Fruit by the Foot)
- 2 cans (16 ounces each) vanilla frosting
- 1 orange fruit slice
- 12 mini chocolate chips
- 2 cream-filled chocolate cookies (such as Oreo)
- 1 thin chocolate cookie (such as Famous chocolate wafers)

1. Heat oven to 350°. Coat bowls with nonstick cooking spray; coat with flour. Place foil liners into muffin-pan indents.

2. Combine cake mixes, eggs, buttermilk and oil. Beat on low speed just until combined. Increase speed to high; beat until smooth, about 2 minutes. Spoon 2½ cups batter into *each* of the large bowls, 1 cup batter into *each* of the medium bowls and ½ cup batter into *each* of the small bowls. Divide remaining batter among the 9 prepared cupcake cups.

3. Bake at 350° until cake is golden and a toothpick inserted in center comes out clean: about 17 minutes for the cupcakes, 22 to 25 minutes for small bowls, 30 minutes for the medium bowls and 40 to 43 minutes for large bowls. Transfer cakes to a wire rack and cool completely.

4. Meanwhile, place the coconut in a food processor and pulse until finely chopped. Transfer to a medium bowl. Cut fruit leather into a 6-inch and an 8-inch length. Fold each in half, pressing to secure, to get 3-inch and 4-inch lengths. Use scissors to cut fringe on narrow end of each piece.

5. Invert cooled bowl cakes onto work surface. Trim flat sides to make level.

6. Place one of the large bowl cakes, flat-side up, on a platter. Spread top with vanilla frosting. Place the other cake layer on top, flat-side down, to create a ball. Spread a thin layer of the frosting all over cake. Gently press the coconut all over to cover. Repeat with the remaining cakes to make 2 smaller balls.

7. Place the medium ball on the large ball. Insert a trimmed chopstick or wooden skewer for support. Place the 2 pieces of fruit leather as the scarf on the middle cake. Add the small ball cake. Add more coconut, if necessary.

8. Cut the orange fruit slice into a ¾-inch triangle for the nose and attach in the center of the small cake. Add the mini chips, pointed-end in, as the eyes and the mouth. For the hat, attach the 2 cream-filled cookies to the flat chocolate cookie with some of the remaining vanilla frosting. Arrange hat on top of snowman.

9. Spread remaining vanilla frosting on the cupcakes, sprinkle the tops with the coconut and serve with snowman.

PER SERVING: 530 calories; 25 g fat (8 g sat.); 5 g protein; 73 g carbohydrate; 2 g fiber; 463 mg sodium; 73 mg cholesterol

PHOTOGRAPHY BY RITA MAAS

celebrate!

DELICIOUS FINGER FOODS AND FUN DRINKS TO GET THE PARTY STARTED.

BY JULIE MILTENBERGER

asparagus rolls and ginger-lemon fizz (nonalcoholic)

MAKES: 12 servings. **PREP:** 20 minutes. **BAKE:** at 425° for 15 minutes.

2 **bunches fresh asparagus**
2 **teaspoons extra-virgin olive oil**
¼ **teaspoon black pepper**
½ **pound thinly sliced prosciutto**

1. Bring a large pot of water to boiling. Cook asparagus for 3 minutes. Drain and toss with olive oil and pepper.

2. Cut slices of prosciutto in half lengthwise. Roll up 2 asparagus spears in each half-slice of prosciutto and place on a baking sheet.
3. Bake at 425° for 15 minutes.
Ginger-Lemon Fizz: In a small saucepan, combine ½ cup sugar, ½ cup water and a 3-inch piece of fresh ginger, sliced. Bring to a boil; simmer for 3 minutes.

Remove ginger and cool. For each drink, mix 2 tablespoons ginger syrup with 1 tablespoon fresh lemon juice and 1 cup seltzer. Serve over ice.

PER SERVING (APPETIZER ONLY): 75 calories; 5 g fat (0 g sat.); 6 g protein; 2 g carbohydrate; 1 g fiber; 335 mg sodium; 0 mg cholesterol

pita wedges and beer

MAKES: 12 servings.
PREP: 10 minutes.
BAKE: at 350° for 15 minutes.

- 6 whole-wheat pitas
  Lemon-flavored hummus
- 1 12-ounce jar marinated roasted
  red peppers, drained and cut into
  ½-inch pieces
- ⅓ cup pitted kalamata olives,
  chopped

1. Wrap pitas in foil. Heat in a 350° oven for 15 minutes.
2. Spread each pita with a few tablespoons hummus, then top with red peppers and olives. Cut into wedges.
Note: Serve with Sam Adams beer, about $11 for a 6-pack.

PER SERVING (APPETIZER ONLY):
123 calories; 3 g fat (0 g sat.); 4 g protein; 22 g carbohydrate; 4 g fiber; 250 mg sodium; 0 mg cholesterol

apple-brie quesadillas and sangiovese

MAKES: 12 servings. **PREP:** 20 minutes.
BAKE: at 425° for 10 minutes.

- 1 tablespoon butter
- 1 Granny Smith apple, peeled, cored
  and thinly sliced
- 8 slices cooked bacon, crumbled
- 8 fajita-size tortillas
- 6 ounces Brie cheese, sliced

1. In a medium skillet melt butter over medium-high heat. Cook apple slices in butter until apples are softened, about 4 to 5 minutes. Add bacon to pan. Cook for 1 minute.
2. Lay 4 of the tortillas on a nonstick baking sheet. Divide apples among tortillas. Top with cheese and remaining tortillas.
3. Bake at 425° for 10 minutes, flipping halfway through cooking time. Cut into wedges and serve.
Note: Serve with Pietra Santa Sangiovese wine, about $18.

PER SERVING (APPETIZER ONLY): 178 calories; 9 g fat (4 g sat.); 7 g protein; 16 g carbohydrate; 1 g fiber; 339 mg sodium; 23 mg cholesterol

Food styling: Liza Jernow. Prop styling: Loren Simons.

With a savvy combination of high-quality prepared and fresh ingredients, these party nibbles and noshes are a snap to make. Paired with the perfect drink, they make an impressive holiday package.

cheese-filled endive and prosecco

MAKES: 12 servings. **PREP:** 20 minutes.

- 8 ounces cream cheese, softened
- ½ cup crumbled blue cheese
- ½ cup chopped walnuts
- ½ chopped sweetened dried cranberries
- 2 tablespoons milk
- 1 head endive

1. In a medium bowl, combine cream cheese, blue cheese, walnuts, cranberries and milk. Stir until smooth.
2. Trim end from endive head and separate leaves.
3. Dollop each leaf with 2 teaspoons of the cheese mixture.
Note: Serve with a medium-dry sparkling wine, such as Santa Margarita Prosecco, about $18.

PER SERVING (APPETIZER ONLY): 140 calories; 11 g fat (5 g sat.); 4 g protein; 7 g carbohydrate; 2 g fiber; 150 mg sodium; 25 mg cholesterol

chive biscuits with ham and a manhattan

MAKES: 12 servings. **PREP:** 25 minutes.
BAKE: at 450° for 9 minutes.

- 2¾ cups biscuit mix
- ⅔ milk
- 2 tablespoons dried chives
- Pinch cayenne
- Honey mustard
- Thinly sliced honey ham

1. In a large bowl, combine biscuit mix, milk, chives and cayenne. Knead on a floured counter five times. Roll to a ½-inch thickness. Cut into 1¾-inch circles, rerolling scraps for a total of 24 biscuits.
2. Bake at 450° for 9 minutes. Cool slightly, then split biscuits with a knife. Spread each biscuit with honey mustard and top with ½ slice of ham.
Manhattan: In an ice-filled glass, blend 2 ounces whiskey, 1 tablespoon dry vermouth and 1 tablespoon sweet vermouth. Garnish with a maraschino cherry.

PER SERVING (APPETIZER ONLY):
182 calories; 7 g fat (2 g sat.); 7 g protein; 20 g carbohydrate; 1 g fiber; 760 mg sodium; 18 mg cholesterol

onion tart and chardonnay

MAKES: 6 servings. **PREP:** 30 minutes.
BAKE: at 400° for 20 minutes.

- 2 tablespoons butter
- 1 Vidalia onion, thinly sliced
- ½ teaspoon fresh thyme
- ¼ teaspoon salt
- 1 sheet puff pastry, thawed
- ¾ cup shredded Gruyère cheese

1. In a medium skillet, heat butter over medium-high heat. Cook onions in butter until browned, about 20 minutes. Add thyme and salt.
2. Unfold puff pastry on a greased nonstick baking sheet. Prick all over with a fork. Bake at 400° for 10 minutes.
3. Spread onions over pastry. Top with cheese. Bake for an additional 10 minutes. Cut into squares.
Note: Serve with Chateau St. Jean Chardonnay wine, about $12.

PER SERVING (APPETIZER ONLY): 289 calories; 21 g fat (5 g sat.); 6 g protein; 19 g carbohydrate; 1 g fiber; 329 mg sodium; 26 mg cholesterol

broccoli bites and peach spritzer (nonalcoholic)

MAKES: 12 servings. **PREP:** 20 minutes.
BAKE: at 375° for 25 minutes.

- 2 refrigerated piecrusts
- 3 scallions, chopped (white and green parts)
- 1 tablespoon butter
- 1 10-ounce package frozen chopped broccoli, thawed
- ½ teaspoon dried dill or 1½ teaspoons chopped fresh dill
- 6 eggs
- ½ cup milk
- ¼ teaspoon salt
- ¼ teaspoon black pepper

1. Roll out one crust. Fit into one half of a 15 × 10-inch rimmed baking pan, pressing into the corners. Repeat with the second crust; press seam together. Prick all over with a fork. Bake at 375° for 15 minutes.
2. Meanwhile, in a medium skillet, sauté scallions in hot butter until softened. Add broccoli and dill. Spoon over partially baked crust.
3. In a large bowl, whisk eggs, milk, salt, and pepper. Pour over broccoli. Bake until set, about 10 minutes. Cut into squares or triangles
Peach Spritzer: In an ice-filled glass, combine ½ cup peach nectar, ½ cup ruby red grapefuit juice and ½ cup seltzer. Stir gently to combine.

PER SERVING (APPETIZER ONLY): 214 calories; 13 g fat (5 g sat.); 5 g protein; 19 g carbohydrate; 1 g fiber; 245 mg sodium; 112 mg cholesterol

sirloin-stuffed mushrooms and gin gimlet

MAKES: 12 servings. **PREP:** 15 minutes. **BAKE:** at 375° for 15 minutes.

- 24 mushroom caps, cleaned
- Nonstick cooking spray
- Salt and black pepper
- ½ pound sirloin, cut into ½-inch pieces
- Butter
- Dash Worcestershire sauce
- Creamy horseradish sauce
- Chopped fresh parsley

1. Place mushroom caps, rounded-side up, on a baking sheet and coat with nonstick spray. Flip over and spray again. Season with salt and pepper.
2. Bake at 375° for 15 minutes, turning mushrooms once.
3. In a medium skillet, cook sirloin in hot butter for 2 minutes over medium-high heat. Add Worcestershire sauce.
4. Spoon a dollop of horseradish sauce into each mushroom cap and sprinkle with chopped parsley. Top with sirloin.
Gin Gimlet: In a shaker, combine ice and equal parts Rose's Lime Juice and gin. Strain into a glass; garnish with a slice of lime.

PER SERVING (APPETIZER ONLY):
105 calories; 7 g fat (2 g sat.); 5 g protein; 3 g carbohydrate; 0 g fiber; 138 mg sodium; 11 mg cholesterol

DINNER IS
served

AN ELEGANT YET SURPRISINGLY
SIMPLE MENU FOR A
PULL-OUT-ALL-THE-STOPS PARTY.

BY CINDY HELLER

Pear Galette
(recipe page 309)
Ripe pears baked in a
buttery, cinnamon-
infused crust is a lovely
way to cap off the meal.

beef tenderloin with blue cheese butter

MAKES: 8 servings. **PREP:** 15 minutes. **ROAST:** at 350° for 45 minutes.

Beef:
1 beef tenderloin (about 2¼ pounds), trimmed and tied
1 tablespoon unsalted butter, softened
¾ teaspoon salt
½ teaspoon black pepper

Blue Cheese Butter:
¼ cup crumbled blue cheese
3 tablespoons unsalted butter, softened
2 tablespoons chopped parsley

1. Beef: Heat oven to 350°. Pat beef dry and spread with butter. Sprinkle with salt and pepper and place on wire rack set in rimmed baking sheet. Roast at 350° for about 35 to 45 minutes or until instant-read thermometer registers 135°, turning roast halfway through cooking.

2. Butter: While roast is cooking, stir together blue cheese, butter and parsley in a small bowl; refrigerate until ready to use.

3. Remove roast to a serving platter and top with one-third of the blue cheese butter. Tent with foil and let roast rest for 10 minutes. Slice and serve with remaining butter.

PER SERVING: 429 calories; 34 g fat (15 g sat.); 29 g protein; 0 g carbohydrate; 0 g fiber; 349 mg sodium; 110 mg cholesterol

Serve this tasty blue cheese-topped tenderloin with Brussels Sprouts and Fingerling Potatoes (Recipe page 309).

roasted vegetable lasagna

MAKES: 8 servings. **PREP:** 30 minutes. **COOK:** 18 minutes. **ROAST:** at 425° for 50 minutes; at 500° for 12 minutes.

- **2 medium-size zucchini** (8 ounces each), trimmed and cut into ¼-inch coins
- **2 medium-size summer squash** (6 ounces each), trimmed and cut into ¼-inch coins
- **2 large sweet red peppers**, seeded and cut into ½-inch slices
- **1 large red onion**, trimmed and cut into 1-inch wedges
- **1 teaspoon salt**
- **1 teaspoon black pepper**
- **8 ounces white mushrooms**, cleaned and quartered
- **1 tablespoon olive oil**
- **3 garlic cloves, minced**
- **2 tablespoons butter**
- **2 tablespoons flour**
- **2¾ cups milk**
- **¼ teaspoon nutmeg**
- **¼ cup minced fresh parsley**
- **2 tablespoons minced fresh basil**
- **12 dried lasagna noodles**
- **6 ounces Fontina cheese, shredded**
- **⅔ cup grated Parmesan cheese**

1. Heat oven to 425°. Coat 2 large rimmed baking sheets with nonstick cooking spray.

2. Spread zucchini, squash, red peppers and onion in a single layer on the prepared baking sheets; coat generously with nonstick cooking spray. Sprinkle vegetables with ½ teaspoon each of the salt and black pepper. Roast at 425° for 30 minutes, stirring halfway through, or until edges are browned. Remove from oven and transfer vegetables to a bowl.

3. Pulse mushrooms in a food processor until finely chopped. Heat olive oil in a large nonstick skillet over medium-high heat. Add mushrooms to skillet. Cook, stirring, for 6 minutes or until all liquid has evaporated. Reduce heat to medium; stir in garlic and remaining ½ teaspoon each salt and black pepper; continue to cook 1 minute.

4. Add butter to skillet and cook until melted. Add flour and cook 1 minute, stirring. Add milk and nutmeg to skillet and increase heat to medium-high. Bring mixture to a boil. Reduce heat to medium and simmer for 8 to 10 minutes or until thickened, stirring occasionally. Remove

skillet from heat and stir in 2 tablespoons of the parsley and all the basil.

5. Meanwhile, bring a large pot of salted water to a boil. Cook noodles according to package instructions, about 9 minutes. Drain, rinse with cold water and set aside.

6. Coat a 13 × 9 × 2-inch baking dish with nonstick cooking spray. Stir together Fontina and Parmesan. Spread ½ cup mushroom sauce into bottom of baking dish, then place 3 noodles in dish. Pour another ½ cup sauce over noodles, then sprinkle one-third of the vegetables and ½ cup cheese mixture over sauce. Repeat layering twice. Top with 3 noodles, pour the rest of the sauce over top and sprinkle with the remaining cheese.

7. Cover dish with nonstick aluminum foil and bake at 425° for 20 minutes. Raise heat to 500°, remove foil and cook for another 12 minutes or until browned. Sprinkle with remaining 2 tablespoons parsley and let stand 15 minutes before serving.

PER SERVING: 348 calories; 17 g fat (9 g sat.); 17 g protein; 33 g carbohydrate; 4 g fiber; 637 mg sodium; 72 mg cholesterol

Ruby-red pomegranate seeds give each bite of this crisp salad a burst of fresh, tart, fruity flavor.

pear galette

MAKES: 8 servings. **PREP:** 20 minutes.
CHILL: 45 minutes. **BAKE:** at 400° for 70 minutes.

Dough:

- 2 cups all-purpose flour
- 2 tablespoons cornstarch
- 1 teaspoon sugar
- ¾ teaspoon cinnamon
- ½ teaspoon salt
- 12 tablespoons (1½ sticks) unsalted butter, cut into ¾-inch pieces
- 7 to 9 tablespoons ice water
  Flour, for dusting

Pear Filling:

- 4 medium-size ripe Bartlett pears (about 2 pounds)
- 1 tablespoon unsalted butter, cut into ¼-inch pieces
- 3 tablespoons sugar
- 2 tablespoons apricot preserves

1. Dough: Place flour, cornstarch, sugar, cinnamon and salt in the bowl of a food processor. Add butter pieces and pulse 10 times or until butter pieces are about ½ inch. Add ice water, 1 tablespoon at a time, then pulse until dough looks ragged and holds together when pinched.

2. Turn dough out onto floured work surface and knead for 30 seconds. Form into a 4-inch square; wrap in plastic wrap and refrigerate for 45 minutes.

3. Heat oven to 400°. Place a piece of parchment on a 12 × 17-inch rimmed baking sheet and sprinkle it with flour; set aside. Place dough on floured work surface and sprinkle with flour. Roll with a floured rolling pin to about 12 × 15 inches. Transfer dough to prepared pan. Roll up a ½-inch border all the way around, pressing edge tightly to adhere to dough.

4. Filling: Peel pears and remove core and stem, then cut lengthwise into ⅛-inch-thick slices. Layer pears over dough, overlapping them slightly. Sprinkle with butter pieces and sugar.

5. Bake galette at 400° for about 70 minutes, or until lightly browned. Meanwhile, stir together apricot preserves and **1 tablespoon water** in a small bowl. Microwave for 30 seconds.

6. Remove galette from oven; cool on wire rack. Brush with apricot mixture.

PER SERVING: 358 calories; 19 g fat (12 g sat.); 4 g protein; 46 g carbohydrate; 4 g fiber; 150 mg sodium; 49 mg cholesterol

walnut-romaine salad

MAKES: 8 servings. **PREP:** 10 minutes.

- 2 tablespoons white wine vinegar
- 1 teaspoon Dijon mustard
- ½ teaspoon sugar
- ¼ teaspoon salt
- ⅛ teaspoon black pepper
- 5 tablespoons olive oil
- 3 hearts of romaine lettuce heads (12 cups chopped)
- 1 cup pomegranate seeds
- 1 cup toasted walnuts, chopped

1. Blend vinegar, mustard, sugar, salt and pepper. Whisk in olive oil until well combined.

2. Place lettuce in a large serving bowl. Sprinkle with pomegranate seeds and walnuts. Drizzle with dressing; toss well to combine and serve.

PER SERVING: 207 calories; 18 g fat (2 g sat.); 4 g protein; 10 g carbohydrate; 0 g fiber; 52 mg sodium; 0 mg cholesterol

brussels sprouts and fingerling potatoes

MAKES: 8 servings. **PREP:** 10 minutes
ROAST: at 400° for 25 minutes.

- 2 pounds Brussels sprouts, trimmed and halved
- 1 pound fingerling potatoes, halved lengthwise
- 2 tablespoons olive oil
- 1¼ teaspoons chopped fresh thyme
- ¾ teaspoon salt
- ¼ teaspoon black pepper

1. Heat oven to 400°. Coat a large rimmed baking sheet with nonstick cooking spray.

2. Toss together Brussels sprouts, potatoes, oil, thyme, salt and pepper. Pour onto prepared pan; roast at 400° for 25 minutes, or until tender.

PER SERVING: 121 calories; 4 g fat (1 g sat.); 5 g protein; 20 g carbohydrate; 5 g fiber; 246 mg sodium; 0 mg cholesterol

Coconut Marshmallow
Patties (recipe page 315)

homemade for the holidays

NO GIFT IS IN BETTER TASTE THAN ONE YOU MAKE YOURSELF.
BY MICHAEL TYRRELL

Food styling: Sara Neumeier. Prop styling: Megan Hedgpeth.

PHOTOGRAPHY BY ANN STRATTON

Banana-Macadamia Nut Muffins (recipe page 315) These fruity, macadamia-laden breakfast treats are like a taste of the tropics on a cold morning.

rosemary asiago-laced bread

MAKES: 12 servings. **RISE:** 2½ hours. **BAKE:** at 400° for 35 minutes.

- 1 package active dry yeast
- 1¼ cups warm water
- 2 teaspoons sugar
- 4 to 4¼ cups all-purpose flour
- 2 teaspoons salt
- 2 teaspoons chopped fresh rosemary
- 2 teaspoons dried minced onion
- ⅛ teaspoon cayenne pepper
- 2 tablespoons olive oil
- ½ cup shredded Asiago cheese
- ½ cup shredded Parmesan cheese
- 1 egg beaten with 1 tablespoon water

1. Sprinkle yeast over ¼ cup of the warm water (105°) in a glass measuring cup. Stir in 1 teaspoon of sugar. Let stand for 10 minutes. Mixture will be foamy.
2. Stir together 3½ cups of flour, salt, rosemary, minced onion, cayenne pepper and remaining teaspoon sugar.
3. Pour yeast mixture into flour mixture. Add remaining 1 cup warm water and the olive oil. Stir to form a ball. Mix together the cheeses and add ¾ cup to the dough.
4. Turn out onto a well-floured surface. Knead for 10 minutes, adding additional flour as needed until dough is smooth and elastic.
5. Lightly grease a large bowl with olive oil. Place dough in bowl and turn to coat. Cover with plastic wrap and let rise in a warm place for 1½ hours, until doubled in size. Punch dough down.
6. Roll out dough into a 20 × 8-inch rectangle on a lightly floured surface. Roll up from a short side. Fold ends under loaf and place seam-side down in a greased 9 × 5 × 3-inch loaf pan. Loosely cover with plastic wrap and let rise in a warm place 1 hour.
7. Heat oven to 400°. Brush top of loaf with egg wash. Sprinkle with the remaining cheese.
8. Bake at 400° for 35 minutes or until loaf sounds hollow when tapped. Remove from pan to rack to cool.
9. Wrap cooled loaf in holiday plastic wrap and tie with festive ribbon.

PER SERVING: 225 calories; 6 g fat (2 g sat.); 8 g protein; 35 g carbohydrate; 2 g fiber; 504 mg sodium; 24 mg cholesterol

minty hot fudge sauce

MAKES: 4 cups (12 servings).
PREP: 10 minutes. **COOK:** 10 minutes.

- 4 ½-pint canning jars
- 1 cup heavy cream
- ¾ cup granulated sugar
- ¾ cup light-brown sugar
- 1 cup cocoa powder, sifted
- 1 stick (½ cup) unsalted butter, cut into 8 pieces
- 6 ounces milk chocolate, chopped
- ¼ teaspoon salt
- ¼ cup crème de menthe
- 1 teaspoon vanilla extract

1. Heat cream in a heavy-bottomed medium-size saucepan over medium-high heat until bubbles form along edge. Lower heat to medium-low and stir in sugars, cocoa powder, butter, chocolate and salt.
2. Continue to heat over medium-low heat, stirring constantly, for about 10 minutes or until smooth. Remove from the heat and stir in the crème de menthe and vanilla. Allow to cool. Pour into jars. Store in airtight jars in refrigerator for up to 2 weeks. To serve, reheat gently.

PER SERVING: 339 calories; 20 g fat (12 g sat.); 3 g protein; 40 g carbohydrate; 3 g fiber; 75 mg sodium; 51 mg cholesterol

The lovely layers of this cookie mix—chocolate chips, nuts and rich cocoa—hold a delicious promise of what's in store when the cookies are baked.

chocolate-walnut cookie mix

MAKES: 36 cookies. **PREP:** 20 minutes.

- 1 wide-mouth canning jar (1 quart)

Dry mix (for the gift):
- 1¾ cups all-purpose flour
- 1 teaspoon baking powder
- 1 teaspoon baking soda
- ⅛ teaspoon salt
- ¼ cup cocoa powder
- ½ cup granulated sugar
- ¾ cup turbinado sugar in the raw
- 1 cup mini semisweet chocolate chips
- ½ cup chopped walnuts

1. Dry mix: In a large bowl, mix together the flour, baking powder, baking soda and salt.

2. Layer dry mix ingredients in jar: Spoon flour mixture into bottom of jar and press down hard to compact (a small spice jar works well for compacting). It needs to be at about the 1¼-cup mark on the jar to ensure that there is enough room for all ingredients. Continue layering with cocoa powder, granulated sugar and turbinado sugar, compacting each layer. Add chips and nuts. Close jar tightly. Store up to 2 weeks at room temperature.

3. Write or type the recipe in the red box, *at right*, on a gift card and attach it to the jar with ribbon.

4. Decorate lid of jar with fabric and tie with ribbon and bows.

PER COOKIE: 134 calories; 7 g fat (4 g sat.); 2 g protein; 17 g carbohydrate; 1 g fiber; 63 mg sodium; 28 mg cholesterol

december

chocolate-walnut cookies

- ¾ cup butter, melted and cooled
- 3 large eggs
- 1 teaspoon vanilla extract
- 1 jar chocolate-walnut cookie mix

In a large bowl, combine the butter with eggs and vanilla. Stir in contents of this jar just until mixed. Refrigerate for 1 hour. Drop by rounded tablespoons, 2 inches apart, onto ungreased baking sheets. Bake at 350° for 13 to 15 minutes or until firm. Cool on baking sheet for 1 minute before removing to wire rack to cool completely. Makes 36 cookies.

Count on being asked for the recipe for Smoky Wild Mushroom Sauce. The rich, slow-simmered sauce is truly addictive.

smoky wild mushroom sauce

MAKES: 2 quarts (12 servings).
PREP: 20 minutes. **COOK:** 38 minutes.

- 2 1-quart canning jars
- 2 tablespoons olive oil
- 1 large onion, finely chopped
- 4 cloves garlic, finely chopped
- 2 Italian frying peppers, trimmed, seeds removed and thinly sliced
- ½ pound shiitake mushrooms, sliced
- ½ pound Baby Bella mushrooms, sliced
- ½ pound oyster mushrooms, sliced
- 1 can (28 ounces) fire-roasted crushed tomatoes
- 1 can (28 ounces) fire-roasted whole tomatoes, broken up
- 1½ teaspoons salt
- 1 teaspoon dried oregano
- 1 teaspoon sugar
- ½ teaspoon black pepper
- 1 tablespoon balsamic vinegar
- ½ bunch fresh basil, torn into bite-size pieces

1. Heat oil in a large stockpot over medium heat. Add onion and garlic and cook 5 minutes, stirring frequently. Add peppers and mushrooms and cook for 8 minutes, stirring occasionally, until vegetables are almost tender.
2. Stir in crushed tomatoes, whole tomatoes, salt, oregano, sugar and black pepper. Bring to a boil over high heat. Reduce heat to medium-low and simmer, uncovered, for 25 minutes, stirring occasionally. Turn off heat and stir in vinegar and basil.
3. Spoon sauce into two 1-quart canning jars. Cool on wire rack. Seal and refrigerate for up to 2 weeks.
4. Arrange in a basket with a package of dried pasta and a wedge of Parmesan, if desired.

PER SERVING: 93 calories; 3 g fat (0 g sat.); 4 g protein; 16 g carbohydrate; 3 g fiber; 608 mg sodium; 0 mg cholesterol

coconut marshmallow patties

MAKES: 36 pieces. **PREP:** 10 minutes.
BAKE: at 350° for 18 minutes.
COOK: 7 minutes. **BEAT:** 14 minutes.

- 1 bag (7 ounces) shredded coconut
- ½ cup confectioners' sugar
- ⅓ cup cornstarch
- 2 envelopes unflavored gelatin
- 1⅓ cups granulated sugar
- ⅔ cup light corn syrup
- ⅛ teaspoon salt
- 1 teaspoon coconut extract

1. Heat oven to 350°. Place coconut on a baking sheet and bake for about 18 minutes, stirring occasionally, until lightly browned. Set aside.
2. Sift the confectioners' sugar and cornstarch into a small bowl. Line a 13 × 9 × 2-inch baking pan with nonstick foil. Coat with nonstick cooking spray. Sift 2 tablespoons of the sugar-cornstarch mixture into the pan, tilting to coat sides.
3. Place ⅔ **cup water** in a large bowl and sprinkle gelatin over the top. Let soften 5 minutes.
4. In a medium-size heavy-bottomed saucepan, heat sugar, corn syrup and salt over medium heat for about 7 minutes, until sugar dissolves. Stir occasionally. Strain into bowl with gelatin and stir in coconut extract.
5. Beat on high speed with an electric mixer until light and fluffy and beaters leave tracks in mixture, about 12 to 14 minutes. Spread into the prepared pan and smooth top. Sprinkle ¼ cup of toasted coconut over top. Let set at room temperature for 2 hours.
6. Lift marshmallow from pan using foil. With a wet knife, cut into 6 squares. Spread remaining sugar-cornstarch mixture onto a baking sheet. Carefully dip bottoms of each marshmallow square in mixture on sheet. Cut each into 6 pieces. Dip cut-sides in remaining coconut. Set on a sheet; allow to set for an 1 hour. Store, loosely covered, at room temperature.

PER PIECE: 84 calories; 2 g fat (1 g sat.); 1 g protein; 18 g carbohydrate; 1 g fiber; 28 mg sodium; 0 mg cholesterol

banana-macadamia nut muffins

MAKES: 12 muffins. **PREP:** 15 minutes.
BAKE: at 375° for 20 minutes.

Topping:
- ⅓ cup all-purpose flour
- ⅓ packed cup light-brown sugar
- 3 tablespoons cold butter, cut into small pieces
- ½ cup salted macadamia nuts, chopped

Muffins:
- 2 cups all-purpose flour
- ¾ cup salted macadamia nuts, chopped
- 1½ teaspoons baking soda
- ½ teaspoon pumpkin pie spice
- ¼ teaspoon salt
- 2 ripe bananas, mashed
- ½ cup granulated sugar
- ⅓ cup milk
- ¼ cup light-brown sugar
- 1 egg

1. Heat oven to 375°. Coat indents of one 12-cup muffin pan with nonstick cooking spray.
2. Topping: In medium-size bowl, combine flour and brown sugar. Cut in butter until mixture is crumbly. Stir in nuts. Set aside.
3. Muffins: In large bowl, whisk together flour, nuts, baking soda, pumpkin pie spice and salt.
4. In a medium-size bowl, whisk bananas, granulated sugar, milk, brown sugar and egg. Make a well in flour mixture; add banana mixture. Stir until ingredients are just moistened.
5. Spoon a rounded ¼ cup of batter into each muffin cup. Evenly crumble topping over each. Bake at 375° for 20 minutes or until a toothpick comes out clean. Cool in pan on rack for 5 minutes. Release muffins with a spatula and cool completely on a rack.

PER MUFFIN: 276 calories; 14 g fat (4 g sat.); 4 g protein; 36 g carbohydrate; 2 g fiber; 256 mg sodium; 26 mg cholesterol

food **university**

FROST LIKE A PRO: AN IRRESISTIBLE CAKE LIKE THIS ONE JUST REQUIRES A LITTLE KNOW-HOW. FOLLOWING A SERIES OF SIMPLE STEPS GUARANTEES GORGEOUS RESULTS EVERY TIME—OUR YELLOW CAKE LAYERS AND MILK CHOCOLATE FROSTING ARE IDEAL FOR PRACTICE. **BY JULIE MILTENBERGER**

PHOTOGRAPHY BY ANN STRATTON

classic yellow cake

MAKES: 16 servings. **PREP:** 20 minutes.
BAKE: at 325° for 40 minutes.

- 3½ cups all-purpose flour plus more for dusting pans
- 1 tablespoon plus ¼ teaspoon baking powder
- ¾ teaspoon salt
- 1 cup (2 sticks) unsalted butter, softened
- 1¾ cups sugar
- 4 large eggs
- 2 teaspoons vanilla extract
- 1 cup milk

1. Heat oven to 325°. Coat two 9-inch round baking pans with nonstick cooking spray. Dust with flour and discard excess. (Or, use a 13 × 9 × 2-inch pan.)
2. Sift flour, baking powder and salt into a small bowl.
3. With an electric mixer set on medium, beat butter and sugar until light and fluffy, 2 minutes (this is called creaming). Beat in eggs, one at a time. Beat in vanilla.
4. On low speed, alternately beat in flour mixture and milk, beginning and ending with flour. Spread batter into prepared pans, dividing equally.
5. Bake at 325° for 40 to 45 minutes or until a toothpick inserted in centers of cakes comes out clean. Cool layers in pans on wire rack for 10 minutes. Run a thin knife around pan edge and turn out cakes to cool completely on racks. Once cooled, spread with Milk Chocolate Frosting.

PER SERVING: 512 calories; 20 g fat (11 g sat.); 6 g protein; 79 g carbohydrate; 1 g fiber; 246 mg sodium; 95 mg cholesterol

milk chocolate frosting

MAKES: about 2⅔ cups. **PREP:** 5 minutes. **COOK:** 3 minutes.

- 4 bars (1.55 ounces each) milk chocolate, broken up
- 1 box (1 pound) confectioners' sugar
- 6 tablespoons milk
- ¼ cup (½ stick) unsalted butter, softened
- 1 teaspoon vanilla extract
- ⅛ teaspoon salt

1. Place chocolate in a small saucepan. Melt over medium-low heat, about 3 minutes. Cool slightly.
2. Combine 1 cup of the confectioners' sugar, the milk, butter, vanilla and salt in a large bowl. Beat with an electric mixer on medium speed 1 minute. Add melted chocolate and beat until smooth.
3. Gradually beat in remaining sugar until good spreading consistency.
4. Use a pastry brush to sweep loose crumbs from one cake layer. Place layer, bottom-side up, on pedestal. Spread 1 cup frosting on top of layer (step A). Brush loose crumbs from second layer; stack on first, bottom-side down. Secure with skewers (step B). With an angled spatula, transfer ¼ cup frosting to side of cake. Quickly spread on side, rotating cake as you spread frosting (step C). Repeat with more frosting, working all around cake. At this point, there should be about 1 generous cup of frosting left for the top. Remove skewers; spread remaining frosting on top of cake. Swirl top with back of spoon, if desired.

A Remove loose crumbs from layers with a pastry brush, then spread about 1 cup frosting over top of bottom layer.

B Brush off second layer; stack on top of first. Secure with skewers so layers won't slide around while you spread on the frosting.

C Use an angled spatula to spread ¼ cup frosting on side of cake. Work your way around layers in ¼-cup increments.

index

In-a-Pinch Substitutions

It can happen to the best of us: Halfway through a recipe,
you find you're completely out of a key ingredient. Here's what to do:

Recipe Calls For:	You May Substitute:
1 square unsweetened chocolate	3 Tbs unsweetened cocoa powder + 1 Tbs butter/margarine
1 cup cake flour	1 cup less 2 Tbs all-purpose flour
2 Tbs flour (for thickening)	1 Tbs cornstarch
1 tsp baking powder	¼ tsp baking soda + ½ tsp cream of tartar + ¼ tsp cornstarch
1 cup corn syrup	1 cup sugar + ¼ cup additional liquid used in recipe
1 cup milk	½ cup evaporated milk + ½ cup water
1 cup buttermilk or sour milk	1 Tbs vinegar or lemon juice + enough milk to make 1 cup
1 cup sour cream (for baking)	1 cup plain yogurt
1 cup firmly packed brown sugar	1 cup sugar + 2 Tbs molasses
1 tsp lemon juice	¼ tsp vinegar (not balsamic)
¼ cup chopped onion	1 Tbs instant minced
1 clove garlic	¼ tsp garlic powder
2 cups tomato sauce	¾ cup tomato paste + 1 cup water
1 Tbs prepared mustard	1 tsp dry mustard + 1 Tbs water

How to Know What You Need

Making a shopping list based on a recipe can be tricky if you don't know
how many tomatoes yields 3 cups chopped. Our handy translations:

When the Recipe Calls For:	You Need:
4 cups shredded cabbage	1 small cabbage
1 cup grated raw carrot	1 large carrot
2½ cups sliced carrots	1 pound raw carrots
4 cups cooked cut fresh green beans	1 pound beans
1 cup chopped onion	1 large onion
4 cups sliced raw potatoes	4 medium-size potatoes
1 cup chopped sweet pepper	1 large pepper
1 cup chopped tomato	1 large tomato
2 cups canned tomatoes	16 oz can
4 cups sliced apples	4 medium-size apples
1 cup mashed banana	3 medium-size bananas
1 tsp grated lemon rind	1 medium-size lemon
2 Tbs lemon juice	1 medium-size lemon
4 tsp grated orange rind	1 medium-size orange
1 cup orange juice	3 medium-size oranges
4 cups sliced peaches	8 medium-size peaches
2 cups sliced strawberries	1 pint
1 cup soft bread crumbs	2 slices fresh bread
1 cup bread cubes	2 slices fresh bread
2 cups shredded Swiss or Cheddar cheese	8 oz cheese
1 cup egg whites	6 or 7 large eggs
1 egg white	2 tsp egg white powder + 2 Tbs water
4 cups chopped walnuts or pecans	1 pound shelled